ROLL CALL TO DESTINY

THE SOLDIER'S EYE VIEW OF CIVIL WAR BATTLES

BRENT NOSWORTHY

CARROLL & GRAF
NEW YORK

Carroll & Graf books are available at special discounts for bulk purchases in the United
States by corporations, institutions, and other organizations. For more information,
please contact the Special Markets Department at the Perseus Books Group,
2300 Chestnut Street, Suite 200, Philadelphia, PA 19103, or call (800) 255-1514,
or e-mail special.markets@perseusbooks.com.

Designed by Linda Harper

Library of Congress Cataloging-in-Publication Data
Nosworthy, Brent.
Roll call to destiny : the soldier's eye view of Civil War battles / Brent Nosworthy.
    p. cm.
Includes bibliographical references.
ISBN-13: 978-0-7867-1747-7 (alk. paper)
ISBN-10: 0-7867-1747-5 (alk. paper)
    1. United States—History—Civil War, 1861–1865—Campaigns. 2. United States.
Army–Drill and tactics—History—19th century. 3. United States. Army—Weapons
systems—History—19th century. 4. Confederate States of America. Army—Drill and tactics.
5. Confederate States of America. Army—Weapons systems. I. Title.

E470.N67 2008
973.7'13—dc22

                                                                    2007036277

10 9 8 7 6 5 4 3 2

To the memory of my loving mother,

Grace Nosworthy

(1916–2004)

CONTENTS

INTRODUCTION

Roll Call to Destiny came about more as a result of "happenstance" than my previous books, which were part of a systematic and long-term effort to fill a perceived void in military history, as it had existed up to the 1980s. Most modern military historical works, regardless of content or focus, have been strangely silent on how troops actually fought. *The Anatomy of Victory; With Musket, Canon, and Sword;* and *The Bloody Crucible of Courage,* in essence a trilogy, were penned to chronicle the development of infantry, cavalry, and artillery tactics during the age of the musket, that is, from roughly the start of the Nine Years War in 1688 until the conclusion of the American Civil War in 1865 (remember, the Enfield and Springfield rifle muskets were, as their name implies, types of "muskets"). Of course, these three studies also attempted to describe the soldiers' combat experience, especially those that related to fighting techniques and practices. Because of the scarcity of anecdotal accounts, this latter proved quite difficult when dealing with early-eighteenth-century warfare. With the increased levels of literacy and the proliferation of published memoirs, it became a much easier task as the focus shifted first to the Napoleonic wars and then to those of the mid-nineteenth century.

While researching the fighting methods and combat experiences of the Civil War, for example, I uncovered literally thousands of regimental histories and published memoirs of Union and Confederate veterans at the New York Public Library alone. Of course, the informational value of these varies widely. Many were little more than pamphlets; some are quasi-fictionalized with the addition of supposed verbatim dialogs, like those found in novels. A few, however, proved to be "treasure troves" that provided invaluable insights into some aspect of warfare or the soldier's experience. Every now and then, these regimental histories or personal memoirs would yield a highly detailed, ultra-vivid account of some engagement in which the writer or unit had participated. Lieutenant Josiah Favill's description of his company's experiences during the Battle of Fair Oaks[1] and Colonel Judson Bishop's account of the Second Minnesota Veteran Volunteer Infantry's conduct during the assault up Missionary Ridge are among the best examples of this type of work.[2]

Highly impressed with the "you are there" feel and perspective afforded by these accounts, I originally intended to include a number of these descriptions, albeit in expanded versions developed with additional supporting materials, as separate chapters in *The Bloody Crucible of Courage*. Unfortunately, the page count of this voluminous work already greatly exceeded the contracted number, so that inclusion of these illustrative narratives was not feasible. Reluctantly, these were removed from the *Bloody Crucible* manuscript.

The result was that the various narratives collected during the research for *Bloody Crucible* remained "at the back of the drawer" for several years. However, these compelling vignettes were too interesting simply to be permanently cast aside, and when the dust settled after the publication of *Bloody Crucible,* it became apparent that the temporarily discarded material provided a convenient basis for a separate book.

However, for a historical analysis to be truly engaging, useful, and informative, prosaic narrative must be enhanced with the compellingly experiential. Accounts limited to dry and technical description of what units were involved and where each moved during the fighting invariably provide a less than riveting reading experience. It is important to include what the men saw, heard, and felt at each stage of the action, as well as the officers' decisions at critical moments, what tactics were used, whether they were successful and why. In *Roll Call to Destiny,* the scope of the narrative was therefore intentionally limited to "small units." Here, "unit" is defined as a group that fights as a monolithic entity and thus undergoes similar experiences, rather than a formally defined level of military organization or size of the fighting force. The goal was to show how events unfolded during an engagement from the point of view of those who shared a single common perspective. Only in this way, when dealing with the First Battle of Bull Run, for example, could one convey the astonishment of the men in the First Rhode Island Infantry when they first came under artillery fire as they worked their way through the last stretch of forest leading up to the battlefield, the reaction of Burnside's men as they lined up opposite their equally green Confederate opponents and came under small arms fire, or what it was like to have friendly artillery race through a regiment's position, disorienting the men and disordering the formation.

At first, the choice of chapter headings was dictated simply by what had already been serendipitously found during previous research dictated by completely different objectives. Favill's account of the Fifty-seventh New York Infantry's participation during the Battle of Fair Oaks, Colonel Judson W. Bishop's account of his regiment's activity at Missionary Ridge, and the feat of Lieutenant Daniel Webster's section of artillery during the assault of Arkansas Post were obvious starting points for chapters. However, as work began it became clear that each of these accounts illustrated a different archetypal battlefield situation. The Fifty-seventh's story at Fair Oaks illustrated the nature of infantry fighting at close range in a relatively thick forest; Webster's guns at Arkansas Post showed what could be achieved with the new rifled artillery, when properly manned and directed, against even a heavily fortified position; the Second Minnesota's experience at Missionary Ridge provided a compelling case study of both the difficulties and the opportunities that could arise when infantry assaulted its enemy counterpart while advancing up a long, relatively steep hill.

The book could no longer simply be a miscellany of interesting but unconnected engagements as experienced by particular units, but had to evolve into a collection of stories that when taken together illustrated many of the facets of fighting during the Civil War. Not only would it be necessary to treat all three arms—infantry, cavalry, and artillery—but it would also be important to show the impact of various types of terrain, and of man-made obstacles such as field works and fortifications. Since the fighting took place over both an extended period of time (four years) and a truly vast area, variations in the combat experience between East and West, as well as some of the developments as the war progressed, also had to be included. Of course, as much as possible there also had to be a balance between the Union and Confederate points of view.

These considerations channeled the direction of subsequent research. It became necessary to include cavalry-versus-cavalry actions, as well as to show an instance of infantry attacking a well-prepared fortified position. Of course, any number of engagements could be used to illustrate these aspects of Civil War combat, and those ultimately selected were largely the result of chance. In several cases, they came about as the result of encounters with Civil War buffs who have spent literally decades researching a particular battle, topic, or military unit. With the benefit of invaluable research generously provided by Lee Sturkey, a lawyer from South Carolina, supplemented by materials from arch-researcher Bryce Suderow, it became possible to provide a step-by-step narrative of what befell Colonel Haskell and the Seventh South Carolina Cavalry Regiment during their charge around the Union right flank during the Battle of Darbytown Road. Dana Lombardy, of History Channel fame, has spent a lifetime accumulating books on Civil War artillery. He was gracious enough to send boxes of these works for perusal and use. The chapter dealing with the Washington artillery's defense against Major General Darius Couch's assault of Marye's Heights during the Battle of Fredericksburg was the result. With fellow author Joseph Bilby's help, I was able to contact Bill Adams, an expert on the fight between Witcher's Thirty-fourth Virginia Cavalry Battalion and various dismounted Union cavalry on the third day of Gettysburg. This eventually, with invaluable help from Scott Mingus, led to a chapter on the cavalry-versus-cavalry engagement that occurred that day on what has become known as the East Cavalry Field. *The Bloody Crucible of Courage* had utilized a number of electronically conducted linguistic searches of the *Official Records*. Among the cornucopia of invaluable data thus generated were a number of detailed reports about General McLaws's assault of Fort Sanders. This formed the basis of yet another chapter.

The last two actions mentioned, the cavalry action at the East Cavalry Field and the assault of McLaws's division against Fort Sanders, might seem oddly placed in a work purportedly dedicated to "small unit actions." However, despite appearances, both are appropriate for the present study. The chapter that deals with Longstreet's attack on Fort Sanders looks at the affair from the perspective of General Lafayette McLaws's entire division. Though numerous Southern regiments took part in this futile Confederate assault, all were concentrated upon the same field; all rushed toward the same rifle pits, entanglements, and Union parapets; and all suffered the same fate. Despite the number of combatants in this case, there is a definite commonality of experience that can be communicated *without shifting perspective*. Thus, there is a single point of focus and this larger formation, from the author's point of view, functions as a "single unit." To tell the story of McLaws's Division in this affair, therefore, is to tell the story of any of the constituent Georgia or Mississippi regiments. The chapter on the cavalry fight on the third day of Gettysburg fits for entirely the opposite reason. Although, once again, there is a sizable force brought to bear by each side, regiments were mostly fed into the engagement piecemeal, so that the fight is largely a series of small unit actions, one following the other. This chapter attempts to describe the experiences of these regiments one at a time as they became involved in the fight.

Of course, as the project neared completion, the treatment and scope underwent several additional transmutations. Early on, it became clear that there was an opportunity to leverage information from the more technical "trilogy." Obviously, it would be useful occasionally to interweave explanations of the "how" and the "why" into the narrative—in other words, explain what is meant by "skirmishing tactics" when the narrative mentioned that a colonel ordered "flankers" to be sent out in front, etc. It became equally apparent once the core narrative chapters were completed that an introductory chapter that explained the developments of weaponry and military practice in the decade leading up to the Civil War was also necessary.

A few words are necessary about terminology. Over the years Civil War historians have adopted a number of nomenclature conventions. Most publishers, for example, abbreviate the names of state volunteer regiments, e.g., "the 57th New York Infantry." Many write about how much of the infantry was armed with "rifles." Though obviously space-efficient, and seemingly harmless, these abbreviations eventually add a filter between the language that was used at the time and how we tend to conceptualize these issues today. In this work there has been a conscious effort to return to the terminology used during the war. So, the official numbers of the volunteer regiments are spelled out, e.g., the Fifty-seventh New York Infantry. The use of Roman numerals to designate Union corps and divisions has also purposely not been utilized, since it is a modern development. Each word in the formal designation of a corps, division, or brigade is capitalized, e.g., Third Division. In the case of Confederate units—but not those of the Union—the commander's name (or that of the original commander) *is* part of its formal designation; thus "Anderson's Brigade" (Confederate), but "Burnside's brigade" (Union). The rifled shoulder arms are referred to as "rifle muskets." This later term is used because both the M1855 Springfield and the Enfield model P53 were officially referred to as "rifle muskets," and this term was used more frequently than "rifled muskets" in official correspondence and after-battle reports.

CAN THIS WORK BE USEFUL?

Unfortunately, any author who claims to proffer new information or a novel point of view regarding the Civil War is likely to appear naive, if not arrogant and prone to braggadocio and hyperbole. After all, the present work at first glance appears to confine itself to well-trodden ground. Books abound on almost every aspect of America's greatest conflict, and a large number of already published books have devoted themselves either to the combatants' experience during this epochal struggle or to the individual battles and engagements.

The Blue and the Gray, a large compendium of vividly written excerpts from soldiers' letters to family members back home, for example, has long been recognized as an invaluable source for those seeking to reconstruct what it was like to fight in this war. Carlton McCarthy's semiautobiographical *Detailed Minutiae of Soldier Life in the Army of Northern Virginia 1861–1865* has proven to be equally useful. In recent years, several excellent detailed studies of the Civil War soldier's experience have also come to the fore: John D. Billings's *Hard Tack and Coffee,* Earl J. Hess's *The Union Soldier in Battle: Enduring the Ordeal of Combat,* Reid Mitchell's *Civil War Soldiers; Their Expectations and Experiences,* and Gerald Linderman's *Embattled Courage: The Experience of Combat in the American Civil War.*

There are an even greater number of in-depth studies of individual Civil War engagements. Not only have large, well-known battles such as Gettysburg, Spotsylvania, Fredericksburg, and Murfreesboro each been the subject of numerous studies, but monographs abound on less-known events. An entire tome, for example, has been dedicated to the attempt by Butler's Army of the James to capture Petersburg on June 9, 1864.[3]

It is hardly surprising, therefore, that most modern readers probably believe that Civil War combat experience has been so thoroughly covered that there is little opportunity for truly groundbreaking work in this area. However, neither the typical battle study nor the fastidious dissection of the soldiers' experiences really touches upon the focus of *Roll Call to Destiny*. John D. Billings and Carlton McCarthy both served during the war, and their excellent works are semiautobiographical. These books are each written in the memoirist's own language, and, when provided, other participants' experiences are extracted from period primary sources and woven seamlessly into the story. Hess's, Linderman's, and Mitchell's works, on the other hand, either are organized to pursue a sociological or psychological theme or are organized into chapters or subheadings, each dedicated to a general topic, such as how the men dressed, the day-to-day experiences of the campaign, etc. In both types of book, selected experiences are extracted from the narrative of battle to serve as building blocks in some larger argument or are manipulated to fit some recognizable schema.

Most battle studies also follow a standardized treatment. Usually starting with a description of the campaign, they typically move on to the armies and commanders involved, before eventually settling upon the actual battle. The description of the fighting tends to move periodically from one part of the battlefield to another as the author attempts to describe how the struggle unfolded on a strategic level. The result is that much of the author's efforts devolve upon providing adequate background; only a fraction of most battle studies is devoted to the actual fighting. Of course, someone interested in the experience of combat from a more detailed point of view can find varying accounts by working his way through a number of works about individual battles or a series of regimental histories and personal narratives. However, this is an ambitious task, requiring one to read hundreds of pages to find and digest a relatively small amount of text that describes a particular combat in detail. One might say there is a high informational overhead, with a much smaller core payload.

This is not to say that books dealing with a series of battles do not exist. William Swinton's *Decisive Battles of the Civil War* and, more recently, the popular *The Civil War Battlefield Guide* or Craig L. Symonds's *A Battlefield Atlas of the Civil War* narrate the events that occurred during the most important Civil War battles. Each chapter in these books is dedicated to a major battle; however, given the limited amount of space dedicated to each, the view is necessarily from "40,000 feet," and is anything but vivid or experiential. The focus is on the commanders' decisions, troop movements, and other strategic issues.

Probably most general readers, and even a large portion of the enthusiast market, would prefer a viscerally pleasing work that paints a more experiential picture. Hollywood has always encountered the same trend. For every moviegoer who wants to see a movie about generals planning the D-day invasion, ten would prefer a movie about the grunts fighting on the front line—witness *Saving Private Ryan*. It is these considerations that lead me to hope that readers will find this work an interesting and useful addition to existing Civil War literature.

I

New Weapons,
New Ways of Warfare

*W*hether because of fervent patriotism, youthful enthusiasm, or simply a sense of adventure born in the humdrum of day-to-day living, there was no shortage of volunteers rushing to the flag after Abraham Lincoln's April 15 proclamation. The omnipresent enthusiasm, however, was mixed with a naïveté and, as it turns out, misplaced optimism, which would prevent the public, politicians, and military leadership from appreciating the nature and scope of the challenge at hand. "It will all be over in ninety days" was the popular cry in print, from the pulpit, and around the dinner table. All over the country camps of instruction sprang up to train the legions of volunteers that now flocked to maintain the Union. Yet, from an operational point of view, these were the halcyon days; there was little fighting during the first ten weeks of what would become the great familial disaccord.

ADVICE IN THE PRESS

Suddenly captivated by the eruption of a national crisis, the public always craves more information about unfolding events. This was as true in the mid-nineteenth century as it is for those watching the horrors of Katrina or the latest crisis in the Middle East today, and during the spring of 1861 almost everyone eagerly awaited the next edition of the local newspaper for the latest developments in the deepening crisis. Weekly newspapers like *Frank Leslie's Illustrated News* not only provided articles on the unfolding events, but also expanded their coverage to include more general military topics such as the latest developments in weaponry, naval designs, etc. This coverage included such topics as French and British experimentation with ironclads and the introduction of breech-loading rifled artillery during the Second Opium War (1856–1860). Some magazines like *Scientific American* at the time a sort of *Popular Mechanics* for American inventors—that ordinarily did not cover news-related items dedicated a special section at the beginning of each issue to the looming military/political crises and related day-to-day events.

The journalists who supplied these articles were not simply producing what they considered to be newsworthy; they were also driven by a sense of patriotism. It was obvious that the large numbers of volunteers rushing to the flag were novices who could not be expected to know even the rudiments of their new occupation. There was a pressing need to explain what otherwise could be acquired only through the painful and sometimes fatal lessons of campaigning. Eager that the next generation would benefit from their experiences, veterans of the Mexican-American War wrote to newspapers, which were only too glad to publish such counsel. A little more than a week after Lincoln's proclamation (April 15), in the *New York Times* an "old soldier" warned the new recruits about the do's and don'ts of guard duty—they were not to sit down even for a moment—the importance of rubbing down their musket every night, and how they should conduct themselves on the march.[1] The very next day in a competing paper, the *New York Post,* another "old soldier" provided advice on how to maintain one's health during the rigors of the campaign. The recruits were cautioned that "more men die from sickness than by the bullet." They were advised to bring along an India rubber blanket and line their wool blanket with "brown drilling" (coarse cotton cloth). To prevent disease, they must wash every day and grow their beards long. Volunteers were especially warned against the dangers of a sudden chill after profuse perspiration.[2] The advice in the popular press was not limited to issues of health and comfort, however; more martial matters were also discussed. During the opening months of the war, articles in *Scientific American* not only explained how to fire the recently introduced rifle muskets accurately, but even described how to disable enemy artillery captured during the give-and-take of battle.[3]

RECENT MILITARY DEVELOPMENTS IN EUROPE — NEW WEAPONS

The press's sudden preoccupation with all things military served a purpose beyond merely providing practical advice to the thousands of volunteers entering service. During the 1840s and 1850s, the pace of technological invention and scientific discovery had quickened, and this was as true for weapons of war as it was of more pacific areas of endeavor. Even though most of these inventions had been developed in Europe, a well-read American would have been aware of many of these innovations.

A number of new weapons that would play an important role in the upcoming war saw their "first use in anger" well before the contending armies amassed after the fall of Fort Sumter. Versions of the new rifle muskets had seen service not only during the Algerian (1830–1847) and Crimean Wars (1853–1856), but in the Indian Mutiny (1857–1858) as well. The Colt revolving rifle first saw action in Texas against Indians in the late 1830s and in Florida during the Seminole Wars around the same time.[4] It was used outside the United States only during the Eighth Kaffir War (1850–1853)[5] and then again during the Indian Mutiny.[6] Breech-loading shoulder arms had been used even earlier; Prussian infantry armed with the needle gun helped quell the revolution of 1848. British officers assigned to siege duty in the Crimea were known to arm themselves at their own expense with the Colt revolving rifle, while some of Garibaldi's forces fought with this weapon during the Italian War of 1859.[7] Some British cavalry had relied upon the Sharps carbine during the Indian Mutiny.

There were two innovations, more than any others, that seemed to capture everyone's imagination: rifled artillery and wooden ships protected by iron armor. The latter for a number of years had been called many names, "armored ships," "mailed ships," "iron protected ships," even "self-propelled floating batteries." However, it was a term that appeared in a British magazine in 1860 that stuck: "ironclads."[8] Although the modern version of the ironclad had been first devised by John Stevens and his sons in Hoboken, New Jersey, in 1812,[9] the French and British became interested in this novel naval technology only in the late 1840s.[10] Though, as would be the case with rifled artillery, it remained for Napoleon III to transform this from a prototype to a fighting ship that actually came under fire (Kinburn, October 17, 1855).[11] Although this action and the unqualified success of this new type of vessel was initially unnoticed by anyone other than professional naval architects and a select coterie of naval officers, the British and French governments eventually were impressed and a series of more sophisticated vessels was soon constructed that did manage to capture the public's attention. In 1859, the French built *La Gloire,* a large armored protected frigate of traditional design. The British admiralty responded with the introduction of the *Warrior* and *Black Prince,* both similar types of vessels.[12] In 1860, when they constructed several "tortoise-shaped" armored gunboats, the French appeared to have reverted to the smaller types of ironclad first proposed by the Stevens family almost fifty years earlier. These were armed with a single, large-caliber rotating cannon,[13] and in many respects were a scaled-down version of the Stevens Floating Battery that had been under construction since the 1840s but was lying unfinished in a Hoboken dry dock.[14]

Another development in weapon technology garnered even more attention, at least in the public's eye. This, of course, was rifled artillery. The period separating the Napoleonic Wars and the American Civil War saw extensive experimentation in this area. In 1816 Captain George Reichenbach, a distinguished mechanic who had served with the Bavarian army, approached the Austrian army with a bronze piece with seven rifled grooves.[15] Joseph Montigny, a Belgian artillery officer, conducted several highly successful trials with his own design before Russian authorities in 1835. M. Ponchara of France, Major Giovanni Cavalli of Sardinia, and Baron Wahrendorf of Sweden also developed working prototypes of the new type of ordnance.[16] All fell victim to the conservatism, indifference, and general lack of vision that permeated all the higher European military circles in the "neoclassical" period that followed the Napoleonic Wars. Once again, it fell to Napoleon III to be the first to officially adopt the controversial weapon. Dusting off a proposal submitted in 1842 by Treuille de Beaulieu, a French colonel, during the mid-1850s the French military tested and then adopted Beaulieu's pattern of rifled artillery. These pieces were successfully employed in the Italian War, to great fanfare in both the European and American press. The next year, the Spanish army had success with its own variety of rifled artillery during the Spanish Moroccan War of 1860.[17] British efforts in the same area were unsuccessful; the Lancaster and the Armstrong guns performed poorly during the Crimean and Second Opium Wars (1856–1860), respectively.

RECENT EUROPEAN DEVELOPMENTS IN TACTICS

If in the late 1850s the American military seemed to be sitting on the sidelines when it came to experimentation with ironclads and rifled artillery, they appeared to keep abreast in the latest developments in tactics. Napoleon III's successes at Magenta (June 4, 1859) and Solferino (June 24, 1859) in Italy ensured that the French army remained the primary role model for the American military. *Scientific American* probably reflected the popular opinion of the day when on January 21, 1861, it declared that:

> Napoleon III, is the ruling spirit who has effected the entire revolution that has recently taken place in the equipment of soldiers, in all armies, with the rifle instead of the musket; and he has given more attention to this subject, perhaps, than any other person living.[18]

However, it was not the new small arms that captured everyone's attention; it was his infantry's use of cold steel, i.e., the determined bayonet charge that was so widely touted in the professional and public press. Four days after Napoleon's glorious victory at Solferino, in the *Military Gazette*, the official publication of the New York State Militia, an officer lauded the time-honored edged weapon:

> Many people supposed that the long range of muskets and rifles would do away with the bayonet charge, but what a mistake! Ah! This deadly, this devilish weapon, how it has become the king of the battles! . . . Gunpowder, crossbows, long bows, rifles, revolvers, and all the missiles they can send, are cast into the shade. Hurrah for the bayonet![19]

This was no lone opinion, the ranting of an out-of-touch military archconservative. In the very next issue, a month later, a brother officer proffered a similar panegyric:

> The Bayonet—The public attention is constantly called to the fact that the bayonet is still a weapon of use, and must be relied on in all exigencies of war. It is always ready. No need of ammunition; no fear of failing in its supply of food. It does its work ever so silently, surely and unfailingly.[20]

It is exactly this sentiment that many Civil War historians have viewed as a myopic and unreflective acceptance of traditional European military doctrine that ultimately would be responsible for the mostly futile, but highly sanguinary nature of Civil War battles.

According to this view, the European military establishment remained hopelessly mired in the methods and doctrine dating back to the great Napoleon's time; methods and doctrine that had become obsolete almost a decade earlier with the introduction of the new rifle muskets, and on a much more limited scale, revolvers and breech-loading shoulder arms. Supposedly, these longer-ranged small arms now allowed the defenders to begin firing at ranges hitherto impractical, and it was inevitable that traditional bayonet charges in which the infantrymen were frequently required to advance without firing would fail.

Unfortunately, this line of reasoning, as logical as it sounds on the surface, ignores both a series of tactical experiments and developments among the more progressive European military circles and pragmatic experience acquired during the Crimean War. There were, indeed, some military thinkers who were quick to appreciate that the new weaponry would have a corresponding effect on tactics. On the theoretical side, there was a small cadre of officers in almost every European army that began to take this view. In Prussia, for example, Captain Wittlich theorized that henceforth firefights would take place at longer ranges and that infantry armed with the new breechloaders would be able to unleash six to eight rounds per minute. The old tactic of rushing up and overwhelming an opponent would no longer be feasible; the defender would be able to inflict too many casualties while the attackers were still at long range. Instead, the attackers first had to deploy and weaken the defenders with a murderous small arms fire. Wittlich also thought that the role of both artillery and cavalry would have to change. Henceforth, cavalry charges would be tantamount to suicide, and cavalry would have to become mounted infantry, dismounting before engaging the enemy and then fighting as normal infantrymen. The amount of artillery on the battlefield would decrease, since skirmishers protected by cover would be able to pick off artillerymen at any range under one thousand yards.[21]

In 1856, Captain Gilluim of the Belgian army went even further than Wittlich, predicting that these new small arms would totally transform the battlefield. Now equipped with the new, more accurate and longer-ranged weapons, the individual soldier would become "a much more effective fighter." Preoccupied with calculating ever-changing ranges and adjusting his back sight accordingly, the infantryman would be calmer than his predecessors. The old practice of "leveling" one's musket at a target or, even worse, shooting randomly would disappear and be replaced by aimed fire.[22]

The Prussians were the first to follow through officially upon these speculations and modify their existing battlefield tactics after the introduction of a limited number of *Zundnadelgewehr* (needle guns) during the early 1840s.[23] As of the 1843 regulations, infantry was still formed up in three ranks, but to offer smaller targets to the new long-ranged weapons, the traditional battalion column was eliminated and replaced by four company columns. In certain offensive situations, two company columns were placed side by side, with the two other columns twenty-four yards on either flank. One-third of each company was known as the "shooting subdivision" and was frequently sent out as skirmishers to cover the front of the battalion.[24]

Bogged down in a series of wars in North Africa, the French decided to raise ten battalions of *chasseurs à pied* (light infantry). Confronted with wily opponents who paid little attention to formality and took advantage of stealth and cover, the chasseurs were to utilize looser, more flexible tactics than had formerly been permitted. These were embodied in a provisional set of regulations (*Ordonnance du Roi sur l'exercise et les manoeuvres des bataillons de chasseurs à pied*) the next year and permanently accepted on July 22, 1845. Intended for light infantry, the maneuvers could be performed at a much quicker pace than that used by traditional regular infantry.

American Adoption of New Methods and Weaponry

During the 1850s, not only was the American military aware of the European experimentation with new military technology, it set up its own program to evaluate and, to a limited extent, adopt some of these new weapons. In Great Britain, just before his death, the Duke of Wellington became interested in a rifle musket that could fire the new "minié balls." His successor, Viscount Hardinge, settled on the .577 caliber Enfield "rifle musket" model P53. Spurred on by Jefferson Davis, who was the secretary of war in the Pierce administration, in 1855 the American military adopted the .580 caliber Springfield rifle musket model 1855, which because of its design and source of inspiration might be called an "unauthorized knock-off" of the British Enfield. The U.S. Ordnance Department was also charged with testing and evaluating breech-loading Burnside and Maynard carbines, as well as the first repeating small arms then making their appearance, such as the Colt revolving rifle. In 1858, Captain Henry Heth set about writing *A System of Target Practice,* which explained how to fire the rifle musket "scientifically." Chiefly a translation of the French *Instruction provisoire sur le tir,* Heth's work remained in use for more than five years.[25]

At this point, the United States infantry still followed the drill and maneuvers prescribed by Winfield Scott's *Infantry Tactics.* First adopted in 1835, this system had been devised in an era when infantrymen were equipped with smoothbore flintlock muskets. Anticipating that the new rifle muskets would lead to both more accurate fire and longer-range firefights, U.S. military authorities recognized that a new drill system, one that allowed quicker march rates and light formations, was needed. The U.S. military decided on the same procedure used to produce *Scott's Tactics*—translate the officially accepted French regulations, in this case, the regulations for the exercise and maneuvering of the chasseur battalions, i.e., the aforementioned *Ordonnance du Roi sur l'exercise et les manoeuvres des bataillons de chasseurs à pied.* Colonel William J. Hardee was appointed to lead the effort. His staff completed the task on July 28, 1854, and the new regulations were adopted by Jefferson Davis's order on March 29, 1855, under the title of *Rifle and Light Infantry Tactics,* soon changed to *Hardee's Tactics.*[26]

Clouds of war swept over Europe once again in 1853 when the British and French allied themselves with the Turks to try to stymie the Russian attempt to gain access to the Mediterranean Sea through the Turkish Straits. To keep abreast of the various European innovations and developments, Jefferson Davis sent three commissioners, Majors Richard Delafield and Alfred Mordecai and Captain George B. McClellan, to follow the hostilities that were certain to come. In his report, penned after he returned to the United States, Major Delafield bemoaned the backward state of the American military:

> Our preparation in material, equipment, knowledge of the art of war, and other means of defense, is as limited and inefficient, as theirs is powerful and ready. . . . As a nation, other than in resources and general intelligence of our people, we are without the elements of military knowledge and efficiency of sudden emergency. . . . We possess a nucleus of military knowledge in the country barely sufficient for the wants of our army in time of peace.[27]

The problem was not so much in small arms, for only limited numbers of breechloaders and rifle muskets had been officially adopted by western European armies. The problem was the sheer volume of innovations being introduced into every aspect of the European art of war—from the engines of war to engineering, transport, and cartography, as well as veterinary and medical sciences. While McClellan's report focused on contemporary European cavalry drill and maneuvers, Delafield's and Mordecai's reports described the various new armaments then being experimented with and adopted by European armies.

Unfortunately, there was little reaction to the three commissioners' reports. The late 1850s saw the return of conservatism and isolationism, at least at the very top levels of the military administration. With the election of Buchanan in 1856, John Floyd was appointed secretary of war. The whole tenure of the administration changed. The energetic, investigative, and forward-looking atmosphere inspired by Jefferson Davis's leadership was replaced with shortsightedness, indolence, and corruption. The experience of Professor Donald Treadwell was typical of many of those who approached either the Ordnance Department or Secretary Floyd with proposals or new ideas. Chagrined that the United States Army seemed to be ignoring the European advancements in rifled artillery, Treadwell approached the Ordnance Department with suggestions as to how metal used to create artillery could be strengthened, but his advice was met with complete indifference. He then went over the heads of lesser officials to Floyd himself. Though treated with courtesy during the ensuing interview, he concluded that the secretary of war "knew nothing, cared nothing" about rifled artillery.[28]

Such shortsightedness and lack of professionalism did not completely permeate the United States Army and related institutions, however. Here and there were cadres of officers and even civilians who sought to learn about the new technical and tactical innovations and have them adopted by the U.S. military. During their travels throughout western Europe on their way to the theatre of war in the Crimea, the three commissioners had acquired a virtual library of the latest European military scientific writings. They returned to the United States with no fewer than 317 different military scientific works.[29] It is clear that these did not sit around gathering dust. Within several years, Cadmus M. Wilcox and John Gibbon, both instructors at the United States Military Academy at West Point, had not only eagerly digested the contents of most of these writings, but published *Rifles and Rifle Practice as an Elementary Treatise upon the Theory of Rifle Firing* and *The Artillerist's Manual,* respectively. Both books were useful and thoughtful syntheses of the newly acquired information. It is equally clear that inspired by these ideas, the instructors modified the syllabus of training to reflect the latest technical and doctrinal European innovations. It is probably no coincidence that a number of American inventors, such as Dr. John B. Reed and Robert P. Parrott, started their work on various artillery innovations after the publication of these works.

There was another source of progressive thinking, one that came from a somewhat unexpected source and which, when internecine war finally broke out, would have an even greater impact on the public and some militia organizations than the United States Army. During the lengthy Algerian War, the already mentioned chasseurs à pied (light infantry) were brigaded with fierce native troops known as *zouaves*. Because of the ignominious performance of some Union zouave regiments during the First Battle of Bull Run, and probably also simply because of their unusual appearance, this type of infantry has often been ridiculed by those unfamiliar with either their origin or the services they rendered during the desultory fighting in North Africa. Nevertheless, these troops added greatly to the overall development of western European and American infantry tactics and did have an impact upon the way both Union and Confederate foot soldiers would conduct themselves during the Civil War.

Not surprisingly, although trained in maneuvers and the use of formations, the zouaves did not completely abandon their traditional fighting methods. When exposed to a heavy fire, zouaves were allowed, even encouraged, to seek cover behind available terrain, rather than stand out in the open, the traditional European practice. When fired upon on open ground, they would immediately fall on the ground to provide less of a target. They were adept at firing while lying prostrate and would reload by rolling on their backs and going through the reloading process. Unlike European-style skirmishing where the men were spread out in extended chains (in open order), zouaves were organized into groups of four comrades. Two of the men would be spread apart in front, while the other two were a distance behind and positioned so that they were in the interval between those in front. When the front two comrades had fired, they would retire and be replaced by the two comrades in back. There was much more emphasis on individual fighting capabilities; these warriors were trained in gymnastics and hand-to-hand combat, not simply how to perform the manual of arms and maneuvers, as had traditionally been the case with European troops. Incidentally, when United States Marine recruits undergo basic training at Parris Island today, they follow a training regimen whose origins lie with these fierce North African fighters.

Such methods naturally appealed to Americans who were familiar with similar methods employed during decades of Indian fighting. The first detailed description of these North African soldiers and their combat methods appeared in January 1858, when a semianonymous article entitled "Modern Tactics" was published in the *Southern Literary Messenger*. Its author, "R. E. C.," was undoubtedly Raleigh Edward Colston, an instructor of French at the Virginia Military Institute who would later command the Sixteenth Virginia Infantry Regiment.[30] Colston concluded that this new system of fighting was particularly suitable to the American population, since it was simply a codification of western "bush-fighting." Colston speculated that if such methods had proven successful for the French, how much more useful would they be in the hands of soldiers who from the start were intuitively familiar with these ways.[31] Colston's words did not fall on barren soil, and a year later Colonel E. E. Ellsworth established the first zouave militia group, the United States Zouave Cadets, in Chicago. After challenging all other militia groups to a contest, Ellsworth and his zouaves embarked on an eighteen-city tour to demonstrate their mastery of the new form of drill and fighting. They received a resounding reception in every city where they performed, but the largest and probably the most enthusiastic greeting occurred when they appeared before ten thousand spectators in front of New York's City Hall.[32] Every exhibit was heralded in major newspapers.[33] As Colton had predicted, the new type of infantry had caught the imagination of the American public.

IT'S WAR!

The assault on and capture of Fort Sumter vitiated all efforts to reconcile with the contumacious states through peaceful political means. On April 15, 1861, Lincoln issued his famous proclamation that called for the raising of seventy-five thousand ninety-day volunteers. These were to be organized in ninety-four regiments, 780 men apiece, to be raised in the loyal states in proportion to their population.[34] The existing state militia units were to serve as the cadres around which the new volunteer regiments would be formed. In New England, for example, the Tenth Massachusetts Infantry Volunteers was formed around the Tenth Massachusetts Volunteer Militia, while the Thirteenth Massachusetts Infantry was based on the Fourth Battalion of Rifles. It quickly became obvious that this force was totally inadequate for the task at hand, and Lincoln issued a second proclamation on May 3 for three hundred thousand volunteers who were to remain in service for three years. However, since all of the prewar militia units had already been involved in Lincoln's first call, other mechanisms for raising and organizing the volunteers had to be found. Many of the new regiments were formed by combining the volunteers from several nearby towns or the same neighborhood in a large city. Another method was to appoint a prominent person as colonel of the volunteer regiment. This person, usually politically well connected, would use his influence and connections to raise the requisite number of men.

Throughout the spring, as more and more men flocked to the colors, training camps sprang up throughout the North and South. Those on Union soil tended to be larger; each regiment was gathered together in a single location, and even when part of a larger military organization, it was surrounded by its own chain of sentinels. The camps of the secessionist soldiers were considerably smaller, usually populated by a single company or so. Those loyal to the Stars and Stripes also enjoyed greater standardization of uniforms and equipment, while their soon-to-be adversaries were attired in a much wider assortment of uniforms: brown, gray, and even blue.[35] The volunteers had to learn the rudiments of soldiering, i.e., how to march in step, handle one's shoulder arm, and perform sentry duty. Next came learning the drills and maneuvers, first by company, then by entire battalion. The volunteer officers, mostly also novices to the military profession, during the day had to master the sword exercises and practice with their pistols, while at night they studied whatever military treatises they could get their hands on.[36]

The received wisdom is that at the start of hostilities, Union infantrymen were equipped with American Springfield or British Enfield rifle muskets, while at first the Confederates were mostly armed with percussion cap smoothbores. In fact, during the opening months of the war there was tremendous variation in shoulder arms distributed even among Union troops. Although infantrymen in the regular army had been using the Springfield M1855 rifle muskets for several years, most volunteer regiments received percussion cap smoothbores. A number of Springfield M1855 rifle muskets had been distributed to individual states prior to the war, and this was probably how the Seventh New York Volunteers came to be armed with this weapon. However, given the numbers of troops being raised, there simply were not enough of the latest models, and most of the volunteer regiments in the eastern theatre of operations had to rely on either percussion cap smoothbores (the Springfield M1842 or the M1816 conversion to percussion cap) or the M1842 percussion cap conversion to rifle musket. Many Union volunteer regiments in the West found it even more difficult to acquire suitable small arms. The Eighth Kentucky Volunteers were able to arm themselves only by disarming local Rebel sympathizers, and as a result initially were armed mostly with small-bore hunting rifles and shotguns.[37]

On the whole, troops espousing the secessionist cause faced an even more difficult situation, and again those in the East were slightly better off than those, for example, in Mississippi, Tennessee, and Alabama, where many infantry were able to secure only old flintlock muskets, squirrel guns, or shotguns.

Initially, there was also variation in the maneuver systems used to deploy into line, form column, and march from one position to another on the battlefield. Some Union volunteer infantry regiments were trained in *Scott's Tactics,* and a few headed by officers who had fought in foreign service even unofficially adopted European systems.[38] Union authorities insisted on the use of *Hardee's Tactics.* However, as the officer for whom these were named had opted for service in the Confederate army, a new maneuver system appeared in 1862, the so-called *Casey's Tactics.* Casey had been the president of the board that sat for "the review, correction, and emendation of the translation of Lieutenant-Colonel Hardee" in 1854. Casey's own work also borrowed very heavily from the French *ordonnances* of 1831 and 1845.[39]

RETURN TO TRADITION

If the early 1850s were characterized by a tentative and cautious willingness to look at new weaponry and begin to think about how these would affect future warfare, the last half of the decade saw a return to traditional methods and a conscious eschewal of futuristic speculation. Two trends in particular beclouded American military thinking and once the Great Rebellion had begun made it more difficult to figure out how the troops could fight most effectively. The more unfortunate trend, one that would place commanders on both sides in a grand tactical straitjacket throughout the Civil War, was the popularization of Baron Antoine-Henri de Jomini's *Art of War* by such American disciples as Henry Wager Halleck. Though a relatively minor player in the Napoleonic Wars, after the return of peace the baron gained recognition first as instructor at the Russian Staff College and then international prominence as the author of *Précis de l'art de la guerre* in 1838, a work that would gain considerable recognition in European and then American military circles and would go through a series of editions. An archconservative in his military philosophy, Jomini was ideally suited for the acridly anti-Napoleon, "neo-classical" atmosphere that permeated all aspects of western European culture in the 1830s and 1840s.

Although in modern literature Jomini is usually portrayed as a seer of Napoleon's art of war, one who was able to communicate the secrets of the great commander to future generations, in reality, the baron was enthralled by the grand tactics and methods of an earlier period, that of Frederick the Great during the Seven Years War (1756–1763). Jomini categorized the recommended grand tactical formations into twelve possible archetypes, known as *orders of battle*.

Most of these were linear formations. A commander who wanted to concentrate his forces to attack an important position along the enemy line of battle could advance with a deployed line reinforced either on a flank or in the center. Concentration was achieved by placing narrower lines one behind the other, or by a series of battalion-sized columns of attack. An enemy flank could be attacked using the very Frederickian oblique attack. Only one of the prescribed twelve orders of battle allowed the use of massed columns, and even then the columns were still to be connected together in a line that stretched across the entire front.[40]

Despite all the hoopla about its being progressive, Jomini's system was, in reality, retrogressive. At its zenith in 1805–1806, French military doctrine placed the emphasis on grand tactical concepts, such as the concentration of superior force at the critical moment, rather than strictly prescribing what formations had to be used. Nevertheless, Jomini's system quickly gained disciples in the United States. As early as 1817 a translation of Colonel de Vernon's *A Treatise on the Science of War and Fortification* was added to the curriculum at the United States Military Academy at West Point. This provided a 105-page summary of Jomini's principles of "grand tactics and operations."[41] But it was Henry Halleck who really popularized this system among the American military. He was sent to France to inspect that country's latest developments in permanent fortifications in 1844. Whether Halleck had been familiar with Jomini's writings prior to this trip is unclear. The next year, Halleck delivered a series of lectures at the Lowell Institute in Boston in which he essentially regurgitated Jomini's opinions.[42] Encouraged by this success, in 1846 Halleck published an enhanced version of the lecture notes as the *Elements of Military Art and Science*.[43] Of course, Halleck would become general-in-chief of the Union armies in late 1862 and was in an ideal situation to encourage subordinate officers to adopt his, and hence Jomini's, approach to war. That this influence had a tangible effect on the types of grand tactics and troop deployment that were used became evident when Couch's Second Corps was ordered to attack Marye's Heights during the battle of Fredericksburg. When

French's and Winfield S. Hancock's divisions assaulted Marye's Heights, each division advanced in three successive brigades in line, two hundred paces apart,[44] a formation described in Jomini's *Art of War*.[45] The mind-set created by Jomini's precepts was one preoccupied with large linear formations and attacks by successive lines, a tactic that one finds used throughout the War Between the States.

The other seemingly retrogressive trend, one ridiculed by many twentieth-century historians, was disillusionment with the long-range capabilities of the new rifle musket and its expected impact on future warfare, accompanied by a renewed enthusiasm for the bayonet charge. As early as 1852, Colonel Chesney of the Royal Artillery, for example, railed against Wittlich's and Gilluim's optimistic beliefs regarding the impending transformation of war, arguing that battles would not degenerate into massive skirmishing duels; instead, massed formations such as lines and columns would continue to be relied upon.[46] Chesney received indirect support from a number of British officers who delivered a series of lectures at the Royal United Service Institute. Lieutenant Colonel Dixon of the Royal Artillery, for example, felt that to be effective small arms fire had to be reserved until the line had approached to within four hundred yards of the enemy.[47] During his lecture, Captain Tyler maintained that infantry firefights would take place at a range of six hundred yards. He reasoned:

> small-arms practice in the field will be less accurate than similar practice at a painted target. The weapon, indeed, will be the same, and its range will be as formidable, but the dust, turmoil, smoke, and excitement of the battle-field will detract from the accurate aim of the men; and irregularities of the ground will much interfere with extreme ranges.[48]

Dixon also pointed out that given the relatively low initial muzzle velocity of the new-style rifle muskets, it was critical to estimate the range of each shot accurately, something that required concentration and sangfroid (literally cold-bloodedness). This was rare among troops in massed formations under fire. Surrounded by smoke and the whistle of shells and bullets flying nearby, most soldiers would become distracted. Some would even shake and wobble on their legs. Their ability to compute ranges, adjust the back sight, and aim accurately would be greatly diminished.[49]

In his forthcoming book on small arms at Gettysburg, Joseph Bilby has uncovered the reason for this seemingly retrogressive trend among some of the more sentient of the British military. Taking advantage of a short respite on their way to the Crimea in March 1854, British Guards engaged in target practice with their new rifle muskets, the P51. The men followed the new scientific method of range estimation and firing and judged ranges by uniform and equipment characteristics (e.g., at 110 yards details such as the buttons or holster of the enemy become visible).[50] At 250 yards a "large proportion" of the shots struck the target. However, despite this auspicious beginning, experience during the war showed that the men and officers did not use these methods but waited until the Russians had approached within traditional ranges, and then resorted to the same methods and tactics developed for the smoothbore musket.[51] Thereafter, the British military entertained lower expectations regarding the rifle musket's actual performance in battle.

Around the same time, French military authorities had also begun entertaining doubts about the long-range effectiveness of the rifle muskets and the so-called scientific method of firing. Experience during the ongoing Algerian wars and then, as with the British, in the Crimea, showed that the average French infantryman failed to use his back sight, and firefights occurred at extremely short ranges. However, unlike the British, the French took concrete action and modified one feature of the new weapons. The back sights on the minié pattern 1850 had been sighted up to nine hundred yards, nearly the effective range of the weapon. Around 1858, however, the maximum range of the back sight was reduced to six hundred yards and the following year further reduced to four hundred yards.[52] In April 1859 the French, allied with the Kingdom of Sardinia, went to war against the Austrians. The new *carbine à tige* that was distributed to the chasseurs à pied did not even have an "elevating" back sight.[53] Preparing his troops for the upcoming fight, Napoleon III cautioned his men against useless long-range fire, and urged them instead to rely whenever possible upon cold steel. The infantry was ordered to advance quickly, withhold their fire, and then charge in with lowered bayonets.[54] French confidence in these traditional techniques did not seem to be misplaced. The engagement at Montebello (May 20, 1859) was finally decided with an aggressive bayonet charge. These tactics also proved successful during the Battle of Magenta (June 4, 1859).[55] It was these tactical successes that captured the imagination of the American military and public alike and led to the already quoted eulogies in newspapers and journals.

Thus, as both sides prepared for war during the late spring of 1861, there was some disagreement about how the war could best be fought. Some, like Captain Cadmus Wilcox, continued to believe in the effectiveness of the new small arms and the significant transformation of war they would effect.[56] However, his fellow instructor at West Point, Captain John Gibbon, espoused the more popular view—that in practice the effective range of the new weapons would be much less than originally anticipated and that traditional methods, for the most part, remained viable.[57] In other words, most accepted Napoleon III's enthusiastic return to resolving the crisis of an engagement with cold steel, i.e., by a determined bayonet charge. This was particularly the case among the southern military, many of whom predicted that "in every battle the southern volunteers will, at any sacrifice, seek the closest quarters possible, and decide the fate of the hour with bowie knife and bayonet." Robert E. Lee seemed to stand alone when he prognosticated that the artillery arm with its new assortment of projectiles (timed fuses, etc.) would play a prominent role. This seemed such an aberrant stance, that one journalist sardonically questioned Lee's intellectual competence in the matter:

The difference in these two opinions [i.e., between Lee and his brother officers] is accountable to the fact that first [that of Lee] comes from purely a theoretical old soldier, who has to do with "man machines" all his life, while the other emanates from those who understand the calibre and spirit of the volunteers.[58]

In the realm of grand tactics Jomini's principles seemed to hold sway. Ultimately, Jomini's influence was far more damaging than an unthinking infatuation with the bayonet, since officers unconsciously employed linear formations with the same bloody but indecisive results that had been experienced in Europe a hundred years earlier when opposing armies faced off against each other along lengthy lines.

The futility of such tactics would eventually become apparent, but this would be a lesson written in the blood of countless young lads from both the North and the South, and one that would take at least three years to digest.

2

BURNSIDE'S FIGHT: THE ADVANCE
TO THE BULL RUN BATTLEFIELD

On July 8, 1861, the hastily thrown-together volunteer regiments that now made up the Union "Army of Northeast Virginia" were finally organized into brigades. One of these, Colonel Ambrose Burnside's second brigade, would play a conspicuous role during the war's first major battle, which has become known as the First Battle of Bull Run or First Manassas. Like all the other units making up McDowell's army, they had to first endure a fatiguing nighttime march that sorely tested their endurance and provided the first indications that volunteers' inexperience and lack of training would limit their performance on the battlefield.

For most of those donning a military uniform, the monotony of parade ground drills and the loss of personal freedom were more than compensated for by the novelty of the situation, a newfound respect from womenfolk, and the expectation that the entire crisis would end after a week or two of campaigning with the defeat of the other side after the very first, but totally decisive, battle. Continuous streams of volunteers flocked to the ever-increasing number of camps set up through both the North and the South. Earlier on, those espousing the Northern cause had a scare, however. Only two regiments of volunteers managed to reach Washington City during the week following the fall of Fort Sumter, and the threat of Maryland secessionists or Virginia Black Horse Cavalry rushing in and seizing the capital appeared real enough. The arrival of 1,500 militia on April 24–25, 1861, improved the situation and the immediate threat had passed. May and June saw the influx or more and more Union volunteer regiments, stationed at various impromptu camps around the city, and by mid-June a veritable army had finally been collected.

Throughout the early summer the mood of the Northern soldiers and citizenry remained optimistic. True, here and there the secessionists had scored victories, such as Major General Kenton Harper's capture of the abandoned arsenal at Harper's Ferry (April 18) and later the defeat of a small Union force at Big Bethel, Virginia (June 10). But these were localized successes, with little if any overall significance, and there was as yet little to indicate the courageousness, resilience, and tenacity that would so characterize Southern troops during the four years of bitter fighting that lie ahead. In fact, there was a rather carefree attitude among both soldiers and their officers gathered around the capital. Passes were freely given to officers and in many regiments the drilling was less than rigorous.[1]

By early June, a Confederate force occupied a defensive line near Washington known as the "Alexandria line." The front line was positioned behind the Bull Run stream, with General P. G. T. Beauregard's headquarters three miles to the rear at Manassas.[2] Seeming Federal inactivity caused a popular uproar and stirred military authorities into action. Brigadier General Irvin McDowell's forces at Washington were to push forward to Manassas Junction, while

Major General Robert Patterson's command was to advance and re-take Harper's Ferry. As it turned out, Patterson was easily able to re-capture his objective, and for the moment there was no need to initiate McDowell's part of the operation. Union forces near the capital thus continued to remain inactive. Nevertheless, it became apparent that McDowell's forces would have to advance out of Washington toward Centreville, and Lieutenant General Winfield Scott asked McDowell to submit a plan of how this could be accomplished. The resulting plan called for thirty thousand men supported by a ten thousand-man force in reserve. This would advance to the enemy line behind Bull Run, turn one of the enemy's flanks, and fall upon his line of communications, thus forcing the Rebels to withdraw. Recognizing that the volunteer officers were totally inexperienced, the general ordered that the regiments "be organized into as many small fixed brigades as the number of regular colonels will admit . . . so that the men may have a fair chance as the nature of things and the comparative inexperience of most will allow." Although the plan was approved and was to be put into action on July 8, there were a number of administrative delays.

The Union army set forth on the afternoon of July 16 and reached Centreville two days later. Here, the foremost division was ordered to wait until the supply wagons caught up. In the meantime, McDowell reconnoitered the extreme left of the enemy position and found that because of unfavorable terrain an attack on this wing was unfeasible. While the commander was thus engaged, Brigadier General Daniel Tyler initiated an unauthorized reconnaissance in force. This ill-advised attack, which would eventually become known as the Battle of Blackburn Ford, consisted of a little more than a brigade of infantry supported by two artillery batteries and was easily repulsed by Beauregard's men. Though only a minor skirmish, this preliminary sparring match buoyed the Rebels' morale while correspondingly lowering the spirits of the Union soldiers.

Of greater consequence, the Union army was forced into two days of inactivity (July 19 and 20). Not only did the supplies have to be replenished, but the men were also exhausted by the heat and rigors of the march. These were not yet the men who would be able to march ten to twelve miles in a day and then fight a battle without food or repose. They were still what Captain James B. Fry would later describe as "civilians in uniforms."[3]

THE APPROACH TO BATTLE

Even though most in the ranks now sensed that the expected "fight to the finish" was finally at hand, the men's routine that Saturday (July 20) seemed little affected by the worrisome prospect. Undaunted by the heat, the soldiers continued to loaf around the camp, write letters to their friends and loved ones, and visit other nearby Union encampments. By late afternoon the mood started to change, however, as formality and grim reality set in. Simon Cameron, the secretary of war, and General McDowell along with his staff entered Colonel Ambrose Burnside's camp where they were joined by William Sprague, the governor of Rhode Island, who presumably had come to encourage those from his state now in the ranks. The men formed a line and were ordered to attention. The expectation was that the army would advance at six o'clock that evening. However, after a brief council of war, it was decided that several key preparations were yet to be completed, and the advance was postponed until the middle of the night.[4] In honor of the high-ranking military officials and governmental dignitaries present, Burnside's brigade was put through a formal dress parade at sunset, followed by the nightly religious services, which, as always, ended with the singing of the Doxology.[5]

Before disbanding, the men were instructed to stay with their company that night, in order to be ready to march at a moment's notice. A little later, just before the tattoo roll call that told them it was time to turn in for the night, the men were informed that they would probably move out at daybreak; they rolled out their blankets and oilcloths and settled down for the short rest that would be allowed them.[6]

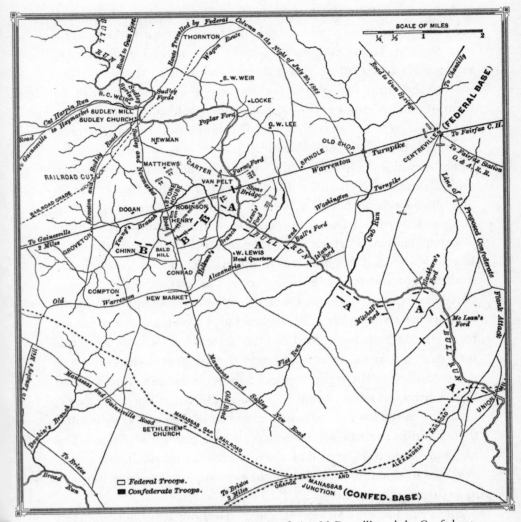

First Battle of Bull Run: The strategic situation facing McDowell's and the Confederate armies on the night of July 2o–21, 1861. *Courtesy of Library of Congress, Online Map Collection (Civil War Maps), Call No.: G3884.M25S5 1861 .S7 CW 571.*

The divisional and brigade commanders, meanwhile, assembled at General McDowell's headquarters at 10:00 P.M. to receive their orders for the next day's operations.[7] The army was to set off at 2:30 A.M. The plan that was unveiled could be characterized as a type of angled "pincer movement." One part of the Union army would swing to the right to pin down the left of the Confederate line, while the remainder went around the pinning force and outflanked the enemy position. To this end, three brigades in General Tyler's First Division were to set off at 2:30 A.M. and move along the Warrenton road to the Stone Bridge. Here, they were to conduct a feint in the form of a heavy cannonade that hopefully would convince the Confederate defenders that this was the main point of the attack. Colonel I. B. Richardson's Fourth Brigade had been temporarily assigned to Colonel Dixon S. Miles's Fifth Division. It also was to conduct a "false attack" (feint) at Blackburn's Ford, while the remainder of Miles's Division would serve as a reserve at Centreville.[8] At the same time, Colonel David Hunter's Second Division, consisting of Colonel Andrew Porter's First Brigade and Colonel Ambrose E. Burnside's Second Brigade, was to march to Cub Run, where it was to turn right and cross the stream above the ford at Sudley Springs. Once across, with Captain Daniel P. Woodbury's engineers in the lead, it was to expand the bridgehead and sweep away any enemy force guarding the lower ford and the bridge on its left. Its objectives now met, it was finally to make way for the next division by once again turning to the right. Colonel Samuel P. Heintzelman's Third Division was to follow behind the Second Division but was to cross Cub Run at the lower ford now secured by the Second Division and then position itself between the stream and Second Division.[9] The night march and the arrival on the intended battlefield at dawn were designed to avoid fighting during the hottest part of the day, as much as to surprise the enemy.[10]

Such was General McDowell's plan. To those at his headquarters that night, it seemed both logical and doable.

THE MARCH

For most, the time for morning assembly and roll call came all too quickly. Albert Sholes of the First Rhode Island Detached Militia would complain in his memoirs that he didn't even have time for the

First Battle of Bull Run: Confederate and Union troop positions during the early stages of the First Battle of Bull Run. Map also shows the terrain McDowell's army had to cross to enter the battlefield. *Courtesy of Library of Congress, Online Map Collection (Civil War Maps), Call No.: G3884.M25S5 1862 .B6 Vault : CW 562.3.*

traditional forty winks before he and his comrades were rudely awakened with the cry "Fall in."[11] According to Charles Clarke of the same regiment, this occurred around 2:00 A.M. Though no one had got a good night's rest, the men nevertheless responded with alacrity and formed into line before the "bugle notes had ceased reverberating among the Virginia hills."[12] On a normal day, before setting off on a long march, the men would have been given time to boil water and drink some coffee, if not eat breakfast. McDowell's plan demanded great expedition and there was no time for even the smallest amenity;[13] their only solace was the hope that along the way they would be able to consume the ration of crackers and canteen full of water they carried.[14] Burnside's brigade was at the head of the divisional column. It managed to set off at the exact time prescribed by general orders (2:30 A.M.) and followed the Warrenton Turnpike leading through Centreville. Colonel John S. Slocum's Second Rhode Island Infantry marched in front. It was followed by Captain Woodbury's engineers guarding a wagon that carried the much-needed pioneer supplies—shovels, axes, and entrenching tools.[15] Next came Captain William H. Reynolds's battery, the First Regiment Rhode Island Detached Militia, the Second New Hampshire Infantry, and the Seventy-first New York Infantry and their howitzers, in that order. Colonel Andrew Porter's First Brigade formed the rear half of the divisional column.[16] Captain Reynolds's artillery, a battery of James 12-pounders, at that stage of the war was attached to the Second Rhode Island Regiment, though it would be detached after the battle and become Battery A, First Rhode Island Light Artillery.[17]

Despite the size of the force, all that could be heard was the tramping of feet, occasionally punctuated by officers giving orders in subdued voices. Augustus Woodbury, the chaplain of the First Rhode Island and one of Burnside's aides-de-camp, remembered that the moon was setting over the hills in the west and there was a cool wind blowing that night. The stars glimmered overhead. Around them could be seen the "lurid light" of campfires in the just abandoned camps, while the baggage wagons and ambulances moving with the column produced a ghostly appearance that suggested "anything but pleasant thoughts."[18]

Nevertheless, overall the men's spirits remained buoyant. There were even those who had rushed to the roll call that morning who had been exempt from active duty. Theodore W. King, for example, had been ill and confined to the hospital for several days. Unexpectedly joining the ranks, he told his comrades in the First Rhode Island, "that if there was any fighting to be done, his place was with Company F." This proved to be a fateful decision. A few hours later, around noon, the young man lay mortally wounded on the field of battle.[19]

For those in Hunter's Second Division, all went well at first and the men continued to march without interruption for the first two miles.[20] Unfortunately, as they approached Centreville, Burnside's men ran into a bottleneck. McDowell's plan had called for Tyler's First Division to occupy the head of the column. The Second and Third Divisions were forced to halt and wait for Tyler's command to advance onto the road in front of them to assume the lead. The troops at the front of Tyler's column appear to have been the last to get into march formation, and so the entire division had to remain stationary until the front of the column was ready to move forward. The delay was greatest for the troops farther back in the column. Officers in the Second Division reported a wait of between one and two hours, while Colonel Heintzelman and his Third Division experienced a three-hour delay.[21]

Finally, the entire army was ready to resume the advance that it was hoped would take the rebellious foe completely by surprise and greatly mitigate the amount of deadly face-to-face fighting needed to achieve the great victory that would restore the Union. The Union force advanced in three parallel columns, the central one following the road, the other two marching in the fields on either side.[22] The road was narrow and rough, with frequent hills. These were sufficiently steep that Reynolds's artillerymen had to chain the gun carriage wheels to prevent the guns from getting loose. Veterans would later recollect passing a few discernable milestones, such as passing through Centreville or crossing over an unstable bridge that spanned Cub Run. Unfortunately, this structure had been designed to withstand much more modest loads. As the column proceeded overhead, groups of infantrymen were seen at work shoring up the structure. Some even helped prop up the slats covering the roadway with their bare hands.[23] Given the weight of the guns, the artillerymen had to be particularly careful.[24] Only one piece was allowed on the bridge at a time. Charles Clarke, ever observant, noted the time was now 5:30 A.M.[25]

It is not clear exactly how much earlier the Second Division passed through Centreville. A few memoirists say they passed through the town "at day break"; others claim it was before dawn.[26] Albert Sholes would write "dawn found us in the midst of a forest, such as few if any of us had ever before seen." The expansive, imposing forest that Private Sholes referred to lay to the north/northeast of the Warrington Turnpike. Two or three miles beyond Centreville, and just a little way past the bridge over Cub Run, there was a fork in the road with a small building. It was here that Tyler and his division parted company with the remainder of the long column. Tyler's force continued for one or two miles along the main road until they reached the Stone Bridge, where his infantry brigades deployed and the artillery unlimbered. The Second and Third Divisions veered to the right at the fork along a country road that led into the foreboding forest. Colonel Oliver O. Howard's brigade in the Third Division halted and remained near the fork in the road. Its role was to serve as a reserve. McDowell arrived in a carriage and established a temporary command post at the small building, remaining there until the column had passed.[27]

The forest was but a momentary obstacle, and the men in Burnside's brigade soon found themselves in a large, open clearing. It was here that the nocturnal portion of the operations finally came to an end as the first rays of sun began to peep over the horizon. Although the troops could now see where they were going, the next leg of the march would prove even more difficult and tiring than the first. Companies K and F of the Second Rhode Island and the carabineer company of the First Rhode Island were thrown out as skirmishers. Some of these at the side of the column acted as "flankers," their role to warn the column of an unexpected flank attack.[28] The men continued to be focused upon the task at hand and their likely fate. As when they had first set off, there was still little or no talking among the ranks. Every man quietly followed his file leader.[29] The silence, however, was finally broken at 6:30 A.M. when two distinct reports from a 30-pounder Parrott gun in Ayres's or Carlisle's battery sent McDowell the prearranged signal. The men breathed a little easier; Tyler's First Division was finally in position and ready to begin its part in the upcoming battle.[30] Moments passed, yet there was no response from the enemy; the nocturnal attempt at surprise just might have worked!

A keen observer might have noticed a seemingly trivial occurrence, one, however, that did not augur well for the Union's fortunes that day. The column's movement had been assisted by a civilian guide riding a gray horse. Suspiciously, this personage abruptly disappeared as soon as Tyler's guns were heard, never to be seen or heard of again![31]

The pathway, which General Beauregard in his own report conceded to be a "tortuous, narrow trace of a rarely-used road," soon meandered back into the forest and the long columns were again confined to the narrow country road.[32] The arboreal pathway had long ago been abandoned. Branches, and even entire trees, had fallen across the path, never to be cleared. Time after time, the column's progress came to a momentary halt as Burnside's men removed the obstacles. When walking alone or in a small group, four miles does not appear much of a challenge. However, when one is part of an immeasurably larger force of thousands of men, forced to stop and start, stop and start, as the ad hoc "pioneers" cleared the way or small bands of skirmishers were sent out to reconnoiter, this seemingly simple task grows immeasurably more difficult and correspondingly fatiguing. The stop-and-go action, coupled with the periodic frenetic activity to clear the way, soon exhausted the citizen soldiers, unused to rigors of actual campaigning. Scores of men dropped by the wayside to nibble at whatever they had in their haversacks or take a short nap.[33]

It was slow going, and it took several hours to proceed a mere two or three miles through the forest. However, by 9:15 A.M. the front of the column had finally regained open ground. Thomas M. Aldrich, who served with Reynolds's artillery battery attached to the Second Rhode Island, remembered the sensation he felt that moment:

> Then it was an inspiring sight, for, as far as the eye could see, it was a level plain with wheat, corn, and all kinds of farm produce which is raised in abundance in that fertile section of country.[34]

As the men passed some "fine looking" farmhouses, the occupants came outside garbed in their "Sunday apparel" to glower at the Yankee invaders.[35] Private Charles Clarke later recalled one woman who was particularly venomous. As his section of the First Rhode Island passed by, she yelled that the Rebel force was ready for them and she hoped that they would "all be killed before night."[36] The men had neither inclination nor time to reply. It was at just about this point that the road finally swung to the left, toward the intended battlefield. A half-hour's march brought Hunter's force to their first objective: the ford near Sudley Church.[37] As they approached the crossing the men's spirits, despite their obvious fatigue, were still buoyant. After all, nothing so far had been heard of their rebellious foe, whom they hoped had been fooled. A rumor quickly spread through the ranks: the night march had been successful and the enemy had withdrawn, all accomplished with no fighting or bloodshed.

These hopes vanished in a heartbeat. Just as the lead elements of Hunter's column approached the ford, between 9:30 and 10:00 A.M., Tyler's guns could be heard firing in the distance for fifteen to twenty minutes, this time in seeming anger.[38]

The morning waxed hot, and by the time General Hunter's column reached the stream near Sudley Springs, the men had been on the march for seven and a half hours. The sight of the pure, cool water proved irresistible to the novice troops. Without orders, the men broke ranks and rushed into the knee-deep stream to fill their canteens or quench their thirst with a cup or two of water.[39] Horses were unharnessed from the artillery limbers and allowed to drink. The number of men was vastly greater than could be supported by the tiny rivulet and within two minutes the pristine waterway had been transformed into a veritable mud puddle. Everywhere was chaos, as officers and NCOs extolled, coerced, and shoved their men back into marching formation, and it was some time before the stream was crossed and the column once again set off to outflank the Confederate force.[40]

In the midst of this confusion General McDowell and his staff arrived. Unfortunately, all was not well. It required little military acumen to realize that the Union army unexpectedly found itself in a potentially critical situation. There were now telltale signs that the Confederates had not retreated, but, on the contrary, were reacting aggressively to the Union attempt to outmaneuver their left flank. First, there was the distant but continuous booming of Tyler's artillery, indicating a stiff fight was taking place at the Red House Ford. Much more ominous were several large clouds of dust along the left portion of the skyline, which suggested the approach of a large body of Confederates. It was clear that McDowell's plan to surprise and roll up the Confederate flank had failed and that it would now be necessary to achieve by feat of arms what it had been hoped to achieve by stratagem.

McDowell's plan had been based upon a swift sweep around the Confederates' left flank. The force crossing the Catharpin Run (a.k.a. Little Bull Run) at the "lower ford" near Sudley Springs had to be in position early in the morning to give the enemy little time to react. In his report after the battle, McDowell singled out two main reasons why his army had been unable to surprise the enemy. The first and most obvious problem was that the debacle near Centreville had destroyed the original timetable. The problem was compounded by the Union failure to reconnoiter adequately the land and roads over which the men had to pass while carrying out the plan. McDowell admitted they had underestimated the distance between where they turned off the Warrenton Pike and the upper ford over Bull Run. The meandering path of the stream also worked against the Union designs.[41] The military engineers and cartographers had thought there was a secondary road that turned off the road that ran through the forest and led directly to the lower ford over Bull Run. Unfortunately, as it turned out, this road did not exist and was the product either of country legend or intentional misinformation on the part of secessionists.[42]

The failure of the Union troops to meet McDowell's schedule, however, must be ascribed to a much more basic and pervasive deficiency than inadequate reconnaissance or inexperienced cartographers. The Union command failed to appreciate how the troops' inexperience—that of both officers and men—would affect every aspect of military operations, and hence neglected to factor this into their plan of operations.

McDowell's proposed grand tactics were based on grand tactical elements first introduced by the Prussians during the Seven Years War (1756–1763) and by the French army during the Napoleonic Wars, and popularized among contemporary military establishments by Baron de Jomini and his American protégé Henry W. Halleck. Drawing upon the experience of near continuous fighting during the 1740s, by the start of the next round of hostilities in 1756, Frederick the Great had devised a method to overpower an enemy by quickly attacking its flank. Utilizing a new, faster maneuvering system, his infantry was able to work its way expeditiously around the enemy's flank in a long but narrow column and very quickly reform line before the opponent had time to take effective countermeasures. More than fifty years later, no longer fettered by a monarchical worldview with the restrictions it placed upon command structure, the French learned that delegation of command to divisional and corps commanders allowed much greater grand tactical flexibility, and it was these heightened capabilities that contributed toward some of Napoleon's greatest victories, such as Austerlitz (December 2, 1805) and Auerstadt (October 14, 1806). Although still strictly bound to follow the commander in chief's plans and orders, subordinate commanders in the new "Napoleonic system" were afforded greater latitude in how their portion of the overall plan was implemented. McDowell's plan of attack was based upon these two qualities: the quick flank attack and the use of discrete division-size forces.

The problem is that the period of relative peace that followed the Napoleonic Wars bred the type of mannerist thinking that naturally asserts itself when the tacticians' theories are left unchecked by the stark realities of actual combat. Gradually, the focus becomes more and more theoretical; the maneuver elements and concomitant grand tactics increasingly complex. Those instructing and nurturing the next generation of officers enthusiastically follow these ratiocinations and, should war break out, unconsciously believe that it is merely a matter of applying these theories on the first battlefield to be encountered. Little thought is given to the level of experience and capabilities of those up and down the chain of command, from the commander's staff and immediate subordinates down to the lowly NCOs. McDowell's plan, although theoretically sound, called for recruits that had been called to service one or two months before to implement what Prussian infantry under Frederick the Great had taken *sixteen years* to master.

A CONFEDERATE RESPONSE

Whether because of Tyler's delay in setting off in the middle of the night, or because the hill upon which the Confederate left was anchored afforded an excellent view of the countryside over which the Union columns had to pass, the Union attempt to outflank the defenders unnoticed was doomed to failure. Much of the credit for thwarting McDowell's stratagem, nevertheless, belongs to two men: Colonel Nathan G. Evans, who commanded the Seventh Brigade of the Confederate Army of the Potomac (later the First Corps), and Captain Edwin Porter Alexander, Chief Signal Officer, who at that point was positioned atop Vanpelt Hill, just north of the Warrenton Turnpike.[43]

Colonel Evans was charged with defending the Stone Bridge across Bull Run. Sometime before 6:00 A.M. the colonel, from his elevated position, became aware of Union activity in his front. He had positioned his small force on the reverse side of the crest of a hill overlooking the rivulet at that point, so the Union shelling had no effect on his troops However, the sheer number of skirmishers thrown out by General Tyler posed a more serious threat. Evans responded by covering his front with two flank companies of Colonel J. B. E. Sloan's Fourth South Carolina Infantry Regiment and one company of Major C. R. Wheat's Special Battalion Louisiana Volunteers, the latter dressed in zouave garb. Despite the lengthy fusillade that ensued, by somewhere between 8:15 and 8:30 A.M., Evans had divined Union intentions. Tyler's motions were but a weak feint, and an ineptly delivered one at that. The real threat would come farther to the left and rear from a force crossing the Catharpin Run near Sudley Springs. Realizing that there were no other Confederate forces in the area to counter these Union designs, and that there was no time to lose, Evans decided to reposition six companies of the Fourth South Carolina and five companies of Wheat's Louisiana Battalion, as well as the two 6-pounders of Latham's battery that had been temporarily assigned to his command. Four companies of the Fourth were left behind to deal with Tyler's seemingly innocuous threat.

Initially, Evans believed the Union forces moving through Sudley Springs were making a wide circular movement to place themselves deep in the Confederate central rear. Accordingly, he deployed his small force on the Brentsville Road about four hundred yards beyond the Pittsylvania (Carter) mansion. However, he quickly, and rightfully, concluded that the Union column was making a much tighter turn to attack the immediate rear of the Confederate left flank. Colonel Sloan was forced to move the Fourth South Carolina a second time, three-quarters of a mile over open fields toward the Manassas road that leads out of Sudley Church. Sometime between 9:00 and 9:30 A.M., Evans arrived in the general location where he would soon engage Burnside's brigade, and it was the dust clouds thrown up by this movement that McDowell and his officers noticed as Hunter's division approached the ford at Sudley Springs.[44] The Fourth South Carolina was placed in a ravine along the Brentsville road, two hundred yards behind a small rectangular-shaped grove of wood. Wheat's battalion and one company of cavalry were positioned to the Fourth's right.[45] Two 6-pounders supporting the two battalions were placed on nearby elevations, one close to the rear of Sloan's men, the other seven hundred yards behind the Louisianans.[46] As a precaution, skirmishers were thrown out onto the hill on the other side of the wood in front of Sloan's Regiment.

Although Evans and his men had been aware of the Union threat since sunrise, it was almost two hours before the Confederate command was appraised of the unfolding situation. Generals Beauregard and Joseph E. Johnston had positioned themselves atop a "commanding hill" to the rear of General Bonham's left. Around 9:00 A.M. Captain Alexander rushed up to the generals to report that Union forces were crossing Bull Run two miles above the Stone Bridge. As proof, he pointed to a large cloud of dust thrown up in that direction. Beauregard responded immediately by ordering Brigadier General B. E. Bee and Colonel Thomas Jackson to move their commands to the threatened flank.[47]

To evaluate the nature of the threat personally and ascertain the lay of the land, General Bee rode to the extreme left of the Confederate position, where he encountered Colonel Evans and his two regiments. He felt that Evans's small force was too isolated and advised Evans to pull his brigade back across Young's Branch, where a much larger force would be assembling.[48] Determined to hold his current position, Evans refused the advice. Bee decided not to abandon Evans, but to bring in a portion of his own command as reinforcements. Bee ordered the Fourth Alabama, the Second Mississippi, and the Eleventh Mississippi Infantry Regiments to join Evans's men.[49]

Though initially surprised and forced to react quickly, Evans and then Bee had funneled enough troops to slow down the Union flanking force while additional reinforcements could be brought up.

3

Burnside's Fight:
The Struggle for Matthews Hill

*B*urnside's four regiments were assigned to Colonel Andrew Porter's Second Division. According to McDowell's plan, Porter's command was to have conducted a flanking movement to outmaneuver the defenders on the left of the Confederate line. Though the Union army failed to surprise the Rebels, as chance would have it, Burnside's men were destined to participate in the first close-range fighting that day and would be one of the few Union organizations that could boast that it had "covered itself with glory" on that hot and sanguinary July day.

PRELUDE TO BATTLE

On his part, McDowell was not slow to realize the significance of the approaching dust clouds. Fearing that Hunter's column would be surprised before the entire division could cross the stream and shake itself out into a fighting formation, McDowell ordered his subordinates to redouble their efforts to restore order and get the men across as quickly as possible. Even then, the danger of surprise and encirclement continued to exist. After reforming, in conformance to the original general orders, Hunter's division, still in route column, followed the road leading south of Sudley Springs. For about a mile the road passed through an oak forest. To the left of the road was "thickly wooded," while the ground to the right alternated between open fields and woods. About a mile from the ford, the ground opened up and for another mile there were large rolling fields all the way to the Warrenton Turnpike.[1]

Of course, columns of route possess little defensive capabilities and are easily enfiladed (taken in flank). McDowell sent aides to instruct brigade commanders to break out of the large column, advance separately from one another, and deploy into line as necessary.[2] Responding to McDowell's latest instructions, the Second Rhode Island Regiment at the front of the column threw out two companies of skirmishers and inclined slightly to the left to break away from the main column while still skirting the edge of the oak forest. All the while, Captain Reynolds's artillery, forced to continue along the road, followed the infantry as closely as possible.

Working their way along the road through the woods, the Second Rhode Island advanced about a mile. Its men still exhibited no sense of immediate danger, continuing to laugh, joke, and occasionally pause to pick berries. But the reality of the situation was about to hit full force. The sounds of sporadic musket fire were soon heard several hundred yards to the front. Company E, one of the two companies detached as skirmishers, had been slowly working its way through the forest on the left. At times, some of its men were as much as a half mile from the road. The company finally reached a cornfield and, now in open terrain, was soon spotted and fired upon by Confederate skirmishers from the Fourth South Carolina who were hiding in a small wood in the middle of the field atop a promontory, known locally as Matthews Hill. Relatively isolated, Company E delivered fire three times while it waited to be reinforced by the other skirmisher company, a quarter mile distant.[3]

Seemingly unperturbed by the approaching tempest, the main body of Burnside's column continued to advance. However, not yet hardened by the rigors of constant campaigning, the inexperienced troops lacked the stamina that their counterparts would enjoy later in the war. Despite their calm demeanor, the men were played out after the morning's long march, and when the front of the column reached a stony road and large huckleberry field on its left front a short rest was ordered. The officers and artillerymen dismounted while many infantrymen threw themselves on the ground. The spot chosen for the short respite, however, was not a fortunate one. Burnside's column was now in the open and hence observable; no sooner had the men begun to relax, than they became the next targets of the Confederates' ire. As if to emphasize the Rebels' determination to protect their left flank, Imboden's battery far away on the right simultaneously joined in.

Elisha Hunt Rhodes, who served with the Second Rhode Island, would later remember his astonishment as the crackling of musketry was heard in the distance, followed a few seconds later by a "whir of bullets" (in reality musket balls; Confederate infantry at this point carried smoothbore muskets) in the branches overhead.[4] Not everybody shared Rhodes's sense of wonderment, and driven by an instinct for survival, most of those still standing unceremoniously joined their comrades already on the ground. Hearing "a cracking of guns and singing of bullets," artilleryman Thomas Aldrich ran up to his lieutenant, William B. Weeden, to inform him that the "pickets" were being driven in. While penning a history of the battery years later, Aldrich admitted because of his "ignorance of warfare" at first he thought this novel experience to be "fun." Weeden, however, was all too aware of the gravity of the situation.

Incidentally, we are indebted to Lieutenant Weeden for noting the exact moment when the main action started on this part of the field. Concluding the short verbal exchange with Aldrich, the lieutenant calmly drew out his pocket watch and noted that it was ten minutes past ten.[5]

The Confederate artillery fired high and shot and shell sailed far over the heads of their intended victims into the woods behind, doing no harm other than unnerving the martial neophytes below.[6] The surprise and resulting paralysis that had gripped most of the men was momentary, however. During the morning's march, Company F of the Second Rhode Island had been serving as the brigade's advance guard. As soon as he heard skirmishers firing on the left, Colonel Hunter rode up to Company F and yelled, "Advance, company front, and let them have it." Company F and the company of skirmishers that had been advancing to the right of the road immediately set off to where Company E was engaging a much larger body of Confederate skirmishers. In a letter written home two days after the battle, Lieutenant Shaw recorded what happened next. They had not marched far when they neared Company E's position and were fired upon by the enemy. The advancing skirmishers stopped, returned fire, and then *à la zouave* fell on their stomachs to reload quickly. This method of loading was the famous French chasseur and zouave practice popularized by Ellsworth's Chicago Cadets during their tour of eastern cities in 1859.

While Hunter's skirmishers were still prone and frantically trying to reload, the Rebels unleashed another volley, but this wave of missiles zipped harmlessly overhead. Having reloaded their weapons, the Union skirmishers jumped up and ran forward. Intimidated by the attackers' determination, the South Carolinian skirmishers chose not to stay and retired quickly up and over the crest of the hill. Following closely, the Union skirmish line ran to the crest, and in the way of offering a bon voyage delivered one last volley. Experienced military men had long recognized that this type of fire, i.e., firing at the backs of the fleeing foe, was always the deadliest. If we are to believe Lieutenant Shaw, "There was one dead for every shot fired."[7] The Rhode

Island skirmishers had succeeded in pushing back the Confederate skirmishers, the first line of defense.

The Battle Begins in Earnest

Just as the Union skirmishers began moving forward, General Burnside received instructions to send the remainder of the Second Regiment forward into the open cornfield to engage the enemy head-on. Not only was this in strict conformity with McDowell's orders to advance and deploy separately, it followed accepted grand tactical doctrine of the time. A hundred years earlier, massive European armies would spend hours stretching themselves across the battlefield before closing in upon one another. Contrary to received wisdom, the French infantry during the late Revolutionary and then the Napoleonic era frequently fought *en bataille,* i.e., in line. However, these were no longer the ultra-wide lines of the linear period, but rather division-, brigade-, even regiment-size lines, according to circumstances and a commander's preference.[8] It was feasible for a French infantry brigade to deploy and then fight as an isolated line with wide gaps on either side, because there was a nearby reserve that could be called up to close these gaps, if required. After 1815, this practice spread to virtually all other European-style armies, and it was this grand tactical concept that guided McDowell and his subordinates as they attempted to shake themselves out of column in front of Matthews Hill.

It fell upon Colonel Slocum, commander of the Second Rhode Island, to implement Burnside's orders. Slocum did not hesitate and gave the order: "By the left flank—MARCH!" The Second Rhode Island responded with instinctive celerity and unison; everyone threw off their blankets and haversacks and set off toward the open field on the left. But first, they had to clear a rail fence on the road's embankment. Much to the amusement of those around, a soldier named Webb clumsily fell off, breaking his bayonet. The life and death aspect of the impending struggle still had not sunk in.[9] Unnoticed,

Burnside's brigade suffered its first fatality. William McCann, Company K of the Second Rhode Island, was struck in the head by a shell fragment and died within a few minutes.[10]

According to Reverend Augustus Woodbury, one of Burnside's aides, Hunter then committed a grand tactical error that stymied his division's efforts to punch quickly through Evans's defensive position on the other side of Matthews Hill. After the battle, Burnside's men would complain that they had been vastly outnumbered, contending with thousands of Rebels. Although a gross exaggeration, it is true that as the Second Rhode Island advanced unsupported up Matthews Hill, it did initially face superior numbers. Faced with two isolated regiments, all or most of one brigade in Hunter's division should quickly have deployed and assaulted the position as the remainder was fed into the fight as needed, or better still, worked its way around the open flanks on either side of the defender's position. The four regiments in Burnside's brigade should have started to deploy simultaneously using a method sometimes referred to as the "adjutant's walk." Instead of each regiment moving into its position in line, one regiment following the other, they instead would fan out and march directly and separately to where they were to form line. This method of forming line from column received its name because in the days when armies deployed in line only after marching processionally across the battlefield, the adjutants left their regiment and took a more direct route following the hypotenuse of the triangle.[11]

Unfortunately for the attackers, Burnside was directed not to bring up the remainder of his brigade, but to position his other regiments as "formations of waiting" in an open field on the right of the road. This was to allow Colonel Porter's brigade to pass by and advance to where the Second Rhode Island was now fighting Evans's command. Now, from a purely military scientific perspective, this makes *absolutely no sense,* since it called for most of the troops at the head of the column to function as a reserve, while the main thrust of the attack was to be delivered by troops in the rear, thus needlessly increasing the time required to get into position. One possible explanation is that Hunter may have had a better relationship with

Colonel Porter, and sensing that this might be the key engagement of the battle, where the most recognition could be earned, he wanted Porter to garner the lion's share of the glory.

Regardless of the merits of the plan and what motivated General Hunter to adopt it, for some inexplicable reason Colonel Porter simply deployed his brigade in the rear of Burnside's men.[12] Adhering to Hunter's orders, the First Rhode Island, the Seventy-first New York, and the Second New Hampshire moved forward to the right of the road. However, finding themselves on the receiving end of galling long-range artillery fire, the regiments were temporarily positioned in a grove in a futile effort to find protective cover. The effect of this grand tactical miscalculation went beyond simply denying Burnside sufficient strength to deliver a quick aggressive assault, or force Evans's men out of their position by a swift flanking maneuver. It would, as we shall see, also affect how some of Burnside's men later conducted themselves under fire.

As if punishing incompetence, fate inflicted the first notable Union casualty. Within moments of riding to the front to superintend the movements of the skirmish line, General Hunter was struck by small arms fire. Despite the pain and disorientation, Hunter maintained sufficient presence of mind to delegate authority. By military protocol, Colonel Porter as commander of the division's First Brigade was next in command, but he was with his brigade in the column behind and thus momentarily unavailable to supervise the forces on the front line. Hunter was forced, therefore, to transfer command to Colonel Burnside, who was nearby.[13]

The main body of the Second Rhode Island, now in line, quickly advanced southward across the open field and up the gentle incline forming Matthews Hill. Although memoirists have left many descriptions of this part of the battlefield, most accounts conflict regarding details such as how far the cornfield extended to the woods on the southern side of the hill.[14] Fortunately, in the days following the battle, John C. Reed of the Eighth Georgia Infantry carefully studied the land, digging out bullets from the trees and measuring the distance between one terrain feature and another. The descriptions found in his journal, coupled with that provided by Gustavus J. Orr, also of the Eighth, allow one to piece together an accurate picture of the nearby landscape. At the top of the hill on the left stood the Matthews House. There were also several smaller outlying buildings, more or less in a line parallel to the woods on the far side of the hill. There was a long fence and a shallow drainage ditch[15] that ran across the top of the hill for several hundred yards. There was also a small icehouse several yards on the other side (i.e., south) of the fence. Here, the hill sloped gently down to a small wood about 125 yards away. These rectangular-shaped woods were directly beyond the Matthews House and about 110 yards wide and covered about three acres. There was a sixty-yard clearing on its right, then a series of smaller woods and thickets extending several hundred yards as one moved farther in that direction.[16] There was a deep valley in back of the woods and then another large hill, on top of which was a Confederate battery.[17]

Once pushed off Matthews Hill, the skirmishers from the Fourth South Carolina withdrew to the cover of the just described rectangular woods. Before the engagement, Evans had issued instructions that his infantry open fire as soon as Union forces approached within "musket range."[18] This term was a somewhat amorphous concept that referred to anything between one and two hundred paces, depending upon the officer who used the term. Despite this defensive fire, which was soon augmented by a Rebel artillery battery that had unlimbered about a mile away near the Lewis House, the Union attackers continued to advance up Matthews Hill in fairly good order until they reached the crest that their skirmishers had secured ten minutes earlier.[19] Looking down, the new arrivals were finally able to see their adversaries, the line of Confederate skirmishers stretched out in front of the woods.[20] Without delay, the Rhode Islanders were ordered to open fire, and, like all attackers who have temporarily had to refrain from using their weapons, they did so enthusiastically.

Up to this point, the remainder of Burnside's brigade had been consigned to the role of mere spectators. With the keen attention born of vested interest, they followed every step of the Second Rhode Island's

The Matthews House: During the fighting, Burnside's men attempted to move the injured to the relative safety of this stone dwelling. *Courtesy of Library of Congress, Prints & Photographs Online Catalog (PPOC). LC-B8184–4227.*

progress up the hill. However, the panorama quickly metamorphosed as the Second reached the crest and began firing. Thick smoke thrown up along the firing line soon engulfed the shooters and obscured the view of the terrain beyond. The rattle of small arms fire became so loud that even those in reserve could no longer hear their officers' orders. All that they could now see in front were rising white puffs of smoke on the extreme right from a Rebel battery in the distance. Any sense of detachment was momentary, however. The Rebel artillery fire, which for a few seconds appeared so innocuous, turned deadly as shot and shell started to rain down near Burnside's reserve, several hundred yards and to the right of the Second's advanced position.[21]

As soon as the Second had been set in motion, Colonel Burnside and the chief engineer galloped up to Captain Reynolds and yelled, "Forward the battery."[22] When Reynolds asked, "In what position?"

Burnside simply barked the same order, but louder.[23] The artillery-men whipped their horses, and the teams of horses and their load set off after the Second Rhode Island at the run. After ten or twelve rods, the teams came up to the fence the infantry had so tentatively scaled a few moments before. Quickly, the artillerymen tore down sections of the rail fence "amid a shower of bullets and canon balls."[24] The battery soon reached the open fields beyond; the artillery teams quickened to a "sharp gallop" and were quickly in advance and slightly to the right of the infantry they were to support. They advanced to a slight elevation in front of the woods containing Rebel forces. As the artillery teams approached the right of the intended firing line, like the Second Rhode Island before them, they were sub-jected to intense small arms fire. The Rebels apparently were firing at them as fast as humanly possible. Captain Reynolds gave the order, "Forward into line of action, front." Not surprisingly, the artillerymen precipitously unlimbered their guns; many had reacted instinctively and not waited for their officers' orders. Despite the rapidity with which the guns were brought into position, the bat-tery and its horses took casualties.[25] Off in the distance a Rebel battery joined in and the Rhode Island artillerymen had more to contend with than minié balls. The lead horse of one team was shot through the chest with solid shot, killing it instantly. Joshua Brown, the driver of another team, was shot in the thigh and through the calf by small arms fire. Preoccupied with their own survival, his comrades were unable to attend him. Though still alive, he was left on the field. A few moments later several more artillery horses were killed by an exploding shell. But the enemy artillery was the least of the Rhode Island artillerymen's problems. Not twenty yards away was a line of Rebel infantry advancing, determined to overrun the battery.[26]

Evans Counterattacks

Until the Second Rhode Island's advance, Major Wheat's battalion of Louisiana volunteers had remained behind the woods with the forward gun of Latham's artillery. However, believing there was now an opportunity to repulse the leading elements of Burnside's brigade just then moving to the top of Matthews Hill, Wheat ordered his men to advance, passing by the woods to his left. There then occurred a problem that both sides would repeatedly encounter that day, a case of mistaken identification resulting in "friendly fire." As the Louisianans left the woods they were fired upon by skirmishers. Supposing these to be Federals, they returned the favor. Major Wheat and Captain Hawthorn, who commanded the skirmishers, soon discovered the error and fortunately only two men were wounded.[27] Wheat's Louisianans resumed their advance, while the skirmishers, no longer at the front of the action, returned to Evans in the rear near the most advanced gun. Once back, they were immediately ordered to return to the front and join Wheat's assault. It was about this time that the Fourth South Carolina approached the contested field. Working their way through the small wood, its men found themselves to the left of Wheat's battalion, then marching in line up the hill. To support the attack, Colonel Sloan ordered his South Carolinians to fire by file (a "file" is a row of men standing one behind the other in the line). Unlike other types of volleys where a major part of the battalion fired at once, when firing by file, the two men in the rightmost file in the battalion fired, then the two men in the next file to the left did the same, then those in the third file. This would continue until every file had fired, then unless otherwise ordered, the men would fire individually, each according to his own whim.

The advancing Louisiana battalion, meanwhile, delivered five volleys of its own during the advance. Finding their position at the crest to have become "too hot," the Rhode Islanders retreated a short distance back to the rail fence, the men, where possible, taking advantage of the cover provided by the shallow drainage ditch. Encouraged by the enemy's retrograde motion, and realizing that the Union force on Matthews Hill would only grow stronger as reinforcements arrived, Wheat decided now was the time to act[28] and ordered his men to charge.[29] The main focus of the attack seemed to be directed against Reynolds's battery to the right of the Second Rhode Island, and it was at this point the artillerymen and horses sustained the greatest number of casualties. It was Wheat's men that the Union artillerymen saw advancing against them. The Union artillery was considerably to Wheat's left, so his regiment had to advance up the hill moving obliquely in that direction. To the Rhode Island infantry along the firing line this appeared to be the crisis of the battle, the moment of truth where one side or the other would break. Despite their inexperience, and momentary wavering here and there along the line, not only did the regiment hold, but the officers were able to get the men to rush forward in a charge. The combined effect of artillery, small arms fire, and then an abrupt charge proved too much for the small attacking force. Wheat's battalion, though managing to approach to within close musket range, at the last moment broke and its men fled precipitously back across the cornfield into the woods.[30] The volunteers from Rhode Island had passed their first test in the bloody crucible of courage.

So far, the burden of stymieing the Union flank attack had fallen exclusively on Evans's small command. But now the first of General Bee's Regiments finally arrived. Colonel E. J. Jones's Fourth Alabama had just entered the small woods when Wheat's battalion had opened fire, and reached the far side that faced the Matthews House just as the Louisianans were running back down the hill. They found themselves a little distance to the left of the Fourth South Carolina. The fleeing Louisianan battalion entered the wood between these two regiments. The Alabamians, however, had never seen a zouave uniform before and thought that the men rushing toward them were Federals. Fortunately, this time their true allegiance was determined *before* shots were fired.[31] The Alabamians now started their own advance up the hill, while the two Mississippi regiments sent by Bee remained in the series of thickets and small woods to their far left. Jones's infantrymen soon espied the heads of the advancing Rhode Islanders as the latter moved over the crest of the hill. According to Lieutenant William M. Robbins, who served in the regiment, the two sides were now only eighty yards apart. The

Second Rhode Island was the first to respond, with a sharply delivered volley, and as almost always happened when troops fired at a target at a lower elevation, the minié balls flew over the Alabamians' heads. Colonel Jones ordered his men to lie down until they could see the Union soldiers down to the waist; then they were quickly got up and unleashed their own volley in turn. If we are to believe Lieutenant Robbins's account, the Second Rhode Island then withdrew slightly to the shallow trench that ran along the northern side of the "long fence" that bounded the sloped cornfield.[32] This, incidentally, would explain an otherwise unfathomable mystery: What became of the Fourth Alabama during the lengthy firefight that ensued, why didn't it sustain as many casualties as the other Confederate troops that would soon line the edge of the woods and join the fracas, and why did it suddenly pop up seemingly from nowhere near the end of this part of the engagement? The southern slope was not flat, but undulated, and here and there were minor depressions, at the time referred to as "hollows." Because of the unevenness of the ground, the Alabamians were probably visible only from certain parts of the hilltop, and thus escaped a devastating concentrated crossfire. Their defensive position improved only when the men were prone. Taking advantage of this, Colonel Jones ordered the men to fire and reload while on the ground.

COUNTERBATTERY FIRE

Freed of the threat posed by the Louisianans, Reynolds's artillerists directed their attention to five guns of the Washington Artillery near the Lewis House, more or less to their front on the other side of the Warrenton Turnpike. Lieutenant John Albert Munroe, who served with Reynolds's battery, would contribute several articles to the journal of the Rhode Island Soldiers and Sailors Society after the war. Benefiting from the wisdom afforded by four years of campaigning, the veteran artilleryman adjudged that Captain Reynolds acted with:

a commendable promptness, but without the caution which a battery commander learns to observe only by experience. . . . [the battery] could easily have been captured and taken from the field by the enemy, before the supporting infantry were formed into line of battle; and two years later under the same circumstances, the entire battery would have been lost; but neither side hardly understood the rudiments of the art of war.[33]

In fairness to Reynolds, his aggressive behavior was probably influenced by the dominant prewar American artillery doctrine: advance boldly to within musket range of the opposing infantry and administer a rapid, destructive, and unendurable fire. Such tactics had been used very successfully by Major Thomas Jackson (who by the end of this very day earned the sobriquet "Stonewall") during the Mexican-American War, and was at this point thought to be irresistible. This probably accounts for the battery advancing considerably beyond the Second Rhode Island Infantry. Ironically, the flaws of such impetuous doctrine would be revealed only hours later by the unfortunate and inglorious fate of Griffin's and Ricketts's batteries, captured by an impulsive Confederate rush.

Unlike their grandfathers during the War of 1812, artillerymen were now equipped with shells that could be set to explode at a preset range (more or less), and it was just such shells that the Rhode Island infantry now had to endure. Some of the men seeing a haystack in front of the line thought that it would afford some protection against the noisy, noxious messengers of death. They were soon disabused of this notion, however, when a shell exploding nearby scattered the hay in all directions exposing those who had crawled underneath. Embarrassed, the men sheepishly returned to their places along the regimental line.[34] The various outlying buildings apparently offered more substantive cover, and infantrymen positioned themselves behind these during the entire engagement.[35]

Despite the incoming fire, the Rhode Island artillerymen furiously plied their trade as they tried to annihilate the Rebel battery on their right with an intensive, prolonged counterbattery fire. Munroe remembers that in their inexperience the artillerymen favored quantity over quality:

> The firing was exceedingly rapid, everyone appearing to feel that the great object was to make as much noise as possible, and get an immense quantity of iron into the enemy's line in the shortest possible space of time, without regard to whether it hit anything or not.

It was a while before they realized that they had to ascertain the effect of each round and then adjust the direction and range of each successive shot accordingly.[36] The more patient approach eventually paid off and the Confederate battery was silenced after about 250 rounds had been fired.[37]

THE SECOND RHODE ISLAND IS REINFORCED

The arrival of Reynolds's artillery did little to alleviate the Second Rhode Island's plight. Burnside realized that he was facing several regiments and that, unless further supported, the attack would bog down. A few minutes after the Second began its advance toward the hill, he ordered the Seventy-first New York Regiment to follow. The New Yorkers responded immediately, and those in Burnside's brigade still standing in reserve watched as the Seventy-first headed toward the crest of Matthews Hill. Then, inexplicably, they saw the regiment halt some distance from the crest and its men throw themselves on their stomachs. Burnside himself was surprised and disappointed; he had ordered the regiment to take its position beside the Second Rhode Island on the crest of the hill. Eyewitnesses later offered conflictingexplanations for the regiment's behavior. Several newspaper accounts appearing during the following week claimed the men in the Seventy-first were ordered to lie down on the ground. The most compelling of these appeared in the *New York Express* and was penned by one of its reporters then serving with the regiment. According to this account, Burnside himself had issued the directive for the men to lie down before they reached the top.

However, as soon as they were on the ground, one of Burnside's aides rode up and screamed for the men to rise and continue their march to the crest. Then, before they were able to get under way, this order was countermanded and they were told to resume their prone positions so that they could remain in reserve near to the firing line without needlessly exposing themselves. A few minutes later, however, a third set of orders provided a second countermand and they were once again ordered forward.[38] Private Clarke of the First Rhode Island offered a less flattering explanation. The men simply refused to advance until they were supported by the two regimental howitzers.[39]

Probably the most detailed, yet most honest explanation has been offered by Josiah Favill of the Seventy-first, whose memoirs are among the most riveting and illuminating of personal narratives penned after the great conflict. Favill recalled that as it set off, the Seventy-first came under intense artillery fire. To the reporter from the *New York Express* it seemed that about once every thirty seconds a solid shot would strike the top of the hill and either ricochet over their heads or plow into the ground before them. Favill poignantly recollected the effect of the artillery fire on the men around him:

> As we slowly ascended the rising ground, suddenly a loud screeching noise overhead sent more than half of the regiment pell-mell the other side of a fence that ran along the road side. Here we crouched down flat on our bellies, just as a shell exploded a little beyond us. It was from the rebel batteries in front, and the first any of us had ever heard, and it certainly did seem a terrible thing, rushing through the air like an immense sky rocket, then bursting into a thousand pieces, carrying death and destruction to everything in its course. The stampede was only momentary, but very funny; the boys jumped back again; in fact, almost as quickly as they had dispersed, and then stood steady in the ranks, watching the advance of the Rhode Islanders.[40]

This initial reaction to artillery was not limited to one color of uniform, and seemed to grip all those being initiated to "the ball." A mile away among the Rebels, John C. Reed would lament that hearing the deadly missiles whistle by overhead was by far "the most trying part of the day."[41]

Regardless of the reason for the snafu, Burnside's first attempt to support the Second Rhode Island had failed. In its exposed position, the regiment continued to be raked simultaneously by small arms and artillery fire for almost twenty minutes. Undaunted, Colonel Burnside next ordered forward the First Rhode Island. Although held in reserve, the First regiment had already undergone its own baptism of fire as enemy shot whizzed around them as they anxiously waited to be brought into action. One round struck just in front of the first platoon; another just in front of Company C, showering the men with dirt.[42] Enemy shot and shell started to rake the treetops, and branches and tree limbs started to rain down on the men below. In a letter written home after the battle, one member of the regiment recalled what it was like to endure the inactivity while in the rear:

> This was the most trying time of all; this forced inaction, while our men were dropping here and there, mangled and dying, was dreadful. This was the moment which, more than any other one, no matter how furious the conflict, puts a man's nerve to the test. The sight of the first dead man, especially if he be one of your own, causes a sickening feeling, not experienced afterwards on the field covered with the wrecks of war.[43]

In his own letter, William Rhodes Arnold, another soldier in the First, also commented upon the general sense of trepidation rippling through the ranks at that point. Struggling to control their own fears, most of the men looked around in astonishment to seek some token of reassurance from their comrades. Arnold remembers his impressions as he looked around at that moment: "many a pale face you see a firm lip and a determination of character which plainer than words [means] we will not flinch when the hour of trial comes, and so it proved."

Before advancing, the men in the First Rhode Island were ordered to unsling their blankets and haversacks and place them on the ground. Despite any misgivings, the regiment marched forward through pastures and over fences. The enemy artillery fire seemed to intensify as they approached one such rail fence shattered to pieces in many places by round shot. Here, they saw Major Sullivan Ballou of the Second Rhode Island lying mortally wounded. One of the men in Company C was knocked out of the ranks by a round shot, but amazingly was not seriously injured. The sound of minié balls whizzing overhead and the increasing presence of small dust puffs rising a few inches from the ground told the men they were now within enemy musket range.[44] The term "musket range" is applicable here in the most literal sense since the great majority of Confederate infantry at this early stage of the war were armed with smoothbores.

The First Rhode Island kept advancing in column. As soon as it had gained the top of the hill, the order "By battalion, left into line" was given and line was formed to the left. Battle line reestablished, the regiment started to move forward once more, but before advancing a hundred yards an event occurred that, though insignificant at the time, would be a source of amusement in later weeks. A single round shot struck the ground in front of the line and ricocheted over the men's heads. In his published memoirs, Albert E. Sholes averred that this shot had passed directly over his head. However, the private had to admit that "every man here today [i.e., in his regiment] will testify that it passed directly over his head, never mind whether he was on the right or left of the line." Coming up to where the men of the Seventy-first were still lying, Colonel Henry P. Martin, who commanded the First Rhode Island, shouted the orders: "Forward double quick!" followed by "Left oblique." The men obeyed reflexively, advancing quickly at an angle to the left, and in a few brief seconds had passed through the Seventy-first and had reached the brow of the hill on the side facing the enemy. The regiment was now positioned between the Second Rhode Island on its left and the Seventy-first to its right and a little to the rear.[45] One of the regiment's officers tried to calm the novice soldiers by theorizing that it took "700 pounds of lead" to kill a single soldier (actually received wisdom was that it required two hundred pounds).[46] A number of men from the various companies had been armed with Burnside breechloaders and grouped together to form a "carabineer company." Thrown out to form a regimental skirmish screen, they now returned to the regimental line. A rail fence ran perpendicularly through the regimental line, so that one half of Company F had to be placed on either side of this flimsy obstacle.[47]

Arnold estimates they were a mere seventy-five to one hundred yards away from the Confederates when the First Rhode Island delivered its first volley. Their muskets now empty, the men fell on their backs à la zouave to reload by order, i.e., by the "nine times" called for by the officially prescribed manual of arms. The fight had now become general. To obtain a better view of the enemy and more accurately assess the situation, Colonel John Slocum of the Second Rhode Island advanced beyond the firing line with its dense billows of smoke, climbed over a rail fence, and stood on the brow of Matthews Hill for several moments surveying the scene below. While retracing his steps he was struck by fragments of a shell as he was climbing back over the rail fence. Several of his men carried him to the Matthews House at the left of the Union line, where a surgeon attempted to dress his wounds. Shortly thereafter he was placed in an ambulance and taken to a field station set up for the wounded in the rear.[48] Unfortunately, he expired on an operating table, as his crushed leg was being amputated. Lieutenant Colonel Frank Wheaton assumed command of the regiment.[49]

Meanwhile, the Union infantrymen had to endure both frontal small arms fire and enfilading artillery that grew increasingly annoying. The line was pestered by the occasional shot and shell. At least once or twice a dexterous soldier was able to escape harm by cutting off the lit fuse with his bayonet before being "blown to atoms."[50] To many, the musket balls passing uncomfortably close to their heads reminded them of bees, to others they sounded like flies. A correspondent for *Scientific American* described his impressions of the sound and fury of a firefight:

You hear a drop, drop, drop, as a few of the skirmishers fire, followed by a rattle and roll, which sounds like a falling of a building, just as you heard the bricks tumble at a great fire.[51]

Most of the infantrymen coped with their anxiety by attempting to fire as fast as possible, the normal tendency when exposed to enemy fire. Of course, unless the musket had been thoroughly cleaned prior to the battle and each ball carefully pushed home, the barrels would quickly clog after a sustained fire. Elisha Rhodes remembered that his smoothbore musket became so fouled that eventually the only way he was able to push the ball to the bottom of the barrel was to hit the top of the ramrod against a fence until it was partially inserted into the barrel. Not only was this a time-consuming process, but there was also a real danger of the barrel exploding during the next shot, if the ball became stuck in the barrel. There was another problem associated with loading small arms before the advent of metallic cartridges, one that has been rarely commented upon in modern-day literature. When loading, the soldier had to bite open the paper cartridges before pouring the loose gunpowder down the barrel. According to *Scientific American,* "It was well known to all soldiers that the tearing of a cartridge with the teeth in battle causes an almost intolerable thirst." The magazine went on to recommend that the infantrymen use the edge of the bayonet to open the cartridge instead.[52]

The Seventy-first New York had faltered during its original advance, and for a time was some distance from the crest of the hill, its men thereby denied any effective targets. A renewed effort was made to bring the regiment forward and onto the firing line. It was ordered to move beyond the two Rhode Island regiments and to the right, where two pieces from Griffin's battery had advanced to support the efforts of Reynolds and his men. Unfortunately, just as the Seventy-first approached its intended line, the right artillery piece advanced hell to leather through the advancing infantry, scattering a large portion of the regimental line. Then, before order could be completely restored, the second piece followed suit, scattering the men a second time. The men in the New York regiment had finally found their mettle, however, and order was soon restored and a brisk fire opened up along the regimental line.[53]

THE EIGHTH GEORGIA INFANTRY ENTERS THE FRAY

When the size of the Union attacking force became apparent, it was obvious that still more Confederate regiments were needed to push Burnside back off Matthews Hill. General Bee sent a courier to Colonel Francis Stebbins Bartow, then near the Henry House, to ask for assistance. Without delay, Bartow personally led the Eighth Georgia toward Evans's command, about a mile to the right. The regiment filed off at the double quick. Though whenever possible the column exploited the hedgerows, thickets, and patches of woods that dotted the area, Reynolds's artillerymen almost immediately spotted the Georgians and fired shells into the protective cover around them, hoping to impede the regiment's movement. They switched to canister as soon as the Georgians approached to within 350 yards. Shot, shell, and "grape" appeared to have little effect, and the regiment continued to traverse the battery's front. However, "friendly fire" once again raised its ugly head as the Eighth, working its way through trees and hedges, approached Bee's Mississippi regiments on the left of the Confederate position in that area. Thinking that troops rushing toward them were repulsed Federals, the Mississippians naturally fired. However, once again the mistake was discovered before too much unnecessary blood was spilt. There was to be no respite for the Georgia troops, however. Burnside's infantry atop the hill had a chance to chime in as the Georgians ran across the sixty-yard clearing beside the small woods that had been the center of Burnside's attention.

Unfortunately for the newcomers, by the time they made it into what they thought would be the safety of the woods, the Seventy-first New York had recovered from its jitters and advanced into position along the hilltop to the left of the First Rhode Island.[54] Reed estimated that the Eighth Georgia needed three hundred yards

frontage to fight effectively in wooded terrain. Instead, the Georgians were cramped into a little more than one hundred yards
loosely interspersed with pine saplings too thin to offer protection
from the storm of minié balls whizzing around them. The ranks in
many places were seven or eight deep and thus perfectly visible to
the Union infantrymen who were within medium musket range.
The Rhode Island and New York men unleashed a crippling cross-
fire that seemed to hit more than five men per minute.

At this point the fight might have appeared to be a "standoff." The
Fourth South Carolina was in the wood to the left of the Georgians,
firing away at the Union line atop the hill. The Fourth Alabama was
still on the hillside, its men firing and reloading from a prone position.[55] There are conflicting accounts about what the Eighth Georgia
did next. Georgia newspapers talked proudly about how the regiment charged up the slope three times,[56] while Reed's journal has the
regiment being decimated in the woods, unable even to form up
because of the sheer volume of enemy fire.[57] There is some evidence
that at least part of the regiment did attempt to advance, but the
heavy Union small arms fire prevented it from getting past the pine
saplings that skirted the small wood.[58]

It may not have been obvious to the Confederates in the wood
below, but Burnside's men were starting to get the upper hand. The
fourth and last of Burnside's regiments finally managed to deploy
along the firing line. While waiting in reserve on the right of the
Sudley Springs Road, the attention of the Second New Hampshire
had been diverted from the struggle on its left front. Noticing some
Confederate skirmishers approaching on their right front, the New
Hampshire men were ordered to fire, and an inconclusive long-
range affair ensued. This sudden threat on the left of the Sudley
Springs Road made Burnside realize that his right flank on
Matthews Hill was also vulnerable. He therefore ordered the Sec-
ond New Hampshire to cross the road and advance to support
Reynolds's battery, which anchored the right flank of the advanced
Union line. Lieutenant Colonel Fiske, who had already worked up
a sweat striding up and down the regimental line, forcefully barked

out the orders, "Attention! Left face—double quick—MARCH!" and the regiment quickly marched to its new position.[59] It advanced up Matthews Hill and positioned itself to the right of the icehouse in front of the long fence and more or less in front of the Fourth Alabama's position on the far hill slope. According to Reed, the Second New Hampshire aggressively crossed over the long fence and deployed along the hillcrest, with its right obliquely thrust forward. Unlike the other three regiments in Burnside's brigade, the New Hampshire regiment was armed only with percussion cap, smooth-bore muskets. They did, however, fire "buck and ball."[60] When using this type of ammunition, the infantryman first loaded three buckshot and then a regular-size musket ball. At close range, the combination of buckshot and musket ball had a deadly effect on opponents in woods, and remained a popular method as long as some of the troops remained armed with smoothbores.[61] This practice, incidentally, can be traced back to the Revolutionary War and was popular among Washington's men.

Soon after the Seventy-first finally managed to get in line, the Second Rhode Island was pulled out of the line and filed to its left in an attempt to outflank the enemy's right.[62] The already deadly Union small arms fire now became more unbearable since the Confederates were being fired at from both front and right. The two companies of the Eighth Georgia, including the Oglethorpe Light Infantry Company, on the right were particularly hard hit. Colonel Gardner, standing in front of the line to dress up the ranks before ordering a charge, fell—his leg shattered by a minié ball.[63]

An event now occurred that would be reported throughout Northern papers during the weeks to come and would spark controversy and outrage. A body of men was suddenly seen approaching the First Rhode Island and the Seventy-first New York. This was the Fourth Alabama, which because of the undulating nature of the slope had been hidden from many of those along Burnside's line. As they apparently appeared out of nowhere, someone in the Seventy-first yelled something to the effect of "Don't fire on our own men." The men in both regiments immediately stopped firing and waited as the unknown regiment continued to approach. Finally, when at close musket range, these men lowered their muskets and delivered a murderous battalion volley. The color-bearer for Company G in the Seventy-first, Sergeant Charles Bercherer, fell, shot through the arm. A soldier nearby seized the colors, which he waved defiantly; however, he too received an arm wound and had to be led off the field. A third man grabbed the flag, which he carried raised with one hand throughout the remainder of the action. Bercherer was a seasoned veteran who had already fought in a European campaign. Though wounded and unable to load his weapon, he elected to stay just behind the firing line. Calmly smoking a cigar, he inspired his comrades by his demeanor under fire.[64] The defenders were momentarily stunned by the sudden volley. Here and there openings appeared in the front rank as men fell or the wounded struggled to get to the rear. The men in the rear rank stepped forward and took their place. Quickly recovering, they started to "give out more than they got." One infantryman, suddenly feeling wind pass between his legs, looked down and was surprised to see that one of his comrades was kneeling behind him and using the space between his legs as a "loophole."[65] Two regiments facing off against one, they were able to deliver a very effective cross fire, and the enemy was soon forced to fall back down the hill and into the woods.[66] One person who was not as easily deceived was the colonel of the First Rhode Island. Realizing that the approaching troops were Rebels, he ordered his men to fire, and after a few moments of hesitation, they did.

It was widely reported in the Northern press that as the unknown regiment approached the Union infantry on the hill, one of its men waved the Union flag so that the Rhode Islanders would think the newcomers were Union reinforcements. However, a combatant in Company C of the First Rhode Island provides a more honest rendition in a letter written to the *Providence Daily Journal*. There is no mention of the enemy holding up the Stars and Stripes.[67] Rather, the cry that they were firing on their own men arose in the Seventy-first, simply because the men approaching them looked as though they were fighting on the same side. As we have seen, this type of "mistaken identity" already had occurred several times that day, although it had led the Confederates to fire on their own men rather than allowing the enemy to approach unopposed. Two factors led to this confusion. At this point during the war, the Confederate troops did not have anything even vaguely resembling a standardized uniform and there was a wide assortment of military garb on the field that day. The second factor, though subtler, was probably an even greater source of confusion. The "Stars and Bars" flag carried by the Southern regiments was similar to the Stars and Stripes of the Union. The design of both consisted of stars and vertical stripes, and they utilized the same colors: red, blue, and white. At distances over two hundred yards it was difficult to distinguish them. Someone watching an approaching regiment apparently flying the Stars and Stripes would certainly be surprised as it got nearer and they saw instead the Stars and Bars. And given human nature, it is natural that they might conclude the opposing regiment had switched flags as a ruse, rather than acknowledge that they themselves had made a mistake. Confederate authorities would later recognize the problem and this led to the adoption of a new flag, referred to as the "Second National Flag."

If there was a debate about the methods the Confederates used, there was no uncertainty about the result of the attack. The men in the Seventy-first and the First New York advanced and the Fourth Alabama fled down the hill. Reinforcements now arrived on both flanks of Burnside's line. Colonel Willis A. Gorman's First Minnesota Regiment, originally slotted to support Ricketts's battery about twenty rods to the right of Reynolds's artillery, was ordered to Burnside's left instead.[68] At the same time, a battalion of regular infantry came up to the right side of Burnside's line and fired a powerful volley at the Rebels in the small woods.[69] To make matters even worse for Evans's and Bee's troops, W. T. Sherman's and E. D. Keyes's brigades had managed to cross Bull Run by a small ford to their right and rear, and were slowly working their way directly behind the advanced Confederate position.[70]

The ranking Confederate officers in the area agreed that a quick retreat was called for and their men quickly left for the rear, at first every man for himself. To distribute ammunition and give his troops a much-deserved rest, Burnside ordered most of his men to the forest that they had traversed when they first approached Matthews Hill. The Second New Hampshire Regiment was sent to support Ricketts's battery, while Reynolds's battery went to assist Porter's brigade as they picked up the fight.

To the Union soldiers who had just fought in the engagement, it appeared that the battle had been won.

THE TURNING POINT AND AFTERMATH

The men in Burnside's brigade had fought bravely. Standing up to the foe, they had exchanged fire until additional friendly forces could be brought up and make the Confederates' forward position untenable. Ultimately, however, this effort would be to no avail. Catastrophe occurred suddenly between 4:00 and 4:30 P.M. Nothing could have prepared even the most veteran Union officers from the regular army for the emotional contagion that suddenly swept through the entire right half of the Union battle line. What had been a series of regimental formations, ordered and controllable, was transformed almost instantly into a mob, as the men, no longer bound by military authority, started to walk off the battlefield. There was no panic during these first moments of the rout; that would come later on the road back to Washington City when the Confederates' belated pursuit finally caught up with the stragglers. It seems as though somehow there was an instantaneous consensus among the rank and file that the fight was over and everyone should just head back to camp. The only visible excitement was among the officers, who made every attempt to rally the men and stop the flow rearward, but their efforts proved completely futile.[71]

It seems paradoxical that troops who had fought and struggled all day, endured extreme heat and the grueling thirst that always accompanies battle, should give up so suddenly. In his *The Outbreak of the Rebellion,* John G. Nicolay attributed the dissolution of the formations to the breakdown of regimental organization as men and officers became hopelessly intermixed.[72] Nicolay's explanation, however, provides only a partial answer, for it fails to address the more basic question: what caused the formations to dissolve? Was it merely a case of lack of control by the officers, so that unchecked the infantrymen left their assigned positions in the line, thereby breaking up the cohesiveness of the formation, or were there more fundamental but less obvious forces at work undermining the men's will to fight?

The answer lies in how inexperienced troops tend to act and react under fire. Of course, if it had been possible to take a modern-style survey on July 20, the day before the battle, few of the Union military would have expressed a concern about the battle preparedness of the Union volunteers. Most of the men, after all, had spent May and June in training camps learning the foundations of their craft. But there is more to effective soldiering than proficiency in the manual of arms and ability to go from column to line, and then back into column. Esprit de corps and battle experience are two essential prerequisites to combat effectiveness. Not only has the veteran learned to draw upon the emotional bond that has been formed with his comrades, but he has developed reactions and instincts that can be acquired only from being under fire. Green troops are often more enthusiastic than those who have already "seen the elephant," as experiencing one's first battle was called. Unable to recognize hopeless or truly dangerous situations, they charge in where seasoned veterans would balk or refuse to advance. On the other hand, green troops have less flexibility, and once broken it is extraordinarily difficult, if not impossible, to rally them. Colonel B. F. Scribner of the Thirty-eighth Indiana Infantry clearly expressed this difference between raw and experienced troops:

Old soldiers when overpowered or taken at a disadvantage may yield ground; but they will keep together as if attracted to each other by a sort of moral gravitation, and will halt when threatened by missiles of the enemy. On the contrary, when raw troops become panic-stricken they cannot be rallied within the noise of battle. Not having acquired the cohesion which long association and discipline give, they will so disperse that much time and effort must be employed to collect them for further duty. But old soldiers will unconsciously reform their ranks, even as cavalry horses are said to have done when abandoned by their riders, who embarked on ships.[73]

This is exactly what happened to volunteers along the Union line late that afternoon.

Esprit de corps develops over time, and usually only after experiencing a series of trials and tribulations.

It would be a long climb upward.

TACTICAL OBSERVATION #1

The extended firefight in front of Matthews Hill had taken place at relatively close range (between eighty and one hundred yards), and three of the Union regiments in Burnside's brigade were armed with the new rifle muskets, while the fourth was equipped with smoothbores firing buck and ball—a devilish combination that maximized casualties. Over the years, much ink has been devoted to explaining how the new rifle muskets were capable of long-range fire and that firefights occurred at much greater ranges than when infantrymen had been armed exclusively with smoothbore weapons. So it is natural that many modern readers might wonder how any of the participants were able to escape unscathed after thousands and thousands of deadly missiles were exchanged during this obstinate struggle.

Burnside's Brigade at Bull Run: Burnside's command on Matthews Hill. The modern reader finds it difficult to understand why it was necessary to fight in these tight formations and why more casualties were not taken. *Courtesy of Library of Congress, Prints & Photographs Online Catalog (PPOC). LC-B8184–4227.*

There were several factors operating on the Civil War battlefield that worked against effective use of the new small arms, and greatly increased the life expectancy of the infantrymen crammed into ordered formations in full view of opponents hell bent on killing them. The first lay in the nature of the new weaponry. Minié balls fired from rifle muskets had a much lower initial muzzle velocity than musket balls fired from smoothbores. The back part of the minié balls were blown apart by the force of the exploding charge and driven against the bore's rifled walls, thus slowing the projectile down. According to ballistic pendulum tests in the 1840s and 1850s, a musket ball fired from a smoothbore initially traveled at 1,500 feet per second[74] compared to 1,115 feet per second for a minié ball fired from an Enfield rifle musket.[75] The result was that minié balls possessed a much more parabolic or "rainbow" trajectory. This didn't make much difference if firing at very close range, say, within eighty yards, but it made it much harder to hit targets at extended ranges. At longer ranges one had to compensate accurately for the rise and fall of the bullet, and elevate the barrel at exactly the correct angle—otherwise the projectile would either under- or overshoot the intended target. The early versions of both the Enfield and Springfield had back sights to assist with this task. However, one still had to adjust the elevation bar on the back sight to the right height; this required accurately estimating the range, a difficult task for all but highly trained marksmen. French trials with the Thouvenin rifle musket showed that this problem increased almost geometrically as the distance increased. For example, to hit a target 273 yards away the soldier had to adjust the back sight for between 218.5 and 306 yards, but when firing at a target 993 yards distant the back sight had to be set for a range between 986.5 and 997.25 yards.[76] In other words, the greater the range, the less room there was for miscalculation or error. Accurate range estimation was an acquired talent that required extensive training and practice, something few of the volunteers rushing into service received. It was a moot point, however. American experience during the four years of fighting would prove very similar to the British and French experience with these weapons in the Crimea and North Africa. Forced into volley fire, where the moment to fire was controlled by the officer and not the individual infantryman, very few ever used the back sight. The most conscientious soldiers would simply look along the top of the barrel; the majority, however, were content to level the weapon at more or less the right elevation. This meant that fire between opposing groups in ordered formations at long range tended to be extremely inaccurate. The firefight in front of Matthews Hill took place at much closer ranges, so range estimation would have played less of a role than if the opposing forces had been separated by, say, five to six hundred yards.

A second factor, however, would have played a very important role, for the shorter the range, the greater its significance. This was the confusion and fear engendered by battle. The smoke, dust, and turmoil, not to mention the irregularities of the ground, made the experience of battle very different from that of the target range, tending to distort both a man's judgment and his aim.[77] But, it was the very goal of combat that had the most profound impact on the soldier's consciousness and thus his capabilities to kill or be killed. In his lecture at the Royal United Service Institute in June of 1857, Lieutenant Colonel Dixon of the British army provides a compelling description of the problem:

Transfer yourself in imagination, to a country of undulating nature, broken, and interspersed with wood and water, a man not only looking to shoot, but to be shot at, hurrying as well as his adversary from one position to another, and excited by every circumstance which in battle may be considered to operate so powerfully to distort a man's judgement [sic] or his aim. . . . [T]he difference in degree of accuracy at ordinary distances of two rifled arms, bears no proportion whatever to the differences which exist in the capability of appreciating distances between two individuals.[78]

Preoccupied with the instinct of survival, most soldiers gave scant attention to the steps required to ensure accurate fire. Frequently, they were barely able to control their muscles, and many would be seen involuntarily bouncing from leg to leg as a result of their nervousness. Others would be oblivious to the events around them and, not seeing that the previous charge had failed to explode, would reload a second, then a third, fourth, fifth charge, etc., all the while thinking that they were firing at the enemy. The most common problem, however, was that many men "fired at the moon," that is, in their nervousness they pulled the trigger before the gun was leveled, let alone aimed. These shots would sail harmlessly over the enemy lines, and this explains why so many soldiers would write about hearing the "buzzing of bees overhead."

All of this had been known from the mid-eighteenth century on. The great French tactician Comte de Guibert estimated that only two shots out of a thousand actually hit an enemy soldier. This was a rather high estimate; Comte de Jean Jacques Gassendi and Guillaume Piobert, two nineteenth-century tacticians, thought that only one out of three thousand (.03 percent) hit.[79] Whether because of increased familiarity with small arms in civilian life or other cultural reasons, there is some evidence that American soldiers achieved much greater accuracy during the Mexican-American War and the Great Rebellion. A British observer noted during the Battle of Churubusco (August 20, 1847) that Mexican infantry inflicted one casualty for approximately every 800 musket rounds expended, while the American infantry were able to kill or wound a Mexican for every 125 rounds. Union military authorities came up with similar conclusions in 1863, when they estimated that during the Battle of Murfreesboro, on average, Union infantry required 145 shots to inflict one casualty.[80]

It was this phenomenon—so few casualties compared to the total number of rounds fired—that led A. P. Hill to observe after the Second Battle of Bull Run (August 29–30, 1862):

I had often thought, how it was possible for so few to be slain when there was such terrific firing. When you consider the great amount of ammunition expended in battles, the loss is insignificant in comparison.[81]

It *was exactly this that led the author of an 1863 article in the* Army and Navy Journal *to conclude:*

> *it certainly robs war of some of its presumed fatality. As I have before remarked the escape of so large a majority of the men, amid such storms sweeping and yelling around their ears, has always been the greatest mystery.*[82]

Actual battle ranges on the fields of the American Civil War, therefore, were often significantly shorter than the theoretical capabilities of the weapons involved. As the war lengthened, and the numbers of experienced veterans increased, effective battle ranges probably did as well, but not by very much. Paddy Griffith's assertion that the average range of the Civil war firefight in 1864–1865 was approximately 141 yards is at least roughly accurate.[83]

4

THE FIFTY-SEVENTH
NEW YORK INFANTRY AT FAIR OAKS

*The Fifty-seventh New York Infantry Regiment was organized in
New York City in October 1861. Arriving at a camp of instruction in
Virginia in December, it participated in General Stoneman's recon-
naissance-in-force around Manassas. The regiment was then shipped
to the York River on the Virginia peninsula and took part in the invest-
ment of Yorktown, as well as the wet and highly uncomfortable slow
advance toward the Confederate capital in May 1862. When Sumner's
division was suddenly thrown into combat to help retrieve a desperate
situation near Fair Oaks, the Fifty-seventh New York found itself at
the very crisis of the battle.*

THE SITUATION—SUMMER 1862

The year 1861 was one of defeat and humiliation for Union forces in the East. The defeat at Big Bethel (June 10) was followed by the even more embarrassing fiascos at Bull Run (July 21) and Ball's Bluff (October 21). In this theatre, the Confederate soldier seemed to be able to outfight his Northern opponent easily and at will. In response, Major General George McClellan spent the winter months of 1861–1862 building up and revitalizing Union forces in the Washington area. His initial plan for the 1862 campaign was to land the Army of the Potomac at Urbana on the lower Rappahannock River and march to Richmond via West Point on the York River. The exigencies of campaigning forced a revision of the plan of attack, however. McClellan shifted his attention to the York and James Rivers as potential bases and lines of operations. On April 2, 1862, McClellan arrived at Fortress Monroe to assume personal command of the Army of the Potomac, much of which was now concentrated at the tip of the Virginia peninsula.

Over the next month, the army's strength was gradually increased to about ninety thousand effectives. The men's daily routine was spent building field fortifications and artillery batteries in front of Yorktown and conducting reconnaissance of the Lower Peninsula. Recognizing that his forward position now faced an insuperable force and a successful defense was no longer feasible, Confederate General Joseph E. Johnston, commander of the Army of Northern Virginia, ordered his men to fall back closer to Richmond, where he planned to put up a fierce defense of the Confederate capital behind the Chickahominy River. Retiring back up the peninsula, the Confederate general occasionally retaliated with rear guard actions, such as at Williamsburg (May 5).

Tentatively, the Union army followed. This advance was not without its trials, however. Closing in upon the coveted Confederate capital proved more difficult than it might have appeared to someone who simply calculated a theoretical rate of march by applying compass to map. First, there was the terrain to be traversed. Despite the pleasant fragrance of magnolia trees in full bloom, much of the ground was deceptively treacherous and posed difficulties unforeseen by Union military planners. While not the obviously rugged mountainous and densely forested country that would later hamper the operations of Sherman's armies at the start of the Atlanta campaign, for example, much of the peninsula between the James and York Rivers consisted of insalubrious bottomlands and swamps that threatened the soldiers' health. Officers of both sides had as yet little practical experience of day-to-day campaigning. For example, despite the daily rations of quinine and whisky, many more men fell to malarial fever than would have been the case had the camps consistently been situated on higher and drier ground. Robert S. Robertson, who served with the Army of the Potomac during this period, recalls the effects of one imprudent choice of campsite:

> The ground upon which we were camped was low, and the back water of the creek, added to by heavy rains, kept us in stagnant water, and of which we could only keep dry by piling up brush for bedding. The drinking water was also bad, necessarily being taken from swamp pools, and nearly all the rank and file as well as the officers were attacked in the rear by an enemy as dangerous as that in our front, and most of us were unfit for duty, even when compelled to take the places of those who were completely disabled.[1]

There were other hidden threats. More than a few men sent out to skirmish, collect wood, or perform some other miscellaneous mission fell victim to the numerous moccasin and copperhead snakes that inhabited these marshy lands.[2] The march up the peninsula was further hampered by poor road conditions made worse by unusually heavy rains for that time of year. According to the regimental history of the Nineteenth Massachusetts Volunteer Infantry, this not only made it more difficult to march but also hampered the troops' ability to rest and regain their strength when a halt was finally ordered:

> The roads were quagmires and constantly grew worse. The march was frequently interrupted to allow columns to pass around . . . in

direct pursuit of the enemy. No sooner was the command "Forward" given than "Halt" would follow and the men would drop their pieces to the ground in disgust. It was impossible to sit down because of the mud and the water, it was irksome to stand, and as the men scuffled along in the brief periods of marching, they slid first to one side, then to the other in the mud. Wagons broke down, horses stuck in the mud, taken altogether the delay was such that in eight hours during the night, the regiment marched only one and three quarter miles. So weary were the men from exposure and the terrible march that some lay down in the mud at every halt, many of which were occasioned by the search for hidden torpedoes.[3]

Despite these tribulations, the men fighting for the Union generally remained in good spirits. Many, if not most, of the Northern men optimistically believed that the war was finally nearing its end.[4]

The Fifty-seventh New York Infantry and the Advance to Fair Oaks

Part of Major General William French's Third Brigade (First Division, Second Army Corps), the Fifty-seventh New York Volunteer Infantry Regiment had arrived on the peninsula in early April. Nicknamed the "National Guard Rifles," it had experiences and duties that were similar to other Union regiments in the area. The slow march toward Richmond had been dreary and, when the rains came, uncomfortable and fatiguing. Nevertheless, like the rest of the army, its men were doggedly optimistic. At the close of each day they were a little closer to the Rebel capital. By Saturday, May 31, they had arrived before the Chickahominy River and, with the rest of Sumner's corps, encamped near the Taylor House, about a mile from the river's northerly (left) bank. Two days earlier it had rained heavily, so the river and its surrounding banks were flooded. That morning, the men in the Fifty-seventh probably hoped for a couple of days' respite while they waited for the water levels to fall before crossing the river and resuming the inexorable march forward.

The men's mood and expectations changed abruptly around 1:00 P.M., when the roar of battle suddenly erupted in the distance. The men knew that General S. P. Heintzelman's Third Army Corps and General E. D. Keyes's Fourth Corps on the far side of the Chickahominy River were now joined in battle with General Joseph E. Johnston's of Northern Virginia and that before long they would be called to support their comrades. Reflexively, the officers in Sumner's corps ordered their men to arms to await instructions from General McClellan that were certain to come. They didn't have long to wait. Instructed by McClellan to prepare to advance to Keyes's support, General Edwin Sumner, commanding the Second Army Corps, ordered General Israel B. Richardson's First Division and General John Sedgwick's Second Division to advance to two bridges (the Upper and Lower Bridges) recently constructed over the Chickahominy, where they were to await further orders.[5] The Lower Bridge, the one closer to Richardson's division, was two miles from Savage's Station. The Upper Bridge, also known as the Grapevine Bridge, was several miles distant, directly in front of General Sedgwick's camp and three miles from Fair Oaks Station.

Though McClellan's orders to advance finally arrived about 2:30 P.M., the men in Sumner's corps soon encountered their first obstacle. The Chickahominy was an annoyance even during ideal weather conditions. Reflecting back upon his experience, Francis Winthrop Palfrey would later muse: "It was hard to say at the best of times where its banks were, and of which no man could say to-day where its banks would be tomorrow."[6] However, the flooding now had transformed the river from a mere obstacle for topographical engineers into a formidable challenge that threatened the viability of relieving Keyes's battered troops.

Part of the Lower Bridge, the one Richardson's division was to cross, had been partially swept away by the swollen river. Nevertheless, the Fifty-seventh New York and the rest of French's Third Brigade at the front of the divisional column were ordered to cross the bridge as best they could. Some of the men managed to work their way slowly across the partially collapsed structure. The Nineteenth Massachusetts

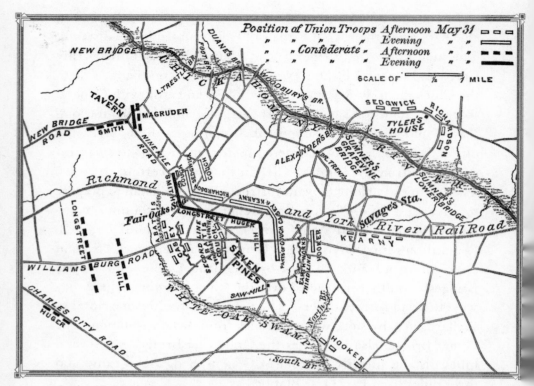

Battle of Fair Oaks: Positions of opposing armies during the first day of the Battle of Fair Oaks. This map allows the reader to follow the route taken by Richardson's division to cross the Chickahominy River and advance toward the raging battle. *Courtesy of Library of Congress, Online Map Collection (Civil War Maps), Call No.: G3884.R5 1862 CW 653.*

Infantry was one of the last units to cross the Chickahominy via the Grapevine Bridge the next day, as this structure also started to break up. The description of its men's experience was probably very similar to that of the Fifty-seventh as it struggled across the collapsing Lower Bridge the day before. According to the Nineteenth's regimental history, the moorings of the Upper Bridge had been damaged by the swollen water. Soon, portions of the bridge began to float freely. Only the weight of the men and artillery kept it temporarily in position. But the bridge's roadway had also deteriorated. It was only with the greatest difficulty that the men struggled their way across: "as the regiment marched along, the logs rolled up in front of the men, much the same way as rough ice does."[7]

Battle of Fair Oaks: This hand-drawn period map shows French's Third Brigade's position along the Union battle line at the start of the second day of fighting.
Courtesy of Library of Congress, Online Map Collection (Civil War Maps), Reproduction No.: Mss5:7 Sn237:1, p. 157.

The Fifty-seventh appears to have encountered the same problem. Seeing the plight of their comrades on the bridge, most of those in French's brigade behind this regiment avoided the structure and chose the more straightforward, yet potentially more dangerous, and certainly more uncomfortable, option of wading waist-deep through the floodwaters. Of course, as they struggled through the stream, the men instinctively held their weapons, powder, and ammunition above their heads. They had yet to learn the value of dry socks! Unlike those later in the war, the infantrymen did not take the precaution of removing their shoes and socks before they entered the water. The trudging of hundreds, if not thousands, of feet stirred up the waters, so sand invariably sifted into the men's shoes to serve as an unwanted abrasive for the remainder of the day. In places, the river depth was up to the men's armpits. General Richardson, as an example to his men, dismounted and also waded across the half-mile swollen river.[8]

Although the Fifty-seventh made it across relatively quickly, it took all afternoon to get the entire brigade to the other side. Once it became apparent that the Lower Bridge was out of commission, Richardson redirected most of his command to the Upper Bridge opposite Sedgwick's camp.[9] As a result, the last troops made it only to the far bank by 5:15 P.M. that evening. However, the men's travails were not over, for they still had to cross a series of small tributaries that flowed into the river and seemingly innumerable deep ditches before the division could regroup. Ascending a hill, they came to open country where the men advanced at the double-quick (i.e., 120 strides per minute, 32 inches per stride). Reaching the Trent House after about a mile, they were ordered to load their (rifle) muskets and continue to proceed forward.[10] Unfortunately, marching along the only available country road, now transformed into a quagmire, proved almost as slow as crossing the river—equally as difficult and certainly more tiresome. What W. H. Morgan wrote about the conditions encountered by the retreating Confederates is certainly as applicable to those who chased them up the peninsula:

No one who has not marched on foot behind any wagon or artillery trains has any conception of what muddy roads are. Horses and

Marching Across Mud: Marching through mud, especially when encumbered with supply wagons and artillery, was one of the most trying situations soldiers faced during the war. *Courtesy of Library of Congress, Prints & Photographs Online Catalog (PPOC). LC-USZ62–79174.*

mules were sometimes literally buried in the mud and left to perish, or shot dead on the spot.[11]

This was exactly the situation facing the Union infantry as it slogged through the mud with the greatest of difficulty. As the infantryman took each step, the forward foot would sink into the shin-deep mud, and it required considerable exertion to extract the other foot, also encased in semiliquid ooze, an altogether enervating and unpleasant ordeal. Sometimes the clay soil became so sticky that the men lost their shoes in the mud.[12] Exhausted, some of the men temporarily fell out; the columns became increasingly disorganized.

What was difficult for the infantry proved to be a disaster for the artillery at the rear of the column. Marching behind the infantry, the gun carriages and caissons sank up to their axles in the mud. The artillerymen double-teamed and then even tripled-teamed the horses to draw the pieces forward; nevertheless, the artillery still became hopelessly mired. Normally, the infantry would have been called in to help extricate the artillery pieces, but they were desperately needed along the battle line. The foot soldiers therefore were ordered to continue on, leaving the artillerymen to their plight.[13] The artillery's fate was sealed by two ambulances that, contrary to orders, left their position at the rear of the column in an attempt to advance quickly to the front to assist the wounded in Casey's beleaguered division. They immediately became completely bogged down, and seemingly glued into position on the road, further obstructing the artillery's advance.[14] The gun crews would have to wait until the middle of the night before the Sixty-third New York from General Meagher's brigade came back to extricate the ordnance stuck in the mud.[15]

It required five or six hours to traverse what would have normally taken an hour or two. As a result, Richardson's First Division only managed to reach the front at eight o'clock that evening, just after dark, and did not take part in any part of the action that day. Richardson was ordered to position his division parallel to the Richmond and York railway tracks near some dense woods between David B. Birney's brigade of Samuel P. Heintzelman's Third Army Corps on his left and General Sedgwick's Second Division on his right. The Fifty-seventh New York was placed in the middle of French's brigade in the first line, with the Sixty-sixth New York on its right and the Fifty-third Pennsylvania Volunteers on its left.[16] The three regiments of General Howard's brigade were placed a hundred yards back along a second line, while General Meagher's brigade was positioned even farther to the rear as a reserve.[17] As a precaution, the Fifth New Hampshire Regiment was sent into the woods as an advance guard to protect the main body of troops.

ACTIVITY DURING THE NIGHT

There would be little rest and no comfort that night. Because of the proximity of a hostile army, scant attention was paid to the amenities of camp life. The men were ordered to "sleep on their arms" in a drizzling rain. Under normal conditions, the men would stack arms and sleep along the regimental line a yard or two from their weapons. In this case, however, the men would sleep with all their accoutrements (belt, cap box, cartridge box, haversack, canteen, and bayonet scabbard) on and their loaded weapons by their side.[18] The precariousness of their position became evident around 2:00 A.M., when the First and Fifth Texas and Second Mississippi Regiments, completely unaware of the nearby Union army, bivouacked "within half-musket shot" (General French says about one hundred yards) of the Fifth New Hampshire in the woods. Upon realizing they were in the presence of a vastly superior Union force, the Confederates quit their position, abandoning that part of the woods entirely.[19]

This did not satisfy General French, whose men were lying along the first line about two hundred yards in front of the woods. The men were awakened and ordered into regimental formations. The front line was wheeled toward the right and the three regiments placed *en echelon*.[20] Even after this maneuver was completed, the men were given little opportunity to fall back to sleep. As a further precaution, at 3:00 A.M. the men were aroused and ordered to form line again. Here they remained until the break of day and the start of the second day's fighting. The men initially stood in line at attention as the colonel and his staff examined their weapons, cartridge boxes, and cap boxes to make certain that all the weapons were clean and in working order and that everyone had the prescribed quota of ammunition (forty rounds). The inspection over, to ease the burden of holding their weapons for a protracted period, they would have been given the "in place rest" command. This allowed the men to place the stock of the gun on the ground in front of them, trigger facing outwards. They could assume any posture, fidget, even whisper to their neighbor in line, but they were not allowed to move from that spot.

As the sun started to rise around 5:30 A.M., General Birney and his staff noticed that a large gap had appeared in the Union line as a result of French's nocturnal maneuvering. This was reported to General Sumner, who in turn authorized French to shift his brigade to the left. Facing that direction, the men marched across the field and over the railroad tracks into the woods in the direction of Seven Pines. Just as the Fifty-seventh New York crossed the tracks, the head of the narrow column came up to the right of Birney's brigade. Halting, facing forward, and reassuming line of battle was but a matter of moments. However, although the brigade had moved laterally only about three hundred yards, the Fifty-seventh had advanced about thirty yards on the other side of the railroad tracks.[21] Most of the regiment found itself standing in dense underbrush and on swampy ground, looking into a dense forest. Company K on the extreme left was about twenty paces to the right of the Fifty-third Pennsylvania Volunteers. The right of the regiment and the Sixty-sixth beside it were still in the open field. Although this end of the regiment, "thrown out in the air," was initially vulnerable to a flank attack, the arrival of Corporal Rufus Pettit's and Frank's artillery batteries put an end to this danger.

THE SECOND DAY OF BATTLE

To fully understand the events that were about to unfold, the story has to be momentarily shifted to the Confederate command. The attack against Heintzelman's and Keyes's forces the day before had been successful to a degree. Two Union divisions had been shattered and Johnston's offensive had overrun a major redoubt and series of abatis and other field fortifications. The most important objective had not been accomplished, however—securing the south bank of the Chickahominy River. The timely arrival of the lead elements of Sumner's corps, along with nightfall, put an end to the Confederate advance. To make matters worse, Johnston, commander of the Army of Northern Virginia, had been severely wounded near the end of the day's fighting, and although his lieutenants knew that he had planned to continue the attack the next morning, some confusion set in. Command of the army temporarily devolved upon Major General Gustavus W. Smith. Around 1:00 A.M., Smith met with General James Longstreet, the commander of the army's right wing. Longstreet was ordered to turn his attention away from an advance toward Bottoms Bridge and to attack northward instead. This meant an

Richardson's Camp at Fair Oaks: Richardson's men in position at his camp near Fair Oaks battlefield. *Courtesy of Library of Congress, Prints & Photographs Online Catalog (PPOC). LC-DIG-cwpb–00191.*

inevitable collision with General Richardson's force along the Richmond and York railway line.

To the immediate right of French's brigade lay a large, rectangular open field, about one thousand yards in depth. The Nine Mile Road (a.k.a. New Bridge Road) intersected a small local road in front of the Fair Oaks railway station at the forward right corner of the field. During the night, Confederate reconnaissance must have reported this area to be inadequately defended. Longstreet's first plan was to drive a column through this field and take both Birney's and Richardson's forces in flank. Unfortunately for the secession cause, Pettit's battery (Battery B, First New York Artillery) had finally managed to reach the battlefield at 4:30 that morning. General Richardson ordered the battery to unlimber along the local road running north of Fair Oaks Station.

Longstreet's first attack was launched about 6:00 A.M. A Confederate column emerged out of the woods and soon began running across the railway tracks, trying to form line. Pettit's 10-pounder Parrotts immediately went into action, first firing shells, then later a spherical case (this projectile consisted of a number of lead balls housed in a tin canister that broke apart in flight). Unable to get into formation, the attackers soon broke and retired back into the woods.[22] The officers and men along Richardson's first line meanwhile continued to wait patiently, vaguely aware of the action on their right. Accounts submitted after the battle suggest there was little agreement among the officers in French's brigade as to the situation they now faced. The general officers, armed with better intelligence, knew that a strong Rebel force had been concentrating in the woods in front of them and that an attack was imminent. The colonel of the Fifty-seventh, Samuel K. Zook, and several of his officers shared this view. A number of company officers, however, mistakenly thought that the Union advance guard had cleared the forest of any potential threat. Whether from lack of vigilance or the broken nature of the ground, both Captains A. B. Chapman of Company A and A. J. La Vallée of Company K later admitted that they and their men were unprepared for the storm about to break. They allowed the men to rest. The men in Company K, for example, broke ranks, threw themselves on the ground near the line, many even with their backs to the forest.[23]

Positioning themselves immediately behind the line in the center of the Fifty-seventh, Colonel Zook, Captain Charles MacKay (Company F), and Lieutenant Josiah Favill anxiously strained eyes and ears to detect any clues as to the enemy's whereabouts in the forest. The Battle of Fair Oaks (Seven Pines) occurred relatively early along the veterans' learning curve, and the realities of warfare had not yet inculcated into officers and men the hard pragmatic spirit prevalent later in the war. For green troops, it is the wait before battle that is particularly trying, as each man wrestles with the demon of self-preservation and the temptation to flee to the rear. Although veteran troops face the same emotional struggle before battle, their anxieties tend to be shorter-lived and not as pronounced. Unfortunately, neither Lieutenant Favill, Captain La Vallée, or Colonel Zook tell us how their men felt and reacted as they awaited their first terrible test of battle. It is reasonable to assume they endured the same emotional crisis as everyone else who has ever had to stare death in the face, and that they used similar physical and psychological techniques to overcome their fears. In this respect, Captain Oscar Jackson's insightful description of how his men prepared for the impending storm during the Battle of Corinth probably is applicable to almost all who had to endure the seemingly endless wait for the "ball" to start in earnest:

> I noticed one man examining his gun to see if it was clean; another to see if his was primed right; a third would stand a while on one foot and then on the other; whilst others were pulling at their blouses and feeling if their cartridge boxes or cap powder were all right, and so on.

Lack of experience also affected the officers' attitudes and behavior. Most officers still believed that their true place was on horseback. Following their colonel's example, the officers in the regiment remained mounted, despite the unsuitability of equestrian motive power in thick underbrush and forest.

Minutes passed, and still no enemy could be seen. The illusion of tranquillity was soon shattered, however. Those near the center of the regiment were the first to be aware of the Rebels' approach in the woods in front. Confederate officers were heard ordering their men into formation. Soon, the Union men could also hear the tramping of feet and the snapping of twigs and crackling of boughs as the Rebels formed up into a necessarily ragged line in preparation for an attack. The men along French's first line, meanwhile, continued to wait. Finally, about a half hour after the regiment had deployed into line, the Confederate storm broke.

Civil War literature provides little information about the forces that French's men were about to encounter. An examination of the positions of the various brigades involved on either side and their experiences during the battle suggest that French's command was opposed by General William Mahone's Brigade. Fortunately, in an upcoming book on the Twelfth Virginia Infantry, John Horn describes the engagement from the perspective of this command, so it is possible to ascertain the Confederate forces involved, how they were deployed, and how they fared during the fighting.[24]

Around the time the Fifty-seventh New York was being deployed into line, Daniel Harvey ("D. H.") Hill was ordering Mahone to move his three regiments quickly forward into the woods occupied by Richardson's Brigade. Before setting off, Mahone asked if any Union forces were in the woods, and if he should throw out skirmishers in front of the advancing line. Hill splenetically responded that he had personally examined the woods and since it was unoccupied there was no need for a skirmisher screen. The regiments in Mahone's Brigade were organized into two lines: the Forty-first Virginia in the lead with the Third Alabama on its right. The Twelfth Virginia, in line, brought up the rear. It appears that the Fifty-third Virginia in Brigadier General Lewis A. Armistead's Brigade briefly joined the fracas.[25] Taking advantage of the thick foliage, the Virginians and Alabamians managed to approach within forty yards of the Union line without being observed. Here, they stopped and delivered a destructive volley.

According to the Fifty-seventh's Captain Gilbert Frederick:

Here we were sitting on the ground or standing around when suddenly, like a clap of thunder, a volley from the Confederate lines threw the regiment into momentary confusion. We knew we were on the line of battle and expected, of course, that something would soon happen, but this was so sudden that some of the men and even officers forgot for the time which way a soldier should face in the presence of an enemy, a little mistake that cost one officer at least his commission. A private in his precipitate retreat fell into the railroad ditch, which on top was covered with brush but underneath was full of water, and, with some difficulty, was fished out of the water by his comrades.[26]

In his postwar memoir, Lieutenant Favill recorded the sensation of coming under fire "without warning":

The noise was tremendous; and bullets whistled about our ears like hailstones, tearing branches, twigs, and leaves from the trees. The horses reared and plunged, and the center and left of the regiment were thrown into some confusion, but most of the men stood their ground, and opened fire.

To encourage the men, Favill turned his horse toward the right flank of the regiment, where Captains MacKay and William A. Kirk (Company G) were likewise engaged. Their efforts paid off, and this part of the regimental line, though wavering for the first few moments, was quickly straightened out. A prolonged firefight immediately erupted.

I noticed the enemy's aim was high, and cautioned the men to aim low. The firing rolled in long continuous volume, now slackening, now increasing, until it seemed as if pandemonium had broken loose, and all the guns in the world were going off at once. With all the frightful racket, I did not fail to notice how few men were being hit, and told the men to take advantage of the little danger, and fire to some purpose.[27]

There are conflicting accounts how the men handled themselves during the first moments of the attack. Somewhat predictably, Colonel Zook later reported to brigade headquarters that his regiment withstood the blast and "instantly returned fire in the coolest manner, causing the enemy to fall back, whereupon we advanced at the 'charge,' driving him entirely from his position."[28] The after-battle reports of Captains Chapman and La Vallée, however, make a convincing case that the initial reaction of the men on the regiment's left was not quite so sterling. The men in Companies A and K were thrown into panic, which fortunately for the Fifty-seventh was short-lived. Many of those in Company K immediately scrambled behind a large log lying near their position and returned fire. Then, either feeling that their current position was untenable or, more probably, succumbing to the fear and panic experienced by

raw troops at the beginning of serious engagements, they retired a second time, albeit slowly. They nevertheless still had enough presence of
mind to reload their rifles. La Vallée and his noncommissioned officers soon managed to reestablish control over their troops, and rallied
the company behind a clump of large trees about thirty paces behind
their original position. Once again in line, Company K advanced
about twenty paces so that it was but ten paces from its original position along the regimental line. Struggling to maintain control over his
charge, La Vallée ordered his men to cease firing after one or two
shots.[29] Also on the regiment's left, Company A experienced a more
transient crisis. Soon after the firing began, its men were pushed back
about twenty feet. Here they rallied, and like the rest of the regiment
soon settled down and handed back as good as they got.

As Favill would point out in his memoirs, there was a definite ebb
and flow of firing along the line. The fire directed against the regiment's left was the first to abate. Unfortunately, this was not the end of
Company K's problems. This time, however, the cause was not the
enemy, but nearby friendly troops. Encountering unexpected
resistance, the enemy directed its wrath against the next regiment on
the left, the Fifty-third Pennsylvania Volunteers, where the firing was
heard to intensify. The right company in the Fifty-third reacted just as
had Companies A and K of the Fifty-seventh. The men quickly fell
back and sought refuge behind La Vallée's men, who having ultimately braved their own test of courage remained firm during this
new crisis. Those fleeing behind Company K, however, in their excitement continued to fire, and the left flank of the Fifty-seventh now
found itself fired upon by friendly troops in their rear. Fortunately,
only a single file closer was struck dead. Before further damage could
be done, Captain La Vallée, Lieutenant Curtis, and two sergeants rallied the stragglers from the adjoining regiment and made them return
to their proper place in their own unit.

The stragglers' fire behind Company K had another undesirable
effect. The enemy's attention was drawn back to the Fifty-seventh's
position and its men soon found themselves again under enemy fire.
Quickly responding, La Vallée's men delivered a volley, but this

almost instantly degenerated into faltering, ragged individual fire. There is a tendency to regard individual fire as potentially more accurate, since, unlike volley fire, the men chose the moment when to fire and theoretically could aim at their targets. Informed opinion during the Civil War took the opposite stance, however. Writing after the war about the lessons to be drawn from the great conflict, the veteran Frederick Whittaker emphasized:

> the men must be taught never to fire before the word. The moral effect of a reserved volley is tremendous. Irregular fire during an advance is both useless and demoralizing. Patience under fire makes veterans so formidable. Their several volleys sweeps everything before it. Thirty or forty feet from the enemy's line is the time to fire, all together and aiming low. Then the reserve of cold steel will come with double the efficacy, real or moral.[30]

The reality was that individual fire quickly became confused and disorganized, and hence tended to be highly inaccurate. Few men attempted to aim. The best that could realistically be hoped for was to have the men point their weapons in the general direction of the enemy. Many men in a near state of panic "aimed at the moon" so that hundreds of shots whistled harmlessly toward treetops. At Fair Oaks, the situation was made worse by the rough terrain. Throughout the exchange, men on either side rarely saw their adversaries. There were a few exceptions, however, that sometimes led to disastrous results not only for those being observed, but ironically for those doing the observing. A Union private named Thomas Ridings spotted a Rebel who he managed to hit. Bragging to the man behind him, Ridings was himself soon shot dead in turn.

THE SECOND CONFEDERATE ASSAULT

The sporadic firing up and down the line continued for about half an hour, then the Rebel fire gradually abated. Of course, if the men along the firing line could not see their opponents, neither side had any idea of the effect their fire had upon their opponents, and memoirs and battle reports are silent on this issue. The Confederates had suffered terribly, however. Colonel Tennant Lomax of the Third Alabama was among those killed. Mahone's first line was forced to fall back.

Not surprisingly, the Union forces assumed the Rebels had withdrawn. However, on the opposing side, Mahone now fed the Twelfth Virginia into the fight. The colonel of the Twelfth barked the orders "Forward, guide center, march!"; the regiment was to dress its line toward the center. The terrain was broken and the skirts of the woods swampy. The line became disordered and the regiment's alignment went askew. The advancing line started to incline slightly toward the left.[31]

Of course, the Union troops were completely unaware of these developments. Once again, egregious inexperience raised its head. Zook and his officers failed a second time to take what by 1863 would be considered the most basic precautions. Keeping all their men in the regimental formation, they also failed to secure their position by throwing out even a few skirmishers.

Taking advantage of the lull in the action, the officers ordered the line be straightened and the wounded removed to the rear. It was at this point that General French arrived on the scene. Riding up to the front line, the general officer quickly dismounted. Relieved of the burden of unthinking subservience to a mistaken sense of honor and duty, the officers of the Fifty-seventh gladly dismounted and finally sent their mounts to the rear.[32]

For reasons not understood, at this point the regiments on either side of the Fifty-seventh began to converge slightly. On his side, La Vallée noticed that a portion of the Fifty-third Pennsylvania started to overlap his own front and he immediately sent Sergeant Richard S. Alcoke (Company K) to communicate this fact to the colonel. Zook responded by moving his regiment slightly toward the right. The Sixty-sixth on the right appears also to have moved across a part of the regiment's front. Feeling his regiment was thus protected by the friendly forces on either side, Colonel Zook ordered his men to lie down.[33] Despite the sporadic nature of the fighting so far, the defenders were probably already exhausted. The officers wanted to take remedial steps so that their men would be ready for whatever came next. Combat experience is extremely enervating, and in mere moments the combatant can be drained of much of his strength. During the second year of the Civil War, a survivor of the Mexican-American War offered the readers of *Scientific American* a vivid description of how one felt by the end of a fight:

> Fighting is very hard work, the man who has passed through two hours' fight has lived through a great amount of mental labor. At the end of a battle, I always found that I had perspired so profusely as to wet all my clothes. I was as sore as if I had been beaten all over with a club.[34]

Regardless of the reasons why the men in the Fifty-seventh were ordered to lie down, this time it proved to be a fortunate decision. Hardly had the men thrown themselves on the ground when the enemy delivered a tremendous volley. Unlike the previous attack when almost all of the shots passed harmlessly over the troops' heads, the enemy's fire was now "uncomfortably accurate," even though delivered from a greater range.[35] The fire whizzed just over the prostrate troops. Had the men been standing, there would have many casualties. As it was Sergeant Henry Stuart, the color-bearer, Lieutenant Henry H. Folger, and several others were killed, while a ball grazed Sergeant Brower's neck and shoulder.[36] The death of Sergeant Stuart was felt as a real loss. A veteran of the Crimean War, Stuart had proven to be a godsend to the Fifty-seventh, teaching men and officers the fundamentals of drill, the art and science of day-to-day campaigning, and castramentation, as the art of laying out camp was called. Sergeant Stuart's death was all the more bitter, because the men believed it could have been avoided. Driven by a strong sense of honor and what many believed was the way men "were supposed to fight," Stuart refused to lie on the ground. Holding the regimental colors erect, Stuart argued it was improper for the flag to be lowered or any part of it to touch the ground.[37]

As soon as the volley was fired, the Rebels, most likely the Third Alabama and Forty-first Virginia, attempted to rush the defenders. Approaching to within thirty yards of the Fifty-seventh, they were finally stopped by a "magnificent fire" that was "steady, effective, and determined." The attackers' fire appears to have been much less effective. Lieutenant Favill recalled:

> Our fellows had no idea of giving way this time, and stood their ground; the trees were riddled, and a heavy shower of branches and leaves continuously fell upon our heads. The air, in fact, seemed full of bullets, and yet so few were hurt we began to think they could not hit us.[38]

Captain MacKay and Lieutenant Favill on the right side of the regiment noticed that the Rebel line on this side did not extend quite as far as theirs. Here at last was an opportunity to turn the Rebel flank, something that, if properly executed, would be sure to embarrass the Rebels and stymie their attack. Favill rushed back to Colonel Zook and reported the situation. Zook acted without equivocation and ordered the two companies on that flank to wheel inward and sweep the enemy's line. Under General French's eye, the operation took but moments to complete. This tactic of wheeling several companies to take an enemy regiment in flank would be used repeatedly during the Civil War, and had been long known to tacticians. We now usually associate this technique with the Duke of Wellington during the Peninsular War (1808–1814), but the practice had been developed by the Dutch during the late seventeenth century and was known as fighting *à la Hollandais*.[39] General James Wolfe and the French Marshal Puységur both had recommended similar tactics.[40] Most American officers were probably unaware of these antecedents and intuitively devised structurally similar methods on their own initiative. The tactic was much more commonly used during the Civil War than in any earlier European war. In Europe most engagements were fought over relatively open terrain, where combatants could see their opponents from afar. One was less likely to be able to "sneak up" and surprise the enemy. This certainly was not the case in America, especially in the western theatre of operations, where a much greater proportion of the fighting occurred on rough, broken, and forested ground. There was thus a much greater chance of approaching an enemy's flank and launching an attack before the opposing force was even aware of its vulnerability.

This was exactly the opportunity handed to the Fifty-seventh at Fair Oaks. The result was everything that could have been desired. Approaching the Rebel line in flank, the Union infantrymen opened fire at an extremely close, deadly range that was "followed up promptly by a bayonet charge."[41] Taken completely by surprise, the Rebels panicked, broke, and fled precipitously to the rear. Years after the fighting, Confederate general William Mahone wrote to his superior, General G. W. Smith:

Meanwhile the Third Alabama had advanced far into the wood on the north . . . [and] hotly engaged the enemy, and doubtless being overlapped and greatly outnumbered, and, having lost its Colonel, was broken and remarched to the open field and reformed.[42]

Meanwhile, Richardson's extreme right wing (Howard's brigade) cautiously advanced through the woods and soon encountered two isolated Confederate regiments that had mistakenly been firing into each other in the general chaos of the combat. One of these regiments quickly fell back in confusion, and the other soon followed.[43] General Richardson arrived on the scene just as the Rebel force was starting to rout. Taking in the scene, and convinced the infantry could do little else barring a general advance through the woods, Richardson decided to let the artillery now have its say. The Fifty-seventh and adjoining regiments were ordered out of the woods. The order to march given, the men exited the woods in quick time and in good order in a column of fours. For them, the day's fighting was finally over.[44] Longstreet's plan had been to attack tentatively and to uncover any weakness along the Union line that could be easily exploited. But his troops having been roughly handled during the first two assaults, he thought it unwise to press the attack further. Although heavy skirmishing would continue throughout the day, for all practical purposes the Battle of Fair Oaks was over.

Attacking ground primarily protected by the Fifty-seventh New York and its adjacent regiments, the Third Alabama had suffered 175 casualties, including Tennent Lomax, its colonel and the adjutant, who had directed the attack. The other two Rebel regiments involved in the attack lost between them nearly 150 more.[45] In contrast, the Fifty-seventh suffered a total of thirty-six casualties—three men killed, eighteen wounded, and fifteen missing.[46]

Though the Union forces under Keyes had been mauled, the reinforcements involved during the evening fighting on the first day and that of the second day showed courage and resolve. The hard-fought affair at Fair Oaks proved to be a poignant prelude to the much larger and even more tenaciously contested struggle that would become known as the Seven Days Battles, destined to begin but four weeks later. During some of the war's earlier engagements Union infantry had initially fought with resolve—for example, Burnside's men at the beginning of the First Battle of Bull Run. Nevertheless, Union infantry in the eastern theatre had lacked the resilience so characteristic of veteran troops later in the war. It is at Fair Oaks that we first see the forging of these essential martial qualities on a large scale. The experiences of the Fifty-seventh New York are illustrative. Several times a part of the regiment vacillated, even broke, but each time its officers were able to regain control and reestablish order. Never again during a head-on, set piece engagement would a Union army be easily pushed aside, psychologically defeated simply by the appearance of the Confederate soldier.

This change was not immediately apparent to their Confederate foe, however. Flushed with victory and the promise of even greater accomplishments during the weeks to come, the Confederate command failed to appreciate that it now faced a more resilient and able opponent than it had confronted the year before. This lesson would only be learned painfully during the bitter and sanguinary fighting that was imminent.

TACTICAL OBSERVATION #2

The manner in which the Fifty-seventh New York ultimately prevailed over its Confederate foe is highly illustrative of one important aspect of Civil War combat. At the start of the war, the popular expectation was that the bayonet would be the ultimate arbiter of much of the fighting. Both sides would rush in lunging and parrying with the long-edged weapons jutting out from the front of their muzzles. By the second year of fighting, infantrymen discovered that "bayonet fighting" rarely, if ever, occurred on the open field. The curious soldier walking around the contested field after the battle invariably would find many who were killed by small arms, others torn apart by exploding shells or mangled by solid shot or canister, but it was incredibly rare to find a corpse with wounds caused by edged weapons. This led many like Captain John William De Forest of the Twelfth Connecticut Infantry to conclude that bayonet fighting existed only in "newspapers and fiction."[47] Statistics compiled by Union medical officers later in the war corroborated these conclusions.

CASUALTIES IN THE ARMY OF THE POTOMAC, MAY–JULY 1864[48]

Cause	Wilderness	Spotsylvania	North Anna	Petersburg	July
SHELL	231	712	95	639	435
CANNON-SHOT	6	37	3	38	4
BULLET	7,046	8,218	959	6,693	2,538
BAYONET	4	14	1	3	14
SWORD	2	1	-	1	1

Disillusioned with their original naive expectations, many soldiers began to regard the bayonet as a useless appendage, something that was useful only to roast meat over a campfire or stick into the ground so that the back end could serve as a candleholder.[49] It is hardly surprising that many later historians picked up on this sentiment, believing that once the new rifle muskets had been adopted, it was folly to think that edged weapons could have any value in future combat.

Unfortunately, this view is based on a confusion of two similar-sounding terms and overlooks what transpired so frequently on the Civil War battlefield. Simply put, "bayonet fighting" and "bayonet charge" are not synonymous and represent two entirely different and, as we will see, diametrically opposed tactical phenomena.

A bayonet fight occurs when opposing sides have closed to contact and the action devolves into a confused melee where individuals attempt to stab their opponents with lunging bayonet thrusts or club their skulls with the musket. A bayonet charge, on the other hand, is a formal tactic that calls for infantrymen to place their bayonets at the end of their muskets and rush in upon the enemy, thereby threatening to "run through" whoever decides to stand up to them.

The bayonet charge as a viable offensive tactic is as old as the musket. Its purpose was to force an immediate decision by destroying the enemy's will to stay and fight, rather than merely to inflict casualties. When executed under the proper conditions, the act of quickly advancing buoyed the infantryman's morale, and frequently so intimidated the enemy that they fled, without a single casualty being inflicted on either side. We are indebted to a British soldier for one of the most compelling descriptions of the psychological effects of participating in a charge:

> *No movement in the field is made with greater confidence of success than that of the charge; it affords little time for thinking, while it creates a fearless excitement, and tends to give a fresh impulse to the blood of the advancing soldier, rouses his courage, strengthens every nerve, and drowns every fear of danger or of death; thus emboldened amidst shouts that anticipate victory, he rushes on and mingles with the fleeing foe.[50]*

Although penned by a veteran of the Napoleonic Wars, these psychological dynamics applied equally to the Civil War infantryman. Looking through Civil War memoirs, one finds veterans recalling that the charge imparted a "careless, reckless indifference" to the danger surrounding them.[51] Conversely, the defenders, especially if they had suddenly taken casualties or found themselves denuded of their fire (for example, if they had no time to reload), would feel powerless to resist, the men would panic, and all cohesion of the unit would be irreversibly lost.

This is exactly what happened to the Third Alabama and Forty-first Virginia when they found themselves suddenly taken in flank by the wing companies of the Fifty-seventh at Fair Oaks. Suddenly attacked from an unexpected direction, they were thrown into confusion and fled when the enemy launched a bayonet charge. This scenario occurred innumerable times during the Civil War. Memoirs, after-battle reports, and letters abound with examples where one side or the other failed to wait until the enemy closed, but instead fled. What are these but examples of successful bayonet charges?

5

Washington Artillery on Marye's Heights (Fredericksburg, December 12–13, 1862)

The Washington Artillery is probably the most famous Confederate artillery unit to emerge from the War Between the States. First organized in 1838, it served during the Mexican-American War and received its regimental flag in August 1846. Its reputation firmly established, it had no difficulty attracting a large number of recruits as the inevitability of civil strife became apparent after the fall of Fort Sumter. It was present at the First Battle of Bull Run and exchanged fire with heavy Union artillery at Antietam. But it was only at the Battle of Fredericksburg that the unit gained international attention, when its role in beating back a series of determined Union charges was reported throughout the European press.

THE ROAD TO FREDERICKSBURG

The bloody Battle of Antietam (September 17, 1862) was followed by six weeks of near stasis as the two contending forces remained within thirty miles of one another. Both armies had suffered numerous casualties and needed time to regroup, receive reinforcements, and be resupplied. On the Union side, it had also become obvious that a change of military leadership was needed. Major General George B. McClellan's overly cautious strategic approach and a series of lost military opportunities created a mood among the government and public that screamed for a more active approach. The general's failure to destroy, or at least substantially compromise, Lee's Army of Northern Virginia during the Maryland Campaign was the "last straw" and made it clear even to the most conservative that a time for change was long past due. McClellan was removed as commander of the Army of the Potomac and Ambrose Burnside took his place.

In a bid to show that he was made of a different martial mettle, Burnside came up with a bold, but what would prove to be an utterly futile, plan of operations. The Army of the Potomac, then at Warrenton, was reorganized into Sumner's Right, Hooker's Center, and Franklin's Left "Grand Divisions," each of which comprised two army corps. Lee's army rested on the other side of the Rappahannock River, Longstreet's First Corps near Culpeper Court House, and Thomas (Stonewall) Jackson's Second Corps in the Valley of Virginia. During the third week of November, Sumner was ordered to move his Grand Division to Fredericksburg, where it was hoped he would surprise the Confederates and cross the Rappahannock unopposed. Lee received intelligence of this movement and on November 18–19 dispatched two of Longstreet's Divisions to proceed quickly to the town to bolster the small Confederate force that was opposing Sumner's thirty thousand men.[1] The lead elements of Sumner's force had arrived on November 17, but the lack of pontoon bridges and other critical engineering equipment prevented the Union force from crossing the river and taking the town by storm. There was nothing for Sumner to do but have his men encamp on Stafford Heights on the other side of the river from Fredericksburg and await the arrival of the remainder of his Grand Division and the much-needed supplies and engineering equipment.[2]

Longstreet's two divisions, meanwhile, arrived at 3:00 P.M. on November 21. By the twenty-sixth it had become apparent to both sides that a great battle would be fought in and around Fredericksburg. Burnside ordered the remainder of the Army of the Potomac (Hooker's and Franklin's Grand Divisions) to hasten to this point, while Lee ordered the remainder of Longstreet's First Corps, as well as Jackson's Second Corps, to reinforce the Confederate troops who had been concentrating along the series of hills and elevations in the rear of the town.

A short description of the town and surrounding environs is needed to understand the events that would unfold several weeks later on December 12–13, and the situation faced by the Washington Artillery in particular. Located on the south side of the Rappahannock River, Fredericksburg is almost equidistant from the capitals of the warring "countries"; the town was fifty-five miles from Washington and sixty from Richmond. Its five thousand inhabitants were surrounded by two series of low hills. Stafford Heights rose from the banks on the opposite side of the river. On the Confederate-held side of town, the hills stretched away forming a semicircular plain, six miles wide and two miles deep. Looking toward the town from the Confederate vantage point, the leftmost of these was Taylor's Hill, close to the Beck's Island area of the Rappahannock above Fredericksburg. On its right rose an elevation known locally as Marye's Heights (sometimes referred to as Marye's Hill), followed by Telegraph Hill to its right. The last mentioned was the highest of these hills and after the battle would become known to posterity as "Lee's Hill." A portion of the hill line took the form of bluffs that were "bold and bare of trees." Most of these hills had originally been wooded and here and there narrow spurs of copsewood still projected down into the plain.[3] The largest of these, known as Bernard Woods, jutted out from the right of Telegraph Hill.[4] The plain itself was intersected by a number of fences demarcating crop fields, gardens, and property boundaries.[5]

Some veterans, such as William Owen, have described Marye's Heights as a type of salient jutting out beyond the surrounding hills.[6] Two roads led out of Fredericksburg and went over this hill: the Orange and Plank Road and to its right the extension of Telegraph Road. Both continued on and went over Guest Hill, an elevation directly behind Marye's Heights. Telegraph Road proper turned almost 90 degrees to the right (from the defender's point of view) just before the hill and followed its contour before turning sharply west and traversing Telegraph Hill on its way to Richmond. Two small streams ran out of the hills, crossed the plain, and emptied into the Rappahannock. Hazel Run ran through the small valley separating Marye's Heights and Telegraph Hill. Deep Run flowed down the right side of Telegraph Hill, initially running parallel to the Orange and Plank and Telegraph Roads, but then snaking left, then to the right into the larger river. An unfinished railway bed ran out of the hills and into the town close to, and generally parallel to, Hazel Run. The Richmond, Fredericksburg, and Potomac Railroad cut across the plain, running more or less parallel to the face of Telegraph Hill and Marye's Heights until it finally turned right and entered Fredericksburg.[7]

As Longstreet's Divisions arrived in the vicinity, they were entrusted with the defense of the hills directly behind the town. Anderson's Division was stationed on the extreme left flank, that is, from the point where the canal flowed out of the Rappahannock in front of Beck's Island, just a little above Falmouth, along the heights up to and including Taylor's Hill. To its right first came General Lafayette McLaws's Division on Marye's Heights and then Pickett's Division, stretching out to the skirts of the woods on the edge of Deep Run Valley on the right side of Telegraph Hill. Hood's Division was placed behind Hamilton's Crossing of the railroad (over Deep Run). Ransom's Division formed the reserve near Longstreet's headquarters behind Marye's Heights.[8] When Jackson's Second Corps finally arrived, it was used to extend the Confederate line to

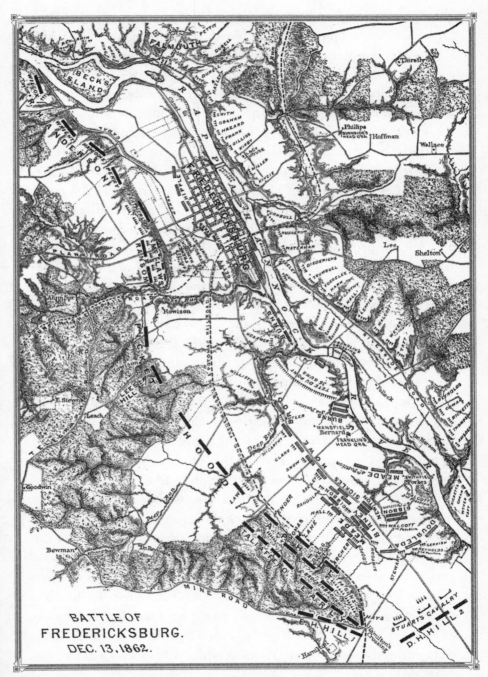

First Battle of Fredericksburg: Union and Confederate positions soon after the start of Couch's grand assault. This map, primarily based on an earlier map belonging to General Burnside, was enhanced with information taken from a Confederate map prepared by topographical engineer Jedediah Hotchkiss for Stonewall Jackson's use. *Courtesy of Library of Congress, Online Map Collection (Civil War Maps), Digital ID No.: glva01 lva00023.*

the right so that the defensive position became a semicircular line with either flank more or less anchored on the Rappahannock River.

It is well known that Jackson objected to the protracted defense of Fredericksburg, arguing that it was preferable for Lee's army to fall back behind the North Anna River. It certainly wasn't because he thought the present position was indefensible; he believed that the Confederates would indeed beat back any Union attack. He reasoned, however, that a Union attack against a position behind the North Anna would also fail, and the terrain there would permit a vigorous pursuit of a defeated Union army. Lee overrode Jackson's objections. Although Lee never left a detailed explanation of his decision, an understanding of contemporary military art and science provides clues. Although Brigadier General William Barksdale's Brigade of Mississippi men were thrown forward in and about Fredericksburg, the main line of defenses as we have seen was positioned on or near the hills on the other side of the plain. A determined defense of the town itself would not only be unfeasible, but also almost certainly suicidal. Lee and his immediate subordinates knew about Brigadier General Henry J. Hunt's large artillery train. Positioned on Stafford Heights these guns could destroy the town, which was within easy range, along with any occupants or defenders foolish enough to stay there during an extended bombardment. This meant the main line of defense had to be away from the river. Though this, in effect, ceded the town, it did not compromise the defensive situation. Although the Union army would eventually be able to cross enough men to take the town, they would still have to attack the main line on the hills. Not only would it be their turn to endure concentrated artillery, but the resulting Union attack would violate one of the cardinal rules of giving battle: never fight a battle with impassible terrain in one's rear. Defeat, and a vigorous pursuit, could lead to the annihilation of the army, bottlenecked on the south shore of the Rappahannock. So, ironically, the Confederate defensive position at Fredericksburg offered exactly what Jackson wanted to obtain behind the North Anna River.

STRENGTHENING THE DEFENSES

During the last days of November, the Army of Northern Virginia started to entrench, making a naturally strong position even stronger. According to General William N. Pendleton, the army's chief of artillery, the artillery trains arrived only on Sunday, November 23. Traversing the prospective battlefield the next day, he observed that although rudimentary groundworks had been started, much still remained to be done.[9] The artillery was assigned positions along the defensive lines and moved into position. McLaws's Division, which would bear a brunt of the fighting in this part of the battlefield, was deployed in front of Marye's Heights so as to offer two lines of defense. The first line was made up mostly of Brigadier General Thomas R. R. Cobb's Brigade of Infantry, and positioned in the "sunken road" at the base of Marye's Heights, specifically from right to left: Eighteenth Georgia, Twenty-fourth Georgia, and Phillips' Legion. The flank of this last unit reached Telegraph Road at the point where coming out of the town it is deflected along the base of the hill. Cobb's front was extended by a fourth regiment, the Twenty-fourth North Carolina, which occupied a ditch or rifle pit north of Telegraph Road. This regiment, though officially part of Ransom's Brigade, had been temporarily assigned to Cobb. The first line of infantry was further bolstered by two guns from Captain V. Maurin's Donaldsonville (Louisiana) Artillery, part of Anderson's Division. These were placed near the Orange and Plank Road.[10]

The responsibility for placing the reserve artillery of Longstreet's Corps fell to General Pendleton, Colonels H. C. Cabell and E. P. Alexander, and Captain S. R. Johnston.[11] Colonel Walton's Washington Artillery was assigned to McLaws's Division and formed the second "line." Posted along a front of about four hundred yards on the crest of Marye's Heights, it overlooked Cobb's Brigade along the road below.[12] Colonel Alexander's artillery battalion was placed beside the Taylor House in Anderson's sector of the defensive line. Benjamin Franklin Eshleman's Fourth Company of the Washington Artillery, with its two 12-pounder howitzers and two 12-pounder Napoleons, was placed on the right next to Telegraph Road, and the two 12-pounder Napoleons of the Third Company, commanded by Captain M. B. Miller, were placed to its left. Next came Captain Charles W. Squires's First Company, with its 3-inch rifle and 10-pounder Richmond model Parrott. These were beside a little brick house and in front of the Welford graveyard. Second Lieutenant John M. Galbraith with the second three-inch rifle from the First Company was positioned on the Orange and Plank Road.[13] The Second Company had been detached and sent over to Pickett's Division.[14]

Temporarily preoccupied with more important priorities, the army's engineers began to entrench the Washington Artillery's batteries only on December 1.[15] It was obvious that the Union army assembling on the far side of the Rappahannock was not ready to attack, and neither the Confederate artillery nor infantry were compelled to continuously man the defensive works then still under construction. It was agreed that upon hearing two reports from the signal guns, two pieces from Captain J. P. W. Read's Battery—positioned on the highest point along McLaws's front—everyone would rush to their assigned positions along the defenses and await the attack.[16] In the meantime, there was ample time for the amenities of camp life, such as writing home to family and friends. The officers of the Washington Artillery even had a Literary and Dramatic Association, which put on plays in camp. Many of the battalion's officers would occasionally meander into town, a depressing experience since most of the townsfolk had fled or were in the process of leaving. The artillery battalion's colonel, J. B. Walton, who had been on leave in Richmond, finally returned on December 9 with several guests.[17]

The work on the Washington Artillery's defenses continued for about a week and a half, the project being adjudged complete only on December 11.[18] The artillerymen, however, were disappointed with the results. They thought that the earthworks were not high enough. Digging the ditch a little deeper, they threw the earth on top of the works. They also carved out embrasures through which their guns could fire. Believing that the gunners were ruining their defenses, the engineers remonstrated. The artillerymen retorted, "We have to fight here, not you; we will arrange them to suit ourselves."[19]

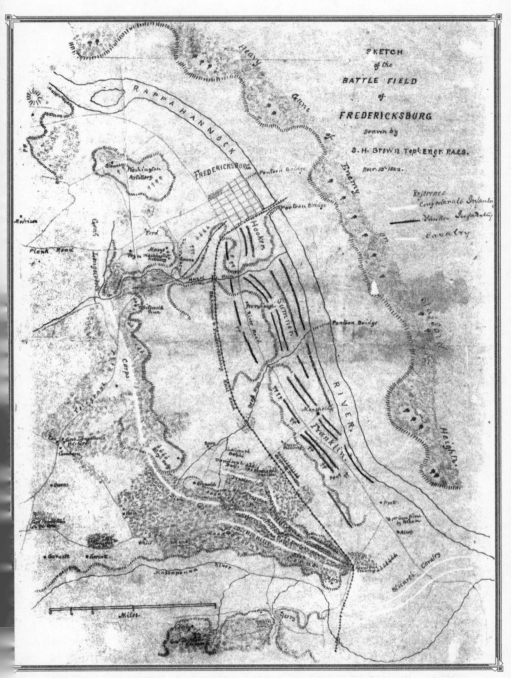

First Battle of Fredericksburg: Confederate and Union troop positions during the early stages of the First Battle of Fredericksburg. *Courtesy of Library of Congress, Online Map Collection (Civil War Maps), Call No.: G3884.M25S5 1862 .B6 Vault : CW 562.3.*

PRELUDE TO BATTLE

The respite from fighting and the horrors of war ended abruptly during the early hours of December 11. At 4:30 A.M. the booming of Read's signal guns told the defenders that the Union army was preparing to cross the river. The buglers sounded reveille and "Boots and Saddles." McLaws's men quickly got up, dressed, and ran to their positions along the defenses. Barksdale's Brigade in Fredericksburg was quick to respond, and small arms fire also could be heard as Confederate marksmen picked off the engineers and infantrymen who were frantically trying to complete a pontoon bridge across the river. The massed Union artillery finally began the long-awaited bombardment at 7:00 A.M., targeting the houses from which the Confederate sharpshooters were firing. However, positioned atop Stafford Heights they were unable to depress their guns sufficiently to hit their intended targets. A few houses were set afire, but the sharpshooters who were so effectively delaying Union plans continued undeterred.[20] The Union artillerymen redoubled their efforts to wreak havoc on the annoying Confederate marksmen. Atop Telegraph Hill (which after this day would become known as "Lee's Hill"), Longstreet had a view similar to those in the Washington Artillery on Marye's Heights:

> [with] their whole available force of artillery on this little city, and sent down from the heights a perfect storm of shot and shell, crushing the houses with a cyclone of fiery metal. . . . The town caught fire in several places, shells crashed and burst, and solid shot rained like hail. In the midst of the successive crashes could be heard the shouts and yells of those engaged in the struggle, while the smoke rose from the burning city and the flames leaped about, making a scene which can never be effaced from the memory of those who saw it.[21]

The Seventh Michigan and the Nineteenth and Twentieth Massachusetts Infantry were now ordered forward to take the town by storm. The Union infantrymen jumped on the pontoons that had not been yet anchored to the bridge under construction and rowed across the river. Ashore, they finally drove off the Mississippi sharpshooters near the riverbank. This deadly threat removed, the Union engineers were finally able to complete the bridge. Oliver O. Howard's Second Division (Second Corps) crossed soon after, followed by Orlando B. Willcox's Ninth Corps. Barksdale's men remained unsubdued and bitterly resisted Union efforts to advance down the streets. However, they faced overwhelming numbers, and as soon as Longstreet felt he was sufficiently prepared, he ordered Barksdale and his men to fall back on the main line of defense. The attackers thus finally succeeded in securing the town.[22] To gain better reconnaissance from the newly acquired advanced position in Fredericksburg, an observer equipped with field glasses was sent up in a balloon that floated high above the buildings.

As the leading elements of Burnside's forces were working their way into Fredericksburg, headquarters for the Washington Artillery was moved up to the Marye House in preparation for the fighting that was now inevitable. The ammunition chests were taken off of the caissons and placed in the traverses that had been dug behind the mini-redoubts and gun positions. For their safety, the teams of horses were led back to a ravine in the rear, which because of its position on the reverse slope would be impervious to enemy artillery fire.

The next day, the twelfth, the weather was overcast and foggy. Those on the heights could see little of what was going on in Fredericksburg, where more and more Union troops were brought in and various preparations made for the impending attack. In mid-afternoon, William Owen says about 2:00 P.M., the weather cleared for a while and the defenders soon espied a Union column crossing the bridge over the Rappahannock. McLaws's Artillery was ordered to fire upon this target of opportunity. Their fire proved accurate, and the column halted, then soon headed back toward Stafford Heights. An hour later, another Union force was spotted approaching near the gasworks on the near side of Fredericksburg. This time, the Confederate artillery fire proved even more deadly and the enemy formation scattered. Their success, however, drew the attention of the Union high command then overlooking the operations from Stafford Heights. The full force of the Union artillery retaliated, and for the next fifteen minutes it was the Washington Artillery's turn to be on the receiving end. Protected by their defensive works, there were few casualties, although Sergeant John Wood, a prominent thespian in the battalion's dramatic company, was badly wounded by an exploding shell and would never return to the battalion stage or active duty.[23]

From their view atop Marye's Hill, when the weather permitted, the men in the Washington Artillery had a clear view of the landscape that stretched before them up to Fredericksburg and on which so many of their antagonists would undoubtedly die once the fighting started. In front of them the hill fell abruptly to Telegraph Road, which followed the contour of the base of the hill. Not only did this road greatly facilitate troop movement, it afforded an ideal defensive position for the infantrymen as well. The twenty-five-foot-wide road had been carved out of the hill and for long stretches was as much as four feet below ground level relative to the side facing the town. A four-foot-high stone fence had been erected on this side. Moreover, along those stretches where the roadbed was sunken it would not have been observable to Union officers when they approached the outskirts of Fredericksburg the next day to ascertain the "lay of the land" for the impending grand assault.[24] From their position on top of the hill, as the Louisiana gunners looked farther out, they would have noticed that the ground quickly leveled out for about 150 yards and then abruptly fell a few feet. This second terrace extended out another two hundred yards until it reached a ravine that contained a millrace, i.e., a canal flowing through a mill wheel. This stream was about twenty feet wide and four feet deep. There was another drop of several feet at this point.

Although the view revealed two open "terraces" leading up to the heights, more or less of equal depth, that could be easily swept by a competently led battery, in reality, there were numerous blind spots where the Union infantry could hide during the maelstrom of death and destruction that was about to erupt. For one thing, the slope was uneven and undulated, especially in the middle of the field—about 150–200 yards from Telegraph Road. This would provide some cover to Union infantrymen who threw themselves on the ground.

Unfortunately, from the defenders' point of view, the days immediately prior to the battle were rainy and foggy, and the defenders could catch only glimpses from time to time of the landscape that extended down to the town.

THE BATTLE

The artillerymen's view was only temporary and the low-lying clouds rolled back in, and on the next morning the intended battlefield was once again completely enshrouded in fog. If their visibility was extremely limited, their sense of sound remained unimpaired. The Louisianans could hear the Union officers bark orders to their men through the mist. Longstreet remembered distinctly hearing the orders "Forward, guide center, march!" The men in the Union regiments were to dress their ranks by ensuring they were even with the colors at the center of each regiment.[25]

As the fog finally lifted between 9:00 and 10:00 that morning, the gunners of the Washington Artillery atop the heights could see Franklin's Grand Division (Union) toward the right disposed in a series of lines near the Rappahannock River. Visibility continued to increase and the fog lifted higher and higher. Eventually, they could discern long columns of Union troops on the road leading down from Stafford Heights, still waiting to cross the Rappahannock in front of Jackson's portion of the battlefield. Reconnoitering the terrain their troops would have to cross, Union officers on horseback rode up the plain to well within artillery range. The continuous rolling of the drums, the bugle calls, and almost frantic scurrying of the couriers and aides on the plain told the experienced veterans of the Army of Northern Virginia that the long-anticipated fight was finally at hand! The Confederate artillery did not respond, however. It was only when the first Union infantry line advanced to take

Bernard Woods at the extreme right of Longstreet's portion of the line that McLaws ordered the seven guns, specially placed to meet this very threat, to fire.[26]

Although most of the defenders' attention was drawn to the Union infantry massing in front of Jackson's Corps, McLaws's men now espied an ominous sight that portended serious consequences on their side of the field. Away in the distance directly in front of them on the other side of Fredericksburg was another lengthy column waiting to cross the pontoon bridge established the previous day. They did not have long to wait before the "ball opened," however. Franklin's Grand Division started to advance in two lines toward the Confederate right. Stonewall Jackson was the first to react. As soon as the advancing Union infantry was spotted, General Stuart, on the extreme right of the line, ordered up a section of horse artillery, which soon unlimbered and began to fire upon the enemy flank from a small mound south of the Massapomax River slightly in advance of Jackson's position.[27] Despite these precautions, two of General A. P. Hill's brigades were driven back upon Jackson's second line and the advancing Union attackers seized a small wooded area in their path. Part of General Early's Division counterattacked and drove the attackers back, reclaiming the woods. The right side of the Union attack enjoyed similar initial success, capturing a small wooded copse in front of General Hood's line. However, these Union soldiers were even more easily dislodged and driven back.[28]

Sensing that there had been a significant buildup of Union troops in Fredericksburg, Longstreet ordered McLaws's artillery to begin firing at the town a little before noon.[29] This fire made it very hot for the Union infantry then marching along the streets. Shortly after the artillery fire began, Sumner's infantry, as Longstreet would say, "swarmed out of the city like bees out of a hive." The attack against the Confederate left had begun.[30]

The staff officers of the Washington Artillery, meanwhile, had been taking advantage of the "calm before the storm" and were smoking their pipes in Marye's yard when a courier from Longstreet approached Colonel Walton with a dispatch ultimately intended for

General Cobb and his infantry along the sunken Telegraph Road below. It instructed Cobb to conform to General Anderson's movements during the upcoming attack should the latter be forced to retire to the second line of defense (where the Washington Artillery was stationed). Handed these orders, Lieutenant William Owen rode down to the general. Cobb responded with expected braggadocio, "Well! If they wait for me to fall back, they will have a long time to wait." Events would soon validate the general's prediction.[31]

The sound of small arms fire was now heard as the Confederate skirmishers in front of Marye's Heights started to be driven in by clouds of Union skirmishers. The leading elements of the Union regiments could be seen marching out of the town at the double as they attempted to cross quickly over the mill-race by narrow bridges along the Telegraph and Orange and Plank Roads. Until they could deploy in the open space beyond, most of these regiments were seen to march by the "right flank, undoubled," that is, in a slender column two men wide.[32] General Hancock would later report that many of the troops were delayed crossing these bridges. Some of the planking, becoming loose, had fallen off, so the men had to work their way slowly over the "stringers," instead of marching along the main roadbed on these structures.[33]

On the other side of the canal there was an embankment that led up to the first "terrace." The Union regiments attempted to take advantage of this relative cover to deploy into line.[34] McLaws and his men watched these developments on his right front with the greatest interest. He noted the Union method of deployment—the color-bearers quickly ran in front of their comrades and planted their standards where their regiment was to form. Although this method had occasionally been used by French troops during the Napoleonic Wars, McLaws was apparently unfamiliar with the practice.[35] The remainder of the men in each regiment would advance quickly and then "file into line on the right"[36] until they occupied the positions indicated by their standard. We learn from a seemingly unconnected source that the Union military had more reason to employ such methods than did their French predecessors.

The embankment in front of them was only three or four feet high, so the men were ordered to lie down to take advantage of this cover. Not necessarily being able to easily see the preceding regiment now lying on the ground, the flags helped the next regiment ascertain where its correct position was to be.[37]

Lieutenant Owen noted that it was now 12:30 P.M.[38]

The pause in the Union advance was but momentary, as General William French's leading brigade of Union troops readied themselves for the assault. A few moments later they appeared, advancing in a "column of brigades." Earlier that morning Major General Darius Couch, commander of the Second Corps, had been ordered to send his two divisions to seize the "heights in the rear of the town." The formations used during the attack were also specified. Each division was to advance in three lines, all of brigade front. Couch was left complete discretion as to the distance to be maintained between each line. The whole was to be preceded by a "heavy line of skirmishers." Couch decided that French's Third Division would lead and be followed soon after by Brigadier General Winfield S. Hancock's First Division; each succeeding brigade was to advance two hundred yards behind the one in front.[39]

The defenders, even those along the second line atop the hill, could hear the Union infantrymen shouting "Hi, Hi, Hi," as they advanced over the muddy ground. They noticed that the Union infantrymen were carrying their shoulder arms at the "right shoulder shift"; the color-bearers carried their standards "aslant" on their shoulders. This means they were probably advancing either at the double (140 paces per minute) or at the run (where they ran as fast as they could). Lieutenant Owen was struck with the strange beauty and grandeur of the sight:

How beautifully they came on! Their bright bayonets glistening in the sunlight made the line looked like a huge serpent of blue and steel. The very force of their onset leveled the broad fences bounding the small fields and gardens that interspersed the plain.[40]

As soon as the Union infantry appeared above the embankment, Colonel Walton barked out the commands, "'Tention! Commence fir-i-ng!!" and the artillerymen commenced their deadly trade. The Washington Artillery batteries immediately belched blue flame. According to Owen, the artillery would "soon warm up to their work and aim and fire coolly and deliberately."[41] Doing so, they were following the time-honored "best practices" of gunnery. Experienced artillerymen had long recognized that effective artillery fire was dependent upon *accuracy* of fire, rather than on *volume*. At West Point, before the war, Captain John Gibbon had cautioned his pupils when firing at distances beyond six hundred yards to fire only once per minute, for example.[42] The initial range was between five hundred to seven hundred yards, thus the batteries atop the hill began by firing solid shot (bolt, in the case of rifled artillery) or fused shell.[43]

In any case, the fire proved deadly. Stationed near Generals Lee and Longstreet on Telegraph Hill, a British artist on assignment for the *Illustrated London News* would recall the effect of the artillery fire on the advancing Union lines: "I could see the grape, shell, and canister from the guns of the Washington Artillery mow great avenues in the masses of Federal troops rushing to the assault."[44] Brigadier General Thomas F. Meagher, commander of the Second Brigade in Hancock's division, noted that when his men went into the fray later that afternoon, there was still a continuous fire of shot and shell, each of which seemed to bring down several men.[45] Although Union and Confederate accounts of the devastation caused by the Confederate artillery on Marye's Heights seem to conflict, it is, nevertheless, possible to reconcile them. From observations made during other engagements, it is known that the men at long, and even medium, ranges could see incoming projectiles, and frequently could move out of the way. From the artillerists' point of view, the effect was something like the "parting of the Red Sea" when the attacker advanced in a deep enough formation; to the gunners it looked as though swathes of men were being cut down, when in fact casualties might be fairly light.

The gunners in the Washington Artillery were both competent and well practiced, and by this point in the war the routine had become instinctive. As soon as the piece was fired, the No. 3 artilleryman moved behind the gun and closed the flow of air by placing his left hand over the vent. He had to be very careful, since if air entered through the vent a premature explosion might maim, even kill, his comrades in front of the piece. Meanwhile, using his sponge-staff, the No. 1 artilleryman cleaned out the residue inside the barrel. He then reversed the staff and rammed down the next round (in the Civil War this was usually a "bag charge" that held the explosive powder), followed separately by the projectile. The gunner aimed the piece, and then yelled, "Ready." The No. 4 artilleryman inserted the primer and the piece was ready to be fired.[46]

Still the Union attackers came on. The Confederate artillerists who had been firing shot or shell switched to canister. The advancing Federal line now finally within effective "(rifle) musket range," the Georgians and North Carolinians in Cobb's Brigade along the Telegraph Road at the bottom of Marye's Heights stood up and after a moment to look along their barrels began to fire. Volley after volley was unleashed upon the advancing Union infantry. This proved to be a truly withering fire, and the combination of small arms and close-range canister fire quickly proved to be too much for the attackers. Once again, gaps began to appear in the Union line, which had now lost its momentum. First, a few men started back toward the rear. This soon turned into a torrent as the men began to run to the relative protection of the canal bank. Brigadier General Nathan Kimball's brigade had been beaten back.

At about 1:00 P.M., Cobb sent a messenger to report that he was running low on ammunition. General Joseph B. Kershaw was ordered to reinforce this portion of the Confederate line with two regiments. Cooke's Brigade from Ransom's Division was brought in. The pause in the action after Kimball's assault was but momentary, however.[47] The other brigades in French's division would do their best to succeed where their predecessors had failed. Andrew's brigade was the next to attack, followed soon thereafter by Palmer's.

All met with the same fate as the first wave.[48] Looking down at the fields in their front, the artillery now could see blue patches where groups of unfortunate Union infantry lay dead or dying.

The success was not without cost, however. Brigadier General J. R. Cooke was severely wounded and General Cobb killed. General Kershaw received a second set of orders to assume command of Cobb's Brigade.[49]

French's division was now completely spent after three successive attacks; next, it was Hancock's turn. His men advanced in the same brigade-size lines seen during the earlier attacks. According to Henry J. Baker, who served as Number 1 on Sergeant William J. Behan's crew, Hancock's men were even more disciplined than their predecessors:

> It was a grand sight to see the perfect discipline and faultless alignment of these well trained Federal soldiers as they steadily and bravely pushed forward regardless of what might come. The progress of Hancock's men was only checked by having to climb over the dead bodies of those who had preceded them.[50]

Cobb's and Kershaw's Regiments withheld their fire until the last moment, and the first wave of Hancock's men, Zook's brigade, seemed to advance farther than any of French's men.[51] Baker remembered a "gallant" Union officer galloping up and waving his sword wildly to inspire his men and urge them forward still. Sergeant Behan promised that he would "check that officer." He calmly sighted his piece and gave the order "Fire." Climbing to the embrasure, Baker saw that the shot had been accurate, killing the horse. Fortunately for the officer, a moment before he had jumped off the horse and was merely holding its reins; unfazed, he ran up and down the advancing Union line flashing his sword and cheering his men on.[52] Remnants of French's lines, checked but not dispirited, joined the attack. Despite all the heroics, however, Zook's attack also proved unsuccessful. Next came Meagher's Irish brigade. Its color-bearers proudly held high the green flag with golden harp, emblematic of Irish pride and hopes. Corporals Payne and Hardie, gunners for the First Company's two rifled guns (a 3-inch rifle and 10-pounder Parrott) then busy at work firing at other targets more directly to their front, were ordered to redirect their guns toward Meagher's brigade. Though their fire proved deadly accurate, the brave Milesian soldiers pushed on. Disregarding the slaughter around, they advanced to within twenty-five yards of the sunken road and its stone wall.[53] But valor alone was not enough, and in the end lead and shell triumphed over spirit and flesh. Hancock was still not done, however. Caldwell's brigade was still fresh, and it advanced in its turn. The result, of course, was the same.

The Union attackers, so far unable to achieve anything by coup de main, next tried their hand at the "long shot." Union sharpshooters edged their way closer and found protection along a "cut" near the base of the hill. A little later, some say as late as 4:30 P.M., Union artillery was also moved forward. Both directed their attention toward the Confederate artillery on the heights.

Meanwhile the Confederate high command had decided that Kershaw's reinforcements were insufficient to meet the waves of brigade-size Union lines that were thrown against them in succession. Around two o'clock Robert Ransom's Brigade was moved from its position in reserve to near the top of Marye's Heights. It stopped on the crest only long enough to deliver a volley at the Union troops approaching Cobb's men below. Then it quickly moved down the hill to join the first line of defenders along the sunken road.[54] Some of Ransom's North Carolinians were killed as they stopped to fire, and the artillerymen in Squires's First and Miller's Third Company had to drag the bodies away from the embrasures in order to be able to fire their pieces unobstructed. Corporal Francis Ruggles, a Bostonian before the war, elated to find a fresh blanket among the corpses, gleefully announced to his comrades, "Boys, this will be a good thing to have tonight."[55]

Unfortunately for Ruggles and the First Company, they soon felt the full force of the Union sharpshooters and nearby artillery. A bolt from a rifled piece scored a direct hit on its redoubt, showering dirt all over the men. Corporal Edwin Kursheedt, a Jewish merchant before the war, playfully picked up the bolt and suggested to his gun crew that they send it back to its original owners, which was quickly done.[56] During the war, it was widely reported that gunners seemed to delight in dueling with opposing artillerymen, though most had nothing but scorn for enemy musket fire.

> Cannon against cannon they appear to delight in; they seemed to feel complimented when the enemy turns his guns upon them; but a musket-ball they despise, and when they begin to hiss about them or strike their guns with a sound like a spat or a splash, they begin to grumble, and think they are not properly supported.[57]

Not surprisingly, all levity immediately evaporated as the artillerists fell victim to accurate sharpshooter fire. Corporal Ruggles dropped as he was ramming a charge down his gun, a minié ball piercing his spine. Private Perry grabbed Ruggles's sponge-staff as it fell out of the fatally wounded artilleryman's hands and stepped forward to take his place, but this lad also was soon hors de combat. The bullet went through his elbow and struck the artillery piece he was working. Ruggles's second replacement met the same fate in short order, and this man, one Private Everett, was placed beside the dying Ruggles in a corner of the redoubt. Everett was still game, however, and offered to cut the fuses from his prone position. In a twist of tragic irony, Ruggles found use for his newfound blanket sooner than he had expected. It was placed over his body as a shroud.[58]

The execution from the deadly sharpshooters continued. A few moments later, Private C. A. Falconer, a planter from Louisiana, was shot in the head near the ear while walking behind a gun; he died instantly.[59] Then Artilleryman J. E. Rodd, who as No. 3 had been holding the vent, also had his elbow shattered. Of course, First Company was not the only one to suffer casualties. By the time the Washington Artillery was relieved, three of its men were dead and twenty-seven wounded. It soon became necessary to remove the casualties from around the gun emplacements. The wounded were moved to a little white brick house just to the rear of Squires's First Company. This proved to be a rather dubious haven, since it also was the target of the Union artillerymen's ire. Rather fittingly, given its new use, it had become so raked with bullets and shot that by the end of the engagement its white walls were so chipped as to be a blood red.[60]

In combination, the Union sharpshooters and artillery had finally managed to decimate Squires's gun crews, and it became necessary to call in nearby infantry to help work the guns. It was getting late in the afternoon when Longstreet directed Major Osman Latrobe to check on how the artillery was doing along Marye's Heights. Once on the hill, he was told that the Washington Artillery was running out of ammunition. Promising that he would relay this information back to General Longstreet, he rode off to Maurin's Battery. Here, he ordered one of its guns brought forward beyond its embrasure where it could more effectively play on the attacking line. But this position was too exposed to enemy small arms fire, and within one minute all of its artillerymen fell killed or wounded; the gun had to be quickly withdrawn to its original position behind the field works. Thinking himself grievously wounded in the chest, Captain Squires asked that John M. Galbraith assume command of his company. However, the bullet that had struck Squires had been spent, leaving only its imprint on his gray jacket. He was soon back on his feet and in control of his unit.

It was at this point that Benjamin Eshleman came over from his battery on the right to explain that he had only a few solid shots left. The officers consulted together and agreed it was time to ask Colonel Edward Porter Alexander to send in more ammunition.[61] However, their superiors decided that the Washington Artillery had served its part, and it would be preferable to replace it with a fresh artillery unit. Colonel Alexander was ordered to send in his reserve artillery. Somewhere between 3:40 and 4:30 P.M. Captain P. Woolfolk's Battery, Captain Moody's Madison Light Artillery of 12-pounders, and two guns from Captain Tyler C. Jordan's Bedford Artillery rushed toward the crest of Marye's Heights to replace the battered Washington Artillery. Yet another Union attack was in progress at the time, and the Federal infantrymen cheered as the heroic Confederate artillerymen started to limber their pieces and quickly pull back over the hill. Buoyed by what they thought was a general enemy withdrawal, the advancing Union infantry continued forward despite their tremendous losses. Seeing that the attackers were now only three hundred yards distant, Alexander's Artillery came in on the gallop amid the proverbial hailstorm of bullet, shot, and shell. All this activity had attracted the notice of the Union artillery on Stafford Heights, which once again now focused its efforts on its counterparts atop the hill. After the battle, Colonel Alexander stated that three-quarters of his losses that day were taken while approaching and unlimbering into position. Despite this, the reserve artillery quickly got into position and opened a "rapid and murderous fire" upon the advancing Union line.[62] In this type of situation, veteran artillerymen had learned a "trick" that allowed the artillery to be fired more quickly. As soon as the gunners saw the flash at the vent, they sprang forward and held the undercarriage wheels, usually reducing the recoil by about 50 percent. This reduced the amount of time relaying and sighting the gun before the next shot could be fired.[63] Regardless of what means Alexander's gunners employed that day, their fire proved effective, and once again the combination of musketry and close-range artillery fire proved too much. This wave of attackers was soon beaten into submission and forced to retire.[64]

Alexander's artillerymen would have to endure one more test of battle that day. Seeing the Washington Artillery moving to the rear, General Joseph Caldwell, whose brigade had been the last to attack, sent word to General Couch, the corps commander, that the enemy was falling back in front of him. Though it was now dark, General Andrew Atkinson Humphreys was ordered to go in with his two brigades, which he promptly did. His men traversed the same ground as French's and Hancock's men had earlier that afternoon. The Confederate line easily beat back the latest assault, and Humphreys's brigade was unable to advance as far as Meagher's command.[65]

Though the Union command didn't realize it at the time, the First Battle of Fredericksburg was over. The Union offensive had completely failed, and Fredericksburg would prove to be one of the

Humphreys's Charge Against Marye's Heights: Humphreys's assault took place after the heroic charge of the Irish brigade. By this point, E. P. Alexander's artillery replaced the Washington Artillery, now exhausted and out of ammunition. *Courtesy of Library of Congress, Prints & Photographs Online Catalog (PPOC). LC-USZ62-139.*

greatest military fiascos of the entire war. In the days that followed, after the Union army had retired, and the Confederates were at liberty to stroll over the hotly contested territory to their front, they would discover the true extent of the carnage inflicted on the Northern soldiers. The correspondent for the *Illustrated London News* would try to convey the horrors of the sight to his readers back in England:

A ride along the whole length of the lines told also a sad tale of slaughter; but when the eye had once rested upon the fatal slope above mentioned the memory became fixed upon the spot, not for fifty-years to come will that scene ever fade from the memory of those who saw it. There, in every attitude of death, lying so close to each other that you might step from body to body, lay acres of the Federal dead. It seemed that most of the faces which lay nearest to Colonel Walton's artillery were of the well-known Milesian [i.e.,

Irish] type. In one small garden, not more than half an acre in size, there were 151 corpses. I doubt whether in any battle-field of modern times the dead have ever lain so thick and close. By universal consent of those who have seen all the great battles of this war nothing like it has ever been seen before.[66]

But the soldiers in blue had fought determinedly and bravely, even when there appeared to be little likelihood of success. A Confederate who could pull himself away from the general jubilation of victory might worry that such men if better led might not always be destined to fail.

6

WEBSTER'S PARROTTS AND THE ATTACK AGAINST ARKANSAS POST

At the suggestion of William T. Sherman, Major General John A. McClernand organized an expedition to capture a Confederate stronghold on the Arkansas River whose forces had been obstructing navigation along the Mississippi River. The plan of attack called for Admiral Porter's gunboats to batter the defenses and neutralize Confederate artillery. The gunboats' performance proved disappointing, and a young lieutenant in charge of two 20-pounder Parrotts was called upon to attempt to silence several large-caliber enemy artillery pieces that had proven to be particularly annoying to the river flotilla and land forces alike. Highly skilled in his newfound martial profession, Daniel Webster and his artillerymen would have an effect on the day's struggle that far transcended the weight of shot fired.

AN OVERVIEW OF THE ATTACK

Spectacular successes at Fort Henry, Tennessee (February 5, 1862), and then at Hampton Roads, Virginia (March 9), when the USS *Monitor* defeated the CSS *Virginia* (a.k.a. the *Merrimac*), ushered in the "age of the ironclad." A few weeks later, Farragut's reduction of Forts Jackson and St. Philip (April 24), followed quickly by the capitulation of New Orleans, seemed to presage a new era in naval warfare, one in which ironclads, gunboats, and mortar ships working in conjunction could batter at will even heavily fortified shore positions into submission. Such an assessment proved unduly optimistic, however, and several river operations of this type were notorious failures, such as the attempted destruction of Fort Donelson (February 12–14) and Farragut's protracted bombardment of Vicksburg (June 26–July 28). The inability of the Union river flotilla to make a serious impression on the Confederate defenses at Arkansas Post was all the more dis-heartening given the duration of the operations and the sheer volume of rounds fired. The Rebel batteries consisted of a mere twenty-nine guns, of which only two were 10-inch Columbiads. The remainder were obsolescent 32- and 42-pounder smoothbores. On the attacker's side, the USS *Brooklyn* alone carried twenty-four 11-inch Dahlgren guns.[1] It is probably difficult for the modern mind to grasp how so many gunboats and mortar ships firing off so many rounds could produce so little damage. Given the original objectives of the Union commanders who planned the operation, it is obvious that the result did not live up to their expectations, and that they failed to appreciate the relative ineffectiveness of gunboat fire against elevated positions, regardless of the caliber of the artillery onboard.

The Union assault and capture of Fort Hindman, or "Arkansas Post," as it was known to Federal forces, although a relatively minor event in the overall Vicksburg Campaign, is highly illustrative in this regard. Occupying a dominating position on the left bank of an oxbow bend, about fifty miles from the mouth of the Arkansas River, military authorities on both sides recognized the strategic importance of Fort Hindman/Arkansas Post. Not only was the

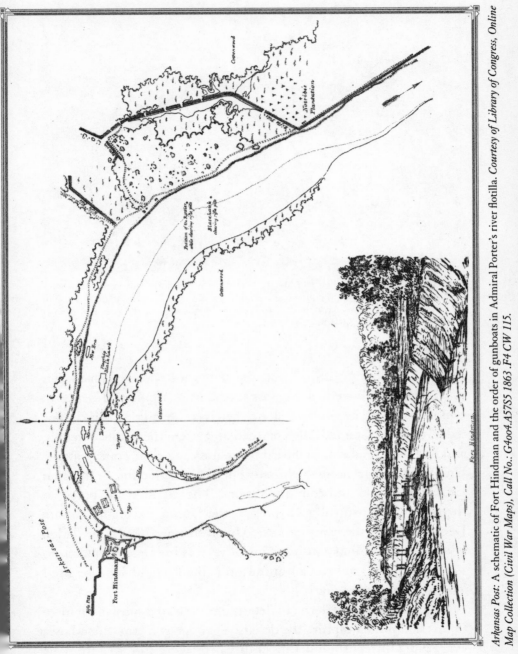

Arkansas Post: A schematic of Fort Hindman and the order of gunboats in Admiral Porter's river flotilla. *Courtesy of Library of Congress, Online Map Collection (Civil War Maps), Call No.: G4oo4.A57S5 1863 .F4 CW 115.*

Naval Bombardment of Arkansas Post: After the war it was popularly thought that the bombardment by the Union naval flotilla had won the day. Illustrations focusing on this part of the engagement became common. *Courtesy of Library of Congress, Prints & Photographs Online Catalog (PPOC). LC-USZC2–1987.*

position the key to Little Rock, the state capital of Arkansas, but downriver it allowed easy assess to the Mississippi and hence to Union traffic plying its way along the river. During 1862 the Confederates had systematically enlarged and strengthened its defenses, and had used it as a springboard for marauding river craft to attack Union navigation along the Mississippi River in an effort to threaten Union operations and communications. The extent of the potential threat became painfully obvious to the Union command in late December with the capture of the Union steamer *Blue Wing,* laden with valuable military stores. This prize was immediately taken to Fort Hindman, and the ammunition gained would soon be used against its original owners.[2]

Major General McClernand determined to lead a substantial force to invest and then capture the defensive works by storm. First, however, the Thirteenth and Fifteenth Corps were to move by river transports to the mouth of the White River on the Mississippi, debark, and then close in on the fort by land. The bitter lessons of the previous year—the need for thorough and timely reconnaissance, the importance of protecting one's position with extensive use of skirmishers, etc.—seem finally to have been appreciated by the Union military. Orders emphatically stipulated that when debarking, the Union forces had to send out quantities of skirmishers and "advanced detachments" in various directions to reconnoiter the ground. Reserves were to be placed at strategic points behind the lines so that they could be moved to counter any sortie that the Rebels might attempt. Finally, each battery was to be accompanied by an infantry company, which was not only to provide protective support but also to assist its movement if necessary.

The two corps began to debark at Notrib's farm late in the afternoon on January 9, 1863. The task was beset with difficulties, however. Not only was there a hard driving rain, but, as it turned out, there was insufficient space to dock the numerous transports. The rain, however, finally cleared up around 4:00 A.M., so that debarkation was able to resume the next day.[3] It was not until noon that all of the troops were back on land and ready to move forward. As the infantry slowly made its way off the transports, Colonel Warren Stewart, chief of cavalry, was ordered to explore the bayou on the right of the fort. Meanwhile, to divert the enemy's attention from the momentarily vulnerable land forces, Admiral David D. Porter and his gunboats were to move up and fire on the enemy fort.

It was soon discovered that the Confederates had already abandoned their first line of defense, a series of rifle pits along a levy that ran perpendicular to the river road. At first, McClernand thought that Sherman's Fifteenth Corps would be able to position itself above the fort near the meandering river by cutting inland by a wide semicircular movement through the woods. However, the road cut through a large swamp, and the only way across one of the bayous was over a narrow old bridge. This route was considered dangerous and probably impassible if opposed by any hostile forces, and, under the best of circumstances, would require too much time for a large body to traverse. Sherman's First Division (Brigadier

General Frederick Steele's), which had been sent forward along the road, was recalled. Countermarching, it returned to the river road and advanced to within one mile of Arkansas Post before turning off to the right a second time. The ground closer to the defenses proved to be less of an obstacle and Steele's division was able to gain the rear of the fort. Brigadier General David Stuart's Second Division eventually found its way to Steele's left. Brigadier General George W. Morgan's Thirteenth Corps followed and deployed between Sherman's Corps and the river. McClernand and his corps commanders had to abandon the original plan of completely investing the fort and be content with a semicircular line that extended from the river below the fort to its rear.[4]

It was dusk when Admiral Porter's gunboats started to bombard the fort. Though the gunboats blazed away for almost two hours, the damage inflicted was minimal. The fort's position on high bluffs made it difficult for the gunboats to fire accurately at their intended targets.[5] It seems that the artillerymen aboard the gunboats underestimated the range of the fort. The fuses were not cut short enough and the shells exploded past the far side of the fort. Other than a few horses rendered hors de combat, there were few casualties, and more importantly little damage was done to either the defenses or Confederate ordnance.[6] To make matters worse, the gunboats seemed to receive more than they were able to hand out. A large gun in the fort's lower casemate was particularly annoying.[7] One of the light draft gunboats, the *Rattler,* had been crippled by a shot that struck her hull.[8] Severely harassed by the three largest Confederate guns in the fort, the gunboats finally had to abort their mission and steam away. The gunboat attack was to be supported by a concomitant infantry assault, but the latter had to be called off; at this point the troops were still making their way up to the fort and were not ready. In fact, portions of the besieging force continued to show up throughout the night and the force was not completely in place until the morning. The defenders, meanwhile, were not idle and hurriedly continued to shore up their defenses. Sherman's men, for example, heard the Confederates

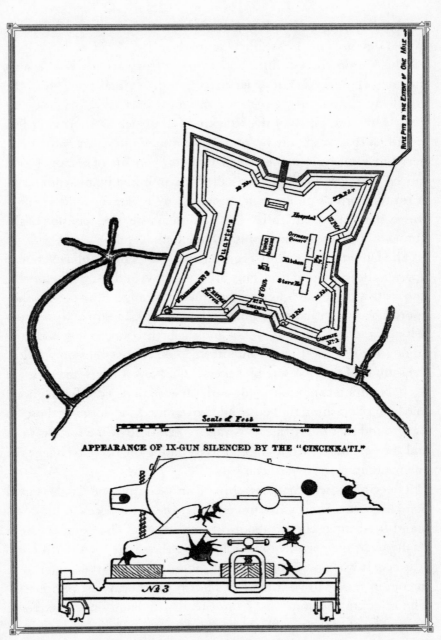

APPEARANCE OF IX-GUN SILENCED BY THE "CINCINNATI."

Confederate Artillery in Fort Hindman: Although the inset shows a 9-inch gun "silenced by the *Cincinnati,*" we now know this gun was destroyed by Daniel Webster's two 20-pounder Parrotts. *Courtesy of Library of Congress, Online Map Collection (Civil War Maps), Call No.: G4004.A57:2F6 1863 .U5 CW 115.2.*

busily chopping and felling trees, a sign that foreboded a determined defense and a possible bloodbath.[9]

The Union forces continued to move forward early the next
morning (January 11) in order to assume their final position in the
attacking formations, which for the most part were brigade-size
lines. Although much of the attacking force, such as Sherman's Fifteenth Corps, was ready by 10:00 A.M., the infantrymen had a long,
nerve-racking wait as the river-based components of the operation
moved into position. The plan called for an initial bombardment by
Admiral Porter's gunboats, augmented by whatever field artillery
was available to the infantry. Three minutes after the cessation of the
gunboats' fire, the infantry was to launch its assault.

The Union attack finally began at 1:00 P.M. as the gunboats moved
upriver and started to fire. This fire was "slow and steady" while the
gunboats were still at long and then medium range. However, as they
approached to within close range the tempo picked up and soon developed into a "hailstorm of shot and shell." Ensconced in woods and
among hedges, most of the infantrymen on shore could only follow
the sounds of the first stages of the action. Nevertheless, the series of
deep, booming explosions, followed a few seconds later by the noisy
mayhem of crashing timber, would have raised the hopes of those on
the ground that this artillery barrage would destroy the fortifications
and the defenders' will to fight, thus obviating the need to engage the
enemy in up-close, mortal combat.

The Union field artillery chimed in near the end of the naval
bombardment. Sherman estimated that the field pieces in his command fired intensely for about fifteen minutes. The bombardment
finally over, the corps commanders gave the order for their men to
advance. It was now about 3:00 P.M., and the Union attackers moved
in concentrically toward the fort's north and northwest periphery.[10]
The attacking formations, from Steele's division on the extreme
right in front of the northwest face of the fort to Osterhaus's division
anchored on the Arkansas River on the left, all set off within a few
minutes of one another. Of course, the form of the attacking formations varied. Sherman's Second Division (Stuart), for example,

advanced at the double-quick in two waves, its second brigade 150 yards behind the first.

The ground immediately outside the fort had been cleared to afford an unobstructed line of fire against anyone with the temerity to rush the defensive works. The land beyond 250–500 yards from the parapet, however, was much more varied; a veritable patchwork of woods, clearings, fields, and paths, with even the occasional marsh. On the Union extreme right there was also the bayou. This meant that each Union brigade had to traverse its own unique per-mutation of changing landscape before entering the open area in front of the fort. The Seventy-sixth Ohio Infantry in Steele's divi-sion, for example, had to struggle mostly through the woods.[11] John M. Thayer's Third Brigade in the same division experienced even greater difficulty crossing over a marshy wooded area, which not only slowed its progress but forced his command out of the larger, division-size formation. Having to work through narrow clearings, Thayer temporarily had to keep his men in a deeper column of reg-iments (i.e., one regiment in line behind the other) until once more on open ground they were able to deploy in line.[12] On the right half of the attacking line, the Sixteenth Indiana (First Brigade, First Division, Thirteenth Corps) had a much easier time; they had to work their way through only about 150 yards of thick underbrush before they came to a large open field in front of the fort.[13]

The task of working their way through woods, across marshes, etc., would pale compared to the experience that awaited them once they neared the fort in the open space. At this time a murderous defensive fire erupted. Many of the attacking columns, enfiladed by artillery and small arms fire, had their progress abruptly checked. In some cases the local commanders, sensing the futility of trying to advance farther in the face of such a withering fire, had their men halt and fall to the ground.[14] Others made a desperate effort to move their men over the remaining stretch of ground, but to no avail. The cross fire proved too much and formations melted away as in-dividual soldiers sought refuge behind whatever ersatz shelter they could find.

We did not open fire upon this column with small-arms until its head was within 80 to 100 yards from our line; then we gave them a very deadly fire, firing by file and with marked effect, as after the first volley those who were not killed or wounded fell back in great confusion to the shelter of the timber, from whence they kept at a very heavy skirmishing fire.[15]

It was at this point that an incredible turn of events occurred. A number of white flags suddenly appeared in the portion of the defenses assigned to the Twenty-fourth Texas (dismounted) Cavalry Regiment.[16] Nearby Union forces took advantage of the lull in firing along this portion of the defensive line. Advancing unopposed, they secured this part of the perimeter. Realizing that the defenses were breeched, the Confederate command had no choice but to surrender the fort and outlying works. From the Confederate perspective the battle came to a sudden and unexpected end.

REASONS FOR THE UNION SUCCESS

Although in his after-battle report McClernand acknowledged that the gunboats and Union field artillery silenced the defenders' artillery, he rather fancifully implied that the actual capture of the fort was the result of the infantry assault that followed the bombardment:

Burbridge's brigade . . . dashed forward under a deadly fire quite to the enemy's intrenchments . . . Colonel Sheldon's brigade being the first to enter the fort. Presenting himself at the entrance of the fort General Burbridge was halted by the guard, who denied that they had surrendered until he called their attention to the white flag and ordered them to ground arms. Immediately after, meeting General Churchill, commandant of the post [sic], and Colonel Dunnington, of the rebel navy [sic], commanding the fort, he referred the former to me, from whom I received the formal surrender of the post, its armament, garrison, and all its stores. Farther to the enemy's left his intrenchments were stormed by General Sherman's command.[17]

The implication, of course, is that the Union infantry managed to storm its way through the murderous defensive fire and approach the walls, whereupon the defenders realized that any further resistance was futile and an expeditious surrender was in order. In reality, the Union effort had been effectively stymied at literally every point along the line, and almost all Union reports acknowledge that the Union infantry were either forced to fall back or stopped in their tracks. The advance to the walls occurred only *after* the white flags appeared. Sherman, in his own report, provides a more honest account, and one senses his surprise at the suddenness of the victory.[18]

Although all three authors of the surviving Confederate after-battle reports were equally surprised at the sudden Confederate surrender, their accounts do mention what probably caused the Texas dismounted cavalry's morale to collapse. Brigadier General Thomas J. Churchill, the commander of the Confederate troops, conceded that "most of the field pieces had been disabled" at the time of the capitulation.[19] Colonel Robert R. Garland of the Sixth Texas Infantry provides further elaboration in his account:

About 4 o'clock P.M. Colonel Dunnington . . . called on me for a re-enforcement of 100 men. . . . I directed Lieutenant-Colonel Anderson to throw the two right companies of his regiment into the fort. While this was being executed two gunboats passed the fort, delivering their fire immediately opposite. The fort and the two guns on this part of the line being silenced, the enemy's batteries and gunboats had complete command of the position, taking it in front, flank, and rear at the same time, literally raking our entire position. It was during this terrific cross-fire, about 4.30 o'clock P.M., that my attention was attracted by the cry of "Raise the white flag, by order of General Churchill; pass the order up the line."[20]

During the war, a number of accounts of this action appeared that did provide a balanced assessment of the Union infantry, artillery, and gunboats' role in the victory. In a two-volume work that began to appear in 1863, Joel Tyler Headley, for example, asserted that the land artillery and gunboat fire were equally destructive.[21] However, armored gunboats were still a novelty and the previous year had gained a measure of fame in the West after the capture of Fort Henry. It was natural that some journalists would attribute, albeit unconsciously, more than their fair share of the credit to the river craft. Although in his book, *War Pictures,* which also appeared that year, James B. Rogers mentions that land batteries were present, clearly his enthusiasm was reserved for the gunboat ordnance, and he quoted a correspondent who had witnessed the gunboat activity during the capture of both forts who considered that the naval artillery had been much more effective at Arkansas Post than it had been a year earlier at Fort Henry:

> The thundering [gunboat] artillery was grand and awful. . . . Round shot and shell tore huge rents in the parapet, dismounted guns, turned others round on their carriages and riddled the embrasures and barracks in the midst of a cloud of dirt and splinters and limbs of men.[22]

Of course, one of those who emerged as a hero after the action was Admiral Porter, who would frequently be lionized in the press. Now, if McClernand in his report had insinuated through omission that the approach of his infantry had induced the Confederates' surrender, Porter exploited exactly the same literary technique to wrestle the credit for himself and his gunboats:

> By this time all the guns in the fort were completely silenced by the *Louisville,* Lieutenant-Commanding E. R. Owen, *Baron de Kalb,* and *Cincinnati,* and I ordered the *Black Hawk* up for the purpose of boarding it in front. Being unmanageable, she had to be kept up the narrow stream, and I took in a regiment from the opposite side to try and take it by assault. As I rounded to, to do so, and the gunboats

commenced firing rapidly, knocking everything to pieces, the enemy held out a white flag, and ordered the firing to cease. The army then entered and took possession.[23]

If one were to believe Porter, his men alone were responsible for the successful conclusion to the entire operation. Of course, his account was completely self-serving and one might say laden with "braggadocio, bombast, and bulls—t." Nevertheless, this was the version that would gain currency in the decades following the War of Secession. Not only would Samuel Schmucker in his *History of the Civil War* (1865) echo Porter's claims that the naval artillery caused the greatest destruction, this author also minimized the contribution of the field batteries onshore: "The chief merit of this conquest was due to the tremendous and destructive firing of the gunboats, whose artillery were much more formidable than those of the Federal land forces."[24] In a June 1888 article in the *National Tribune,* W. T. Michael of the U.S. Navy would claim, "The gunboats dismounted every gun in the fort." This was a theme that would be picked up by numerous general histories, such as *Military and Navy History of the Rebellion* and A. T. Mahan's *Gulf and Inland Waters.*[25]

Just around the time these works appeared, two events occurred that would forever alter the way the War Between the States would be treated. This, of course, was the appearance of a truly vast number of articles in the *Century Magazine* from November 1884 to November 1887, later assembled and published as *Battles and Leaders.* The other was the United States War Department's publication of *The Official Records of the War of the Rebellion,* later known as *The War of the Rebellion: A Compilation of the Official Records.* This had a cascading effect, and ultimately generated many articles in newspapers and magazines, such as those in the *National Tribune.* Of course, the most avid readers were the veterans themselves, most of whom were now in their fifties and early sixties. Many of the former soldiers were horrified at what they read, feeling that many of the reports were self-serving or otherwise inaccurate. The result was that a relatively large number of men set out to write their own memoirs to try and correct these inaccuracies.

One of these was Daniel Webster. Webster had proved to be a more than competent artillerist, and served most of the war as a lieutenant and the de facto commander of the First Wisconsin Battery of Light Artillery. Promoted to captain in November 1864 in recognition of his talent and organizational skills, he was appointed acting chief of artillery for the Department of the Gulf on January 23, 1865.[26] It was, in fact, during the affair at Arkansas Post that Webster first attracted the attention of senior officers. After the war, Webster grew increasingly indignant that history had given the artillerymen, especially those in his section, such short shift and that few recognized their role in securing this victory. Working with a comrade in his artillery unit, Donald Cameron, the former Wisconsin cannoneer collected and analyzed accounts and memoirs of others who were present that day. The work was finally published in 1907 as the *History of the First Wisconsin Battery of Light Artillery*. The story told differs from the period histories not only in its explanation of what materially contributed to the Confederate defeat at Arkansas Post, but in the level of detail provided.

WEBSTER'S PARROTTS DURING THE ASSAULT

It was clear to the Union command that bombardment by the gunboats during the evening of the tenth had produced disappointing results, and it would be necessary to augment their firepower during the upcoming assault planned for the next day. As a result of the previous evening's fiasco, Admiral Porter ordered that a light field battery join the assaulting forces.[27] The left section of the First Wisconsin Battery, consisting of two 20-pounder Parrott rifled guns commanded by Captain Foster, and an infantry brigade were placed on the opposite bank from the fort. Their duty was to prevent any of the Rebels within the fort from escaping; later the artillery would also be ordered to play on the Rebel sharpshooters in the rifle pits. Another two guns from the

20-Pounder Parrotts: This illustration shows the type of ordnance Lieutenant Webster and his men used to bombard Arkansas Post. *Courtesy of Library of Congress, Prints & Photographs Online Catalog (PPOC). LC-DIG-cwpb–01028.*

Wisconsin battery, the right section under Lieutenant Webster's command, were ordered to approach quietly to within about one thousand yards of the fort on the same side of the river as the assault. There they were to remain concealed until the gunboats made their appearance. Then, these two guns were to concentrate upon neutralizing the two 8-inch guns in the casemates. Written orders handed to Webster specifically forbade him from firing his guns at the 9-inch gun *en barbette*. This was to be destroyed by the gunboats with their heavier armament.

The First Wisconsin Battery, at this point, like so many other organizations, was but at partial strength. Webster's section was undermanned, and some gunners had to be temporarily recruited from the center section, which was to be inactive during the upcoming engagement. Moreover, several sergeants were either sick

or otherwise unavailable, so the individual guns would be commanded by senior gunners, rather than NCOs. These problems
notwithstanding, by noon Saturday, Webster was able to move his
section to within six to eight hundred yards of the fort. Taking advantage of some young growth, the two guns were placed behind a
large sycamore log without drawing the attention of the defenders
in the fort.

Lieutenant Webster's two guns were to begin fire only as the first
gunboat passed their left flank. One of the lead drivers would later
recount how the sections managed to get into position with time to
spare, and Webster had ample opportunity to ensure that everything
was according to regulations. He upbraided the chief in charge of the
left caisson for not properly aligning the wagon perfectly with its gun
in front. The gunners, meanwhile, took advantage of the temporary
respite and crawled cautiously to the front of the woods to get an idea
of the work that was in store for them. The gunners soon returned
and were seen shaking their heads and whispering among themselves.
Approaching one of the men, the driver soon learned the source of
their apprehension. One of the men was overheard to bemoan: "Loose
grape. They'll throw a bushel of it. . . . When we open fire. The Rebels
will knock us into pie."[28] In the battery history that Webster would
later coauthor, the lieutenant would claim that the section was a mere
six hundred yards from the fort, in other words, well within canister
range of the largest defending guns. The gunners feared that in an artillery duel between large guns firing canister well ensconced within
fortifications, and the unprotected 20-pounder Parrott field guns, the
latter would quickly come off the losers.

The gun crews did not have long to wait, and soon the first gunboat, the *Benton,* reached the designated position on the section's left
flank. Yelling "pieces by hand to the front," the lieutenant ordered his
small command into action. However, before the two guns' wheels
were able to take "scarce a half dozen revolutions," a white puff of
smoke was seen ascending over the left casemated gun in the fort.
The shell burst high over the battery, but the fragments continued
their course. Two men were killed outright and another two injured

in the infantry regiment placed slightly to the rear in support of the artillery pieces. The already quoted lead driver would recall thinking: "Bless the man that cut that fuse, and why didn't Webster wait until the gunboats drew their fire. . . ." For a brief moment the guns in the fort continued to fire rapidly and three more shells burst in short order. Fortunately for Webster's artillery, the defending gun crews overcorrected the first shot and these burst harmlessly too far in their front. It was a matter of moments before the two guns in the section were finally wheeled into position, loaded, and fired. Webster's section had only a few solid shots, and so began exclusively firing shells. Like the first Confederate shot, their first round was too high. The second round fired was too low. The third, however, went straight to the target and entered the left gun's casemate and knocked it immediately out of service. The Rebels' 9-inch gun en barbette was not inactive during this time and hazarded a few shells at the two First Wisconsin guns. But they also missed their mark. Fortunately, the gunboats at last were in position and started to play upon the defenders, who turned their attention from the two small field pieces to the large 9-inch and 10-inch guns on the ironclads in the river. This proved to be a fatal error, the worst of the day. The two guns supervised by gunners Gabe Armstrong and Ira Butterfield fired shot after shot right on target. Sergeant McKeith recounts how one of his functions was to watch each shot carefully and inform Armstrong of the results, so that the proper adjustments in aim and length of fuse could be made. This information "was not difficult to give, as I would see every shot from the time it left the smoke of the gun, until it struck."[29]

Soon another Rebel gun, just to the right of the disabled casemated gun, was directed to counter the land-based artillery threat. Only a few rounds were exchanged before one of the Wisconsin guns hit the axle of the Rebel gun and dismounted it. Another round hit its caisson in the rear, blowing it up and killing all six horses.[30] While this was happening, the Confederate 9-inch gun en barbette was making a nuisance of itself with the Union fleet, and the gunboat *De Kalb* with its 10-inch gun began what proved to be a short-lived duel. The land-based gun, with stable platform, soon fired a round through one of the *De Kalb's* portals, setting the boat afire and temporarily disabling it. Brigadier General P. J. Osterhaus, the commander of the Second Division (Thirteenth Corps) that had been assigned to assault the fort, felt the entire fleet was now in danger, and he immediately sent one of his orderlies with verbal instructions to Webster to "silence that gun, or it will sink the fleet." Webster eagerly complied and ordered his guns to switch to solid shot. The Wisconsin gunners enjoyed the same success as they had with the two casemated 8-inch guns. Within three minutes several rounds scored direct hits against the largest Rebel gun. One round bit into the carriage's cheek, while another round, which McKeith claims was fired from Armstrong's gun, hit the muzzle and tore off about one hundred pounds of iron. With all heavy artillery resistance snuffed out, the few Confederate field guns posed no real threat to the small Union fleet. The gunboats were now able to continue their operations undisturbed, and sensing the ultimate futility of the situation the men in Colonel F. C. Wilkes's Twenty-fourth Texas Cavalry held up white flags that soon led to the capitulation of the entire defending force.

Despite Admiral Porter's claims, which for the most part were accepted by the public and press, the crucial damage had been inflicted by the two guns from a field battery. In a relatively short time, the two-gun 20-pounder Parrott section was able to fire a total of sixty-three rounds at the guns in the fort, all but the first two hitting near or directly on their mark. General L. A. Sheldon, the brigade commander, and General Osterhaus would both later attest to the accuracy of these field guns and the tremendous damage they had been able to inflict. Sheldon, for example, had personally witnessed the destruction of one of the casemated 8-inch guns, the dismounting of the 9-inch gun, and the explosion of the caisson. In his after-battle report, he delivered even higher praise for Webster's accomplishment:

> This cannonade lasted fully two hours, during the whole of which time I was near Lieutenant Webster's section of artillery, my presence not being necessary at any other place, and I consider it my duty to state that I never saw a better officer or better men serving artillery.

Cool, deliberate, and intrepid, they sent their deadly shot against the enemy's stronghold, their commander controlling every round and its effect, the men quietly obeying his orders without the very superfluous huzzaing and yelling, which is incompatible with the dignity of the arm of artillery. I heartily congratulate Lieutenant Webster and his men on their great success. The reduction of the lower casemate and the silencing of three or four formidable guns are their exclusive merit.[31]

The Confederates who were interviewed after the fort's surrender agreed with this assessment. A Confederate officer stationed in one of the lower casemates during the artillery engagement was heard to say: "That little battery on the bank did us more harm than all the fleet, as it would not let us work our guns."[32]

At first glance, the section's success appears amazing, in fact, almost unbelievable. It is natural to assume that the gunboats armed with a greater number of guns, all of larger caliber, would necessarily have inflicted many times more damage than two 20-pounder Parrotts. One doesn't have to look far for the reasons why the reverse was true, however. Interviewed soon after surrendering by W. C. Paddock, a reporter for the *Chicago Tribune,* the fort's commander would note:

When those two guns came there in front of the fort we did not pay much attention to them; the gunboats were what we feared most. But those two guns damaged us more than all the fleet. . . . "1st shot high, 2nd low and the 3rd—oh, God! look here, pointing to the dead gunners lying by the side of the gun."[33]

The rest of the explanation is provided by Lieutenant Webster himself. For one thing, the smaller Parrotts served by veteran cannoneers could be fired much more quickly than the larger guns in the fort. Webster estimated that his men enjoyed a three-to-one advantage in rate of fire. A much more important advantage was the accuracy of the fire: "With us every condition requisite for accurate shooting was favorable, and when the range was once obtained it was maintained to the last."[34] Obviously, given the results of the initial artillery exchange, the fort's gunners couldn't make the same boast. And any significant reduction in accuracy usually proved fatal to the side thus disadvantaged. (The following year the officer in charge of the construction of the canal at Dutch Gap near Petersburg, Major Ludlow, would remark that: "It requires the nicest manipulation and a real interest in every shot to make average correct shooting. One good shot is worth a dozen bad ones. . . .")[35]

The artillerists on the gunboats were even more disadvantaged than those in the fort. Gunboats, because of their very nature, were always denied one of the prerequisites of accuracy: a stable platform. Despite all efforts to remain stationary, it was never possible for the gunboats to remain still. This made it difficult for the gun crews both to acquire the proper range and then to maintain it. Gunboat fire was notoriously inaccurate. At the siege of Petersburg, an officer implored Colonel Henry L. Abbot, commander of the siege train and artillery of the Army of the Potomac, to use his influence to stop the fire of the ironclads in the James River against land-based targets since "they do more damage to us than the rebel batteries."[36]

However, an even larger obstacle to accurate shooting was the difference in elevation between the gunboats and the targets at which they aimed. The foundation of the fort was thirty feet above the shoreline, and the 9-inch gun en barbette was ten feet higher still. Observers on the shore would note how frequently the gunboats would have to back away in order to gain sufficient elevation, and how throughout the engagement they would pour broadside after broadside harmlessly into the riverbank below the fort. Inevitably, the tendency was then to overcompensate for the shortfall, and the result, as occurred here, was that the projectiles fell harmlessly on the other side of the targeted area, doing no damage to either fortifications or personnel.

Of course, the assault had been a resounding success and the Union focus was on victory and giving thanks. As always occurs in such situations, shortcomings were ignored, and once again the difficulties in using river craft to attack heavily fortified shore positions were overlooked.

7

CAVALRY VERSUS CAVALRY AT GETTYSBURG — JULY 3

Scott Mingus, Coauthor

The Battle of Gettysburg in many respects marked the turning point of the fighting in the eastern theatre. A series of uncharacteristic errors in judgment by several key Confederate commanders, repeated miscommunication, poor timing, lack of coordination, and determined fighting on Northern soil by Union troops all added up to a tactical and strategic defeat for Robert E. Lee. On July 1, 1863, elements of the Second and Third Corps of the Confederate Army of Northern Virginia overwhelmed outnumbered Union defenders north and west of Gettysburg, driving them back through the borough's streets to the hills and ridges south of town. In a debatable decision, the day's successes were not followed by attempts to seize Cemetery and Culp's Hills late in the afternoon. On day 2, sledgehammer attacks by much of Lee's army gained territory on both flanks, but failed to dislodge the Army of the Potomac. The following day, savage fighting on Culp's Hill preceded what became celebrated as "Pickett's Charge." Among the many lessons learned by both Lee and Meade at Gettysburg was newfound respect for the fighting ability of the cavalry of the Army of the Potomac.

THE FEDERAL CAVALRY COMES OF AGE

The Gettysburg Campaign was a turning point in the fortunes of the Union cavalry in the eastern theatre. Since the beginning of the war, this branch of service had generally been outgeneraled, out-maneuvered, and outfought with embarrassing regularity by the Confederates, most notably by Major General J. E. B. Stuart. As the war began, the regular U.S. Cavalry was understaffed and scattered throughout a multitude of posts—primarily on the western frontier. They had been reassembled in the East and augmented with scores of volunteer state regiments, many of which comprised men with little or no cavalry experience. As a result, Southerners, often with much more experience riding horses, had early advantages in tactical combat in the East.

The first signs of improvement among Union cavalry in this theatre occurred during two weeks of fighting in the Loudoun Valley in October–November 1862. The gap in capabilities continued to close during the campaigning leading up the great conflagration that would take place at Gettysburg. As Lee's army began its movement toward Pennsylvania in early June 1863, Stuart's cavalry was surprised at Brandy Station by Major General Alfred Pleasonton's Union forces. This battle, and the earlier cavalry fights in the Loudoun Valley, helped raise the confidence level of Pleasonton's troops. Additionally, a series of recent organizational changes at the division and brigade levels had brought in fresh leaders, many of whom were young and aggressive. Stuart's plan to circle behind the Union army to cause mischief and confusion before rejoining Lee's main force was approved, and he and his cavalrymen set off on the night of June 24–25. However, his force was checked at the June 30 Battle of Hanover and forced to circle ever farther to the right in a fruitless effort to rendezvous with Lee's Second Corps. A rearguard action at Hunterstown on July 2 again demonstrated that the Federal cavalry was now a worthy match for Stuart's vaunted cavaliers.

Stuart's cavalry was in no shape to fight another prolonged battle as they wearily arrived at Gettysburg on the late afternoon of July 2.[1] Men and horses were exhausted by days of endless riding over the undulating Maryland and Pennsylvania terrain. The two previous days had seen a hard fight at Hanover and two successive forced all-night marches. Ammunition was running low, and many of his men were mounted on the more than one thousand horses stolen from York County farmers. Few of these replacement mounts were suitable for military usage, and none had been exposed to the terrors and confusion of combat. In some regiments, manpower and officers were greatly reduced by the endless series of battles and marches.

On the Union side, horseflesh was generally in better condition and the regiments were generally well supplied and armed, mostly with effective breech-loading carbines, although some Michigan troopers carried Spencer repeating rifles. The many changes in generals and leadership had not yet been tested to a great degree, but a number of the previous commanders who had been replaced were not competent or popular, and morale generally had been raised further by these changes instituted by Pleasonton.

Gregg and Custer Reach the Battlefield

Early on July 3 as both sides prepared for the third day of bitter fighting, the commander of the Army of the Potomac, General George Gordon Meade, worried about a fresh Confederate attack against his right near Culp's Hill, appealed to his cavalry commander for help. Major General Alfred Pleasonton responded at 6:00 A.M. by sending an officer with orders for Second Cavalry Division commander

Brigadier General David McMurtrie Gregg, whose troops were bivouacked along White Run and the Baltimore Turnpike. Pleasonton directed Gregg's cavalry and artillery to march along the Baltimore Turnpike toward Gettysburg until they reached the bridge crossing Rock Creek. So important was this position that Pleasonton emphasized that it had to be held "at all hazards."[2]

Fortunately for the Union, David Gregg was a highly professional, veteran officer with prewar combat experience, who had led the Eighth Pennsylvania Cavalry before assuming command of his own cavalry division.[3] Unlike so many of his brother officers, Gregg displayed an unusual degree of grand tactical acumen and was intuitively able to sense not only the combat implications of terrain, but also how the enemy was most likely to interact with Union dispositions. General Gregg felt strongly that Pleasonton's proposed movement was a very bad idea, because there was a larger threat farther to the army's left in the area around Brinkerhoff and Cress Ridges, immediately east of Gettysburg along the Hanover Road. The previous evening, two of his regiments had skirmished with the enemy in this area. Though it had been a relatively light affair, it did portend a more serious Confederate effort in this part of the field. Gregg explained his fears to Pleasonton's messenger and requested that he be permitted to guard the extreme right flank. The messenger returned a second time and reported that Pleasonton remained adamant: his original orders stood. However, he would allow one of General H. Judson Kilpatrick's brigades to move to the area about to be vacated by Gregg's cavalry.

As it happened, George Armstrong Custer's Michigan cavalry brigade (Second Brigade, Third Division, Cavalry Corps) would be singled out for this task. Major Luther S. Trowbridge, who commanded a battalion of the Fifth Michigan Cavalry, would vividly remember the events of that morning. At 7:00 A.M., he and his fellow officers were awoken by a senior officer he had never met before. Trowbridge realized it was General Kilpatrick, their divisional commander. The men and officers, sensing the importance of Kilpatrick's visit, dressed, ate breakfast, and saddled up with proverbial "alacrity." The division commander was there, presumably, to ensure that the brigade speedily followed Pleasonton's initial instructions. The

East Cavalry Field (Gettysburg—July 3): The fields to the northwest of the Hanover Road/Low Dutch Road section would see one of the largest cavalry-versus-cavalry actions of the war. The area would eventually become known as the East Cavalry Field. *Courtesy of Library of Congress, Online Map Collection (Civil War Maps), No.: G3824.G3S5 1863 .B5 CW 328.*

brigade proceeded westerly along a road for a while and then turned around and countermarched toward the extreme right flank instead. Reaching the neighborhood of the junction of Hanover and Low Dutch Roads, about three and a half miles east of Gettysburg, the brigade temporarily halted.

Custer's next actions can be understood only by carefully examining the terrain that now confronted the Michigan cavalrymen. The two roads intersected almost at right angles at the George Howard House, the northwest corner being slightly obtuse. The Hanover Road, or as it was alternatively known, the Bonaughtown Road, ran east-southeast along this stretch, while the Low Dutch or Salem Road coursed roughly toward the northeast. There were a number of houses spaced out along both roads. Cress Run, a small meandering stream, ran parallel to the Low Dutch Road, with a small tributary branching off south of the road. The latter, known as Little's Run, crossed the Hanover Road between the Reever and Little Houses. It ran northward through a woods up to its source near the Rummel farm and was closer to the Low Dutch Road. Sandwiched between the Lott and Rise Houses was a woodlot about a mile from the intersection along the Low Dutch Road on the west side. Adjacent to this was a large open field that extended about a mile westward to Little's Run and the Rummel farm. It was bounded on the west by the wooded Cress Ridge, north and west of the Rummel barn. Though the field was relatively level with only minor undulations, it was crisscrossed with a number of sturdy wooden fences.[4]

When determining how to position his command, Custer had two different factors to consider: the expected line of approach vis-à-vis the terrain and his troopers' armament and associated tactics. Custer's brigade consisted of two different types of cavalry. The First and Seventh Michigan Cavalry were armed with sabres and carbines and were expected to utilize traditional cavalry methods—that is, to execute quickly delivered mounted charges with outstretched sabres or to exchange carbine fire at short range with the enemy. The other two regiments, the Fifth and the Sixth, were the first Army of the Potomac regiments to be armed with the new seven-shot Spencer

Cavalry Deployed as Skirmishers: This is the type of loose extended order Custer's skirmishers would have adopted as they reconnoitered the land in front of Rummel's farm before the cavalry-versus-cavalry action began. *Courtesy of Library of Congress, Prints & Photographs Online Catalog (PPOC). LC-USZ62–14916.*

repeating rifles.[5] To achieve anything even remotely resembling accurate fire, these troopers had to dismount.

Custer realized that the enemy could approach either from the north or the west, and he positioned his command accordingly. The responsibility of protecting the flanks, reconnoitering, and forming the first line of defense fell to those armed with Spencers. The sabre/carbine regiments were held in reserve in a central position. Detachments from the Sixth Regiment were placed on either flank along Hanover Road. The First and Fifth Michigan Cavalry were stationed next to the Low Dutch Road just north of the intersection. The Fifth, armed with repeaters, was in a "double column closed in mass" and occupied the frontal position. The main body of the Sixth and all of the Seventh Michigan Cavalry was stationed south of the Hanover Road, behind the Reever and Spangler Houses, respectively. This last-mentioned building was about two hundred yards west of the Howard House and the intersection.[6] The main body of the brigade was preceded by a skirmish line along Little's Run. This was formed from Captain George Maxwell's company of the First Michigan.[7] Lieutenant Alexander Pennington's six 3-inch rifled guns, Battery M Second U.S. Artillery, were positioned in the southwest corner of the junction. It was now about 8:30 A.M.[8] Two detachments from Trowbridge's battalion were sent out to reconnoiter the surrounding area.

THE ARRIVAL OF McINTOSH'S BRIGADE

While Michigan troopers were scouting the area north of the intersection, General David Gregg's concern about the vulnerability of the Union right flank continued to grow. This anxiety only increased when his Third Brigade, led by his cousin Colonel J. Irvin Gregg, reported to Colonel Meade's headquarters and then was ordered to move up Taneytown Road to scout Rebel positions inside Gettysburg. Given the number of Rebel sharpshooters in that area, this assignment was tantamount to a suicide mission. The mission was cancelled at the last minute, but Pleasonton then ordered part of Irvin Gregg's brigade toward the Twelfth Corps at Wolf's Hill. Acting on his own, Irvin Gregg decided that despite his orders he had to remain in the vicinity of the Hanover/Low Dutch junction. Around 10:00 A.M., he ordered his First Brigade under Colonel John B. McIntosh to move to the rear of Custer's position near the intersection.

UNION CAVALRY
IN JULY 3 EAST CAVALRY FIELD BATTLE

FIRST BRIGADE, SECOND DIVISION (COL. JOHN B. McINTOSH)
Purnell (Maryland) Legion, Company A, Capt. Robert E. Duvall
First New Jersey, Maj. M. H. Beaumont

Third Pennsylvania, Lt. Col. E. S. Jones
First Maryland, Lt. Col. James M. Deems

SECOND BRIGADE, THIRD DIVISION (BRIG. GEN. GEORGE A. CUSTER)
First Michigan, Col. Charles H. Town
Fifth Michigan, Col. Russell A. Alger
Sixth Michigan, Col. George Gray
Seventh Michigan (10 companies), Col. William D. Mann
Battery M, Second U.S. Artillery was assigned to this brigade

Note: The First Massachusetts Cavalry Regiment had been temporarily detached and was not present in the fight.

There is some uncertainty as to exactly how the day's cavalry engagement began. The history that has been passed down to posterity is full of controversy, ambiguities, omissions, and, one suspects, subtle but purposeful deceptions, as well as occasional outright lies. One does not have to go beyond how the engagement started to find an example. Many late-nineteenth-century accounts, such as Luther Trowbridge's *The Operations of the Cavalry in the Gettysburg Campaign,* claim that the opening shots occurred when Stuart ordered Griffin's battery on Cress Ridge to fire in different directions in an attempt to entice hidden Union artillery to respond and thus reveal their position.[9] Now, such an action seems to fly in the face of Stuart's goal of surprising the Union forces on this flank. Stuart, in his own after-battle report, says little about the matter except that the Confederate artillery had "left" the ridge soon after a strong Union skirmish line advanced against the Confederate forces at Rummel's barn and along Cress Ridge. Several detailed Union accounts state that the action began as opposing dismounted cavalry faced off, rather than being initiated by Confederate artillery.

Although the first signs of the impending action became noticeable as early as 9:00 A.M., as the men in Gregg's division were ordered "to horse," the leading elements in the form of Colonel

John B. McIntosh's brigade (First Brigade, Second Division, Cavalry Corps) reached Custer's position on the far right Union flank only between noon and 1:00 P.M.[10] Rendezvousing with Custer in an open field between the Reever and Lott Houses (three-quarters of a mile to the west of the intersection of the Hanover and Low Dutch Roads), McIntosh informed the blond-haired general that he had been ordered to replace the Michigan brigade on that flank. All seemed perfectly quiet, not even picket fire could be heard. When McIntosh asked Custer if he had any knowledge of the enemy's position, Custer calmly replied that the enemy had been moving a heavy cavalry force to the Union right flank, and the newcomers could expect a hot engagement any moment from that direction. As Custer and his cavalrymen set off to report to General Kilpatrick's headquarters on the other side of the Union line, McIntosh seemed up to the challenge and immediately started to position his forces accordingly.

The First New Jersey Cavalry was deployed slightly behind on the skirt of the woods to the right of Jacob Lott's house, itself a short distance west of the Low Dutch Road. To the left of the First New Jersey, the Third Pennsylvania and First Maryland Cavalry, drawn up in a column of squadrons, took their place in a clover field southwest of Lott's house.[11] A section of Captain Alanson M. Randol's four-gun battery, Battery E, First U.S. Artillery, momentarily remained on the Hanover Road near the intersection. The entire brigade faced a large open field at the other end of which, about a half mile distant, was the large Rummel barn and, to its right (northwest), the "wooded knoll" on Cress Ridge behind which Stuart had concealed his forces.[12] General Gregg, meanwhile, set up his headquarters in the Reever House.[13]

A little after 1:00 P.M., the sound of artillery erupted along Seminary Ridge, far to their left. This was the great "barrage," to use a neologism, that preceded Pickett's charge. The sheer volume of guns firing was unprecedented during that war. The ground shook and the repeated booming of the Confederate artillery was so loud it was as if Custer's and McIntosh's men were beside the gun batteries.

In the distance smoke began to rise, and it seemed to one Pennsylvania trooper as if "thousands of acres of timber were on fire."[14]

THE CONFEDERATES MOVE TO BATTLE

The "heavy cavalry force" that Custer had referred to was Major General James Ewell Brown (J. E. B.) Stuart's Cavalry Corps. Jones's and Robertson's Brigades were not present. Prior to the Pennsylvania campaign, Stuart's cavalry had consisted of three brigades, commanded by Wade Hampton III, Fitzhugh Lee, and W. H. F. "Rooney" Lee (later replaced by Colonel John R. Chambliss, Jr., after Lee was wounded at Brandy Station). They were normally supported by Griffin's Maryland as well as Captains James Breathed's and William M. McGregor's Virginia Batteries.[15] However, given the scope of the intended operations, in late May, Stuart's force had been strengthened by the temporary addition of Brigadier General Albert G. Jenkins's and Beverly Robertson's Brigades. Robertson's Brigade was left behind to guard the mountain passes in the Shenandoah and Cumberland Valleys while Stuart's three brigades were off on their independent mission. Jenkins's Brigade was with Ewell's Corps and had led the advance into Pennsylvania. Upon his belated arrival in Gettysburg in the late afternoon of July 2, Stuart took command of Jenkins's Brigade again, which was commanded that day by Lieutenant Colonel Vincent A. Witcher, a twenty-seven-year-old attorney and former partisan ranger whose bold and irregular actions had galvanized parts of western Virginia in 1861 and early 1862. General Jenkins had been wounded and was out of commission, and the senior colonel, Milton J. Ferguson, was not present. A significant portion of Jenkins's Brigade was on detached duty. Captains Smith's and Morgan's companies of the Thirty-sixth Virginia Cavalry Battalion were serving as vedettes guarding some roads on the army's flanks. They were stationed near where Griffin's Battery had initially been positioned, that is, at the intersection of the lane leading north up Cress Ridge (present-day Gregg Lane) and the farm lane leading to the Daniel Stallsmith farm. A number of companies from the Four-teenth Virginia Cavalry were guarding Union prisoners taken on the first day of fighting, while a part of the Sixteenth Virginia Cavalry under Colonel Ferguson was still on the Fairfield Road. This left only five companies of the Thirty-fourth, and four each from the Fourteenth and Sixteenth Regiments, available for action.[16]

J. E. B. STUART'S COMMAND (JULY 3, 1863)

WADE HAMPTON'S BRIGADE
First North Carolina
First and Second South Carolina Cavalry Regiments
Cobb's Georgia, Jeff Davis's & Phillips's Georgia Legions

FITZHUGH LEE'S BRIGADE
First, Second, Third, Fourth, & Fifth
Virginia Cavalry Regiments

W. H. F. LEE'S BRIGADE (LED BY CHAMBLISS)
Second North Carolina, Ninth, Tenth,
& Thirteenth Virginia Cavalry Regiments

JENKINS'S BRIGADE (ALL ARMED AS MOUNTED INFANTRY)
Fourteenth, Sixteenth, & Seventeenth
Virginia Cavalry Regiments
Thirty-fourth & Thirty-sixth
Virginia Cavalry Battalions

ARTILLERY
McGregor's, Breathed's, & Jackson's Virginia Batteries
Baltimore Light Artillery (Griffin's) Battery

Note: The Thirty-fourth Battalion of Virginia Cavalry was attached to Jenkins's Brigade for this campaign only.

The ground in front of the Cavalry Corps, broken and wooded in parts, was not suitable for cavalry operations, so late during the evening of July 2 Lee ordered Stuart to move his men to the left and slightly in front of Ewell's Corps, which at that point was in front of the Union position on Culp's Hill. To facilitate an early start, his men should remain in the saddle all night. Stuart dutifully passed these instructions on to his subordinates. His men were thoroughly exhausted, however, and understandably so. Not only had they been in the saddle almost continuously for four days, they had fought two engagements (Hanover, June 30, and Hunterstown, July 2) with Kilpatrick's cavalry as they rode around the Pennsylvania countryside in a frustrating search for Lee's army. Colonel Richard L. T. Beale of the Ninth Virginia Cavalry quickly informed Stuart's messenger:

> the request would be cheerfully complied with; but that the utmost verge of endurance by men and horses had been reached, and that whatever the morrow might bring, [it is feared] that neither horses nor men could be used either to march or fight.[17]

Realizing that unless permitted to get a few hours rest his command would be useless the next day, Stuart quickly countermanded these instructions.

Although Stuart's forty-five hundred cavalrymen had been called to arms early that morning, according to Major Henry B. McClellan, Stuart's assistant adjutant general, they remained immobilized for several hours where they had bivouacked near Rock Creek (north of Benner's Hill) as they replenished their ammunition. They were finally able to set off around noon. Chambliss's and Jenkins's Brigades took the lead; Hampton's and Fitzhugh Lee's Brigades followed. Two of Stuart's Batteries, those of Breathed and McGregor, could not be resupplied and had to be left behind.[18]

Stuart's Cavalry, now in a lengthy column of route, moved along the York Turnpike one or two miles to the east of their original position. Reaching a cross-country road about two and a half miles from

Gettysburg, the column turned right along a narrow road that led through a forest. After about a half mile, they came to a large rolling field around the Stallsmith farm.[19] Once there, they began to form a line of battle on the far side of the field near a wood on a low—but in parts steep—rise, known locally as Cress Ridge. It was obvious to Stuart that this area was potentially of extreme strategic importance. He found himself on a "commanding ridge" that looked out over a wide expanse of farmland stretching from Hanover to the base of the mountain spurs then occupied by Union forces in the throes of the great battle.[20] The position appeared to be the gateway to a seemingly exposed Union right flank.

One unit in Jenkins's Brigade would play a particularly prominent role in the events about to unfold. This was the Thirty-fourth Battalion, Virginia Cavalry, which upon Witcher's ascension to leadership of the brigade was now commanded by Major John H. McFarlane. The previous evening, it had been moved up to Brinkerhoff's Ridge on the flank of a part of Lieutenant General Richard S. Ewell's Second Corps, a mere three hundred to five hundred yards from where the cavalry fight would start. Moving from its own bivouac that morning, it met up with the head of Stuart's column as the latter emerged from the woods near the Stallsmith farm and Cress Ridge.

Jenkins's Brigade made its way to the ridge overlooking Rummel's farm. The Thirty-fourth Battalion was the first to reach a stone fence on the near side of a barn. Arriving at the front, Stuart ordered the remainder of Jenkins's Brigade to support the Thirty-fourth.[21] Wade Hampton's and Fitz Lee's Brigades were positioned to the left of Chambliss's men, who were roughly in the middle. Jenkins's Brigade formed the right of the line. The line formed an obtuse angle with the apex roughly in the area of the John Rummel farm.[22] One of Chambliss's squadrons dismounted and advanced three hundred yards in front of the line.

The Thirty-fourth, like much of Jenkins's Brigade, was armed with U.S. Model 1841 "Mississippi" rifles, and some Confederate Richmonds and Enfields, plus revolvers (both .44 and .36 caliber

Colts) instead of the traditional cavalry weapons—carbines, pistols, and sabres. Jenkins's men functioned as scouts, but tended to fight as mounted infantry. The regiment had been raised in early June 1862 in Wayne County in the mountains of western Virginia, and the men were a tough hardy lot. Several were from eastern Tennessee and Kentucky, as well as western North Carolina. Many of the men were well known to Federal authorities in the region as bushwhackers and guerillas. They had been pressed into service in the Army of Northern Virginia early in the campaign to protect Lee's right flank as his army advanced northward toward Maryland and Pennsylvania. Portions of Jenkins's Brigade on July 2 were in Gettysburg guarding Union prisoners or scouting the flanks. The rest of the brigade rejoined Stuart, many mounted on fresh horses secured from Pennsylvania farmers.[23]

Stuart rode up to Lieutenant Colonel Vincent A. Witcher and ordered the Thirty-fourth Battalion to occupy the Rummel barn and a stone fence in front of it. Complying, the battalion immediately dismounted. Its line stretched from the barn on the right to Captain Jacob Baldwin's Company at the Rummel springhouse and some bushes on the left.[24]

Stuart sent for Generals Hampton and Fitzhugh (Fitz) Lee so that they could report the situation and receive orders. Hampton, however, failed to appear, and events, starting to take on a life of their own, demanded immediate action.

In his after-battle report, Stuart would explain that he attempted to engage the enemy with a line of "sharpshooters" while moving his cavalry "secretly through the woods . . . to effect a surprise upon the enemy's rear."[25] However, he admits that Hampton's and Fitz Lee's Brigades had unfortunately wandered out into the open while they had been moving in column along the York Turnpike. Union pickets on Cemetery Hill spotted this long line of enemy horsemen, artillery, and ambulances. General Oliver O. Howard, commander of the Eleventh Corps, immediately notified General Meade, who, in turn, passed this information on to General David McM. Gregg, commander Second Division, Cavalry Corps.[26]

THE ENGAGEMENT BEGINS:
THE DUEL BETWEEN DISMOUNTED CAVALRYMEN

While Stuart and his troopers started to move up to the Rummel farm, McIntosh had been busy acquiring an accurate "lay of the land" and positioning his regiments. In order to ascertain the size of the enemy force he knew lay hidden in his front, around two o'clock McIntosh ordered Major Myron H. Beaumont to dismount a portion of the First New Jersey. They were to spread out as skirmishers in front of the position just vacated by Custer's men. However, the New Jersey men were slow to execute McIntosh's orders to advance. Beaumont claimed that he was ill—something that, suspiciously, had happened several times before other major engagements. Enraged, McIntosh yelled at an aide, "Damn them, bring them up at a gallop." Now led by Major Hugh H. Janeway, a nineteen-year-old known never to run away from danger, the 150 dismounted troopers from the First New Jersey immediately began to advance.[27] On the other side, Stuart was quick to respond. As the dismounted Jerseyites moved forward, they soon spotted a Rebel skirmish line south of Rummel's barn, comprised of some of Witcher's dismounted western Virginia riflemen. The advancing Union line was a little oblique to the Confederate line of defense, and Janeway's men changed direction slightly to form a line parallel to their adversaries. Succumbing to the near irresistible urge to strike at a threat looming ever larger, both sides unleashed small arms fire.

The intense fire continued unabated, and both sides quickly started to take casualties. Realizing the importance of the engagement to his plans, Stuart ordered up reinforcements. The Confederate line was strengthened by eight companies. The four companies from Major Benjamin F. Eakle's Fourteenth Virginia Cavalry Regiment were now in the center of the line with McFarlane's Thirty-fourth on the left and the four companies from Major James Nounnan's Sixteenth Regiment on the right.[28] From the start, the fight was a hot one. The vivid description of an intense cavalry fight at Shelbyville, Tennessee, penned by General Joseph Wheeler's staff after the war probably accurately reflects the men's experience on this occasion:

> The carbines and rifles were flashing and banging away at times, and scattering shots, when the game was at long range, and then when the charge came on and the work grew hot, the spiteful sharp explosions swelled into a crackling roar like that of a canebrake on fire, when, in a single minute, hundreds of boiler-joints have burst asunder. Add to all the whizzing, angry whirl of countless leaden missiles which split the air about you; the hoarse, unnatural shouts of command—for in battle all sounds of the human voice seem out of pitch and tone; the wild, defiant yell and the answering huzzas of the opposing line; the plunging and rearing of horses; the charges here and there of companies or squadrons which seem to be shot out of the main body as flame shot out of a house on fire; here and there the sharp, quick cry from some unfortunate trooper who did not hear one leaden messenger—for only those are heard which have passed by; the heavy, soggy striking of the helpless body against the ground. . . . All these sights and sounds go to make up the medley of a battle-field.[29]

Witcher's men soon found themselves running out of ammunition. Although in his report Stuart would claim that the Thirty-fourth Virginia had begun the engagement with only ten rounds apiece, he was in error. The Virginians started off with the normal allotment of ammunition. Several men were sent in succession to the woods in the rear to bring up more cartridges, but all of these were picked off by the Union firing line. Witcher's Battalion, no longer able to fire, had to fall back to the stone fence in the rear. Its right flank was now behind the Rummel barn while its left rested upon a road. The rest of the Confederate line still able to fire held in its original position. Charles Edwards, the Thirty-fourth's adjutant, had been wounded earlier in the action near the Rummel springhouse, so Witcher had no choice but to go to the rear himself. Borrowing Major Nounnan's horse, the colonel dashed through "shot and shell." Witcher did not have to go all the way to the woods, however. He came across one of the men he had dispatched earlier to get ammunition. The man had been wounded while returning, but had the needed ammunition.[30]

It was during this phase of the fighting that Griffin's battery dashed to the edge of Cress Ridge, quickly unlimbered, and began to fire at the Union attackers. The Federal response was not long in coming. The Union artillery batteries were still limbered and on the Hanover Road when the first cannon shots were heard. Lieutenant Kinney's two-gun section of Randol's Battery E moved off of the road and unlimbered into "battery" on the highest part of a ridge in an orchard east of the Howard House.[31] Randol would remain with Kinney's guns through the upcoming fight. Lieutenant James Chester's section unlimbered just south of the Lott House.[32] Pennington's three two-gun sections also moved off the road so that they could unlimber and return fire. Lieutenant Clarke's section was south of the Hanover Road about five hundred feet west of the intersection. Hamilton's and Woodruff's sections moved to rising ground about one thousand feet from Joseph Spangler's large barn. Hamilton later characterized this as a "commanding position," ideal for artillery, and the two sections of artillery remained there throughout the fighting that day.[33] A commanding position, incidentally, did not mean a lofty height. In fact, artillery officers were enjoined not to place artillery on high mounds or hills, since this produced a plunging fire and, in the days of smoothbore artillery, deprived the gunners of their most effective tool—ricochet fire. Even after the advent of rifled artillery this advice remained valid.[34] Plunging fire was much less accurate, and as the enemy moved forward, they could move into temporary dead zones for a short respite from the defenders' artillery fire.

After the war, popular literature generally accredited Randol's battery with quickly knocking out the Rebel battery on Cress Ridge, but letters written by officers in Pennington's battery to Colonel John Bachelder during the 1880s suggest that Pennington's gunners also had a significant hand in the affair.[35] Given the distance separating the opposing batteries, the Union gunners opted for percussion shells. After the war, Lieutenant Pennington would always recall one particular shell that exploded amid the Confederate guns, silencing several guns.[36] Another shot hit a wheel of a gun carriage and left a number of gunners hors de combat.[37] Stuart's adjutant, Major McCellan, in his memoirs would attest to the accuracy of the Union artillery fire. According to McClellan, almost every shot, from the very first, hit the mark, and Griffin was soon forced to withdraw out of harm's way.[38]

No longer threatened by Griffin's Baltimore Light Artillery, the Union artillerists were now ordered to turn their attention toward a number of sharpshooters within Rummel's wooden barn. Some Union artillery officers, such as Lieutenant James Chester, Battery E, would claim after the war that they made short work of this target, driving the Confederate shooters from this structure, and, in fact, several Federal artillery rounds passed through the wooden barn but did not explode.[39] To this day, there is a perfect side profile of a Schenkl projectile punched through one of the barn beams, indicating that the round struck sideways and the percussion fuse did not detonate. More honest veterans, however, conceded that the artillery fire against the barn proved entirely futile. Lieutenant Frank B. Hamilton from the same battery conceded, "So far as our shots were concerned we did not appear to make much impression."[40]

By this stage of the war, officers had learned that in order not to stand out as a target, it was far safer to dismount and advance on foot like the rest of the men. Nevertheless, Major Janeway with reckless abandon rode up and down behind the New Jersey line "encouraging, warning and directing" his skirmishers. The Confederate skirmish line continued to be incrementally reinforced, and it was all Janeway and his men could do to hold on to their ground. Forced to lay out a heavy volume of fire, they also soon depleted the ammunition for their carbines and resorted to their revolvers. Realizing that they would be unable to hold out much longer, Janeway rode back to Major Beaumont and requested more ammunition and reinforcements. Beaumont, in turn, relayed this information to the brigade commander.[41]

McIntosh soon realized that the Confederate force he faced was more powerful than his brigade. He sent a staff officer asking General Gregg to send reinforcements, specifically asking if Colonel J. Irvin Gregg's brigade could be sent to his assistance "at the trot."[42] What happened next was the subject of controversy among veteran officers during the decades that followed the war. Opinion appears to have been divided according to whether the author's sympathies lay with Custer's or McIntosh's brigade. One suspects that each side was unconsciously trying to maximize the importance of their unit's contribution to the affair by establishing that they were there first, or were involved in a larger portion of the fighting, etc. Both camps agree that Custer did, in fact, receive orders to report to General Kilpatrick at the other end of the Union line, and he did start to prepare to comply with these instructions. The question is whether he and his men, at least temporarily, vacated the field of battle and then returned because they were ordered to do by General Gregg. Major Luther Trowbridge, who served with the First Battalion of the Fifth Michigan Cavalry during the battle, adamantly insists that the Michigan cavalry regiments never left the field, and the decision to stay, at least before General Gregg's arrival, was courageously taken by Custer himself.[43] In letters written to General Bachelder after the war, McIntosh provides a more prosaic and far less heroic version. As he passed General Gregg's makeshift headquarters at Two Taverns moving away from McIntosh's position, Custer was stopped and ordered to return to the field he had just left.[44] This is by far the more credible explanation and the one that most modern historians have accepted.

The growing threat posed by ever increasing numbers along the Rebel skirmish line meant that McIntosh could not wait for the reinforcements he requested. He had to reinforce the attacking Union line quickly.[45] Two squadrons of the Third Pennsylvania Cavalry, under Captain Charles Treichel and Captain William W. Rogers, respectively, were ordered forward to the left of the First New Jersey skirmishers. What happened next is the subject of yet another controversy. If we are to believe Henry Pyne, the First New

Jersey's chaplain, the Third Pennsylvania at first advanced to within only one hundred yards of the Jersey skirmish line. There, intimidated by the heavy volume of fire, they were unwilling to advance farther. Even Colonel McIntosh's threats and admonitions at first had no effect. Fortunately, they overcame their jitters and started off once again.[46] They crossed a small stream known as Little's Run that traversed the battlefield and arrived at Rummel's farm. Reaching a small declivity in the ground slightly behind the intended line of battle, the men dismounted. Their horses, protected by the higher ground in front, were relatively protected from the deadly missiles that flew above their heads.[47] Treichel's and Rogers's men continued their advance on foot. Robert Duvall's Maryland troop (Company A of Purnell's Legion) was required to move even farther to the left and anchor the moving line.[48]

McIntosh showed himself to be an experienced cavalry officer, and he was not deceived by the Confederate show of force to his front. He knew that, given the lay of the land, his right flank was potentially at risk. Captains James W. Walsh's and F. W. Hess's squadrons of the Third Pennsylvania moved out from the woods beside the Jacob Lott House and wheeled to the right to protect that flank. Captain William E. Miller's squadron from the same regiment next faced the same direction. It stretched from the woods, near where the regimental monument now stands, to the country lane that led to the Stallsmith House. As a result, half of the Third Pennsylvania found itself on the right flank of McIntosh's line, while the other half was advancing on the extreme left. The First Maryland, still drawn up in a column of squadrons, remained in reserve near the Lott House to cover the intersection of the Hanover and Low Dutch Roads.[49]

Noticing Rebel cavalry forming in the distance to charge, Colonel McIntosh decided to call in his reserve, the First Maryland Cavalry. Realizing the urgency of the situation, he rode back to the Lott House to order these troops into action. However, much to his chagrin, as he neared the Low Dutch Road the regiment was nowhere to be found. General Gregg, now alerted to the escalating action, sent orders for Irvin Gregg's brigade to move his command to Spangler's house.[50] The general also decided to ride up to where the action was unfolding and take charge himself. Once there, he ordered the First Maryland to the intersection of the Low Dutch Road and a work pike.[51]

By this point, Custer's troops, massed in column, were to the rear and left of the left of the Union skirmish line.[52] It was now the turn of the dismounted cavalrymen from the First New Jersey and Third Pennsylvania regiments to run out of ammunition. On the other side, the Confederate line continued to grow stronger as another regiment from Chambliss's Brigade, the Ninth Virginia Cavalry, dismounted and joined the fight.[53] Lieutenant Colonel R. L. T. Beale of the Ninth Cavalry would later testify to the intensity of the firefight at that point and admit it was all the officers could do to hold their men in position.[54]

During a lull in the firing between the opposing skirmish lines, the men in the first and second battalions of the Fifth Michigan dismounted and advanced across Little's Run, accompanied by a part of the Sixth Michigan. Reaching a fence, the Sixth stopped and began to return fire with their Spencer rifles.[55] To help bolster this new left flank, Captain Randol (Battery E, First U.S. Artillery) sent the two guns of Lieutenant Ernest Kinney's section to the left and rear of Custer's position.[56]

What happened next again is subject to debate. In the Union version of events, the First New Jersey and Third Pennsylvania reluctantly started to withdraw. Though closely pursued by the Confederates for a distance, they preserved complete order and were able to turn around and chase the following Confederates away.[57] Not surprisingly, several Confederate eyewitnesses offer a very different account. Both Beale and McClellan attest to a determined Confederate charge that drove the New Jersey and Pennsylvania cavalrymen back in disorder.

This fire did not check our men, but, advancing steadily until close upon them, they rushed at the enemy with a hearty yell, which was echoed down the entire line, and the men in blue, running from all points, were pursued by our men so rapidly and with such ardor that they could not be recalled in time to save them from the charge of a mounted regiment which, passing through them, captured some.[58]

The intense firefight continued, and the dismounted men of the Fifth Michigan Cavalry, now bearing the full weight of the Confederates' ire, sustained numerous casualties—among them Major Noah H. Ferry, who was shot down by a rifleman of the Thirty-fourth Battalion of Virginia Cavalry. Eventually the men of the Fifth suffered the same fate as those who had manned the skirmish line before them; they also started to run out of ammunition. Told of the crisis, Colonel Russell A. Alger, the regiment's commander, sent Lieutenant Harris to find quartermaster Thurber, to instruct him to send a wagonload of additional ammunition. Unfortunately, Harris was unable to find Thurber and returned empty-handed.[59] According to most Union sources, Alger was forced to order his men to fall back to their horses, comforting his troopers by explaining that the saber would now replace carbine and revolver in settling the matter.[60] Witcher provides a different account of the retreat, one that is less charitable to the Michigan troopers:

> Recrossing the fence and formed the 34th Battalion in the wheatfield. The 5th Michigan in line of squadrons having reached the fence, the 34th Battalion, which had alone rallied with me, opened upon the 5th Michigan, sweeping down its ranks with a most deadly fire, killing its major, capturing its colors, and covering the ground with the killed and wounded men and horses of the 5th Michigan. Our cavalry charging his rear, Alger took to his heels.[61]

With the last of the Union skirmishing line falling back, the Confederates sensed victory and surged forward, attempting to catch up to the retiring Fifth Michigan. Veterans of the regiment would afterward claim that this retreat, though performed expeditiously, was orderly and not a rout. However, in a letter written to Colonel Alger after the war, even Major Trowbridge acknowledged that to an out-sider it had all the appearances of an uncontrolled flight. As the men of the Fifth retired to regain their horses, they passed a colonel who commanded a regiment from some other brigade. The colonel, thinking the men had panicked, was infuriated. He angrily attempted to rally the men. It was not until Trowbridge approached and explained that they had orders to fall back that the officer calmed down and suggested that the men in the Fifth Michigan stop and give a cheer to the enemy to show they were still not defeated. According to Major Trowbridge, he complied and commanded his men to halt, march back several rods, and deliver three "ringing cheers."[62]

Whether or not the men along the Fifth Michigan's skirmish line had routed, or whether they were conducting a hasty, but controlled, retreat was a moot point, the effect on nearby friendly troops, not to mention the enemy, was the same. The stalemate appeared to be bro-ken. In a seeming effort to throw a wedge between the Union troops being pushed back from Little's Run and McIntosh's uncommitted troops around the Lott House, Stuart ordered the First and Second Virginia Cavalry from Fitz Lee's Brigade forward.[63]

General Gregg, sensing the urgency of the situation, decided to take immediate action and leave his headquarters at the Reever House to get closer to the fighting. Riding over to Colonel D. Mann, he ordered the colonel to take his Seventh Michigan, then in reserve in a close column of squadrons near the Hanover Road, to charge the oncoming First Virginia Cavalry, which was then threatening to run down the retiring dismounted Michiganders.[64] Custer, who until a few moments before had been near the Spangler House, rushed to the head of the cavalry column now headed to the right of the Fifth Michigan near Little's Run. As his horse broke into a gallop, Custer yelled to his men, "Come on, you Wolverines!"[65] Some witnesses say that the right part of the Fifth Michigan swung back to get out of the horsemen's way; others such as Trowbridge claim this charge was as much as fifty rods to the right of the Fifth's position.[66]

In the years after the war, some veterans of the Seventh would por-tray the charge as a complete success, first slashing through the Ninth

Virginia and advancing up to the First and Thirteenth Virginia Regiments.[67] This would be contradicted by a markedly different version proffered by the likes of Lieutenant William Brooke Rawle, Third Pennsylvania Cavalry, and Major Luther S. Trowbridge, First Battalion of the Fifth Michigan. Trowbridge and his men, heartened by the mounted reinforcements so eagerly rushing into the fray, stopped to watch what they hoped would be a successful outcome. In the already alluded to letter to Colonel Alger, the major recalls their horror upon witnessing what happened next:

> To our astonishment and distress we saw that regiment, apparently without any attempt to change direction, dash itself upon a high staked and railed fence, squadron after squadron breaking upon the struggling mass in front, like the waves of the sea upon a rocky shore, until all were mixed in one confused and tangled mass.[68]

Some witnesses claim that the Seventh had originally charged toward clear terrain, but a change of direction had been effected by the horses rather than by their riders. Those in the leading squadron changed direction, despite the cavalrymen's exertions to stay on course.[69] Whatever the reason, the leading elements soon found themselves crushed against an immoveable, tall fence that some characterized as a high "stake-and-rider" fence, while at least one officer in the Seventh described it as an "impassible stone wall and high fence."[70] Unfortunately, historians have been unable to even pinpoint the exact location of this fence, let alone how it was constructed. In his study of this action, Michael Phipps concluded that it was about fifty yards northwest of the Michigan cavalry monument that now stands on this portion of the battlefield.[71]

The men on each side, finding themselves literally staring the enemy in the face, unleashed an intense and destructive carbine and revolver fire. Those who could dismounted, so as to fire more accurately and more quickly. The men in the First Virginia Cavalry initially had the advantage, for many of the Union troopers lucky enough not to have been bowled over by their comrades still had not managed to extract themselves from the unexpected entanglement. Cavalrymen on both sides now dismounted, rushed the fence, and frantically tried to pull it down. But the fence was "there to stay."[72] The fire was so intense that many of the dismounted Confederate troopers had to lie down.[73] It was now Colonel McIntosh's turn to intervene. He rode up to a squadron of the Third Pennsylvania Cavalry and ordered it to move up to another fence that ran perpendicular to the one being so hotly contested.[74]

Suddenly enfiladed, it was now the First Virginia's turn to endure a superior fire, and their formation started to lose cohesion. Sensing his men were nearing their breaking point, Colonel Chambliss sent one of his aides to Fitz Lee for reinforcements. Realizing that time was of the essence, this officer instead approached Brigadier General Wade Hampton, who was closer. Hampton complied with his brother officer's request; within moments the First North Carolina and the Jeff Davis Legion were advancing to succor the hard-pressed Virginians.[75] Like its predecessors, the Seventh Michigan was forced back after a hard fight. Emboldened, the Confederate dismounted cavalry advanced into the vacated Union position on the other side of the fence.[76] Colonel McIntosh says they were able to move up to "a point somewhere opposite the Howard House."[77]

CONFEDERATE CHARGE
VERSUS UNION COUNTERCHARGE

Like two boxers clinching to catch their breath and regain their strength, a sense of inactivity fell over both sides. It was now around three o'clock. The First North Carolina and the Jeff Davis Legion had advanced too far in pursuit of the Union cavalry and was in an exposed position. General Hampton rode forward to rally his men.[78] However, as he did so, his aide, Captain T. G. Barker, thought that he wanted the rest of his brigade to follow, and so he ordered it to advance.[79] As he approached the troops he had come to rally, Hampton noticed Barker and the remainder of the brigade emerging out of the woods on Cress Ridge in front of the Stallsmith farm and advancing toward him. Though shocked, he maintained enough presence of mind to realize that his command was "past the point of no return," and there was nothing to do but make the best of the situation—he must deliver one final, devastating attack to end the matter once and for all. The brigade advanced in a close column of squadrons at first at a walk. Believing that Hampton's force was insufficient to overthrow the Union forces in its front, Fitz Lee now ordered the remainder of his brigade to follow. The Fourth Virginia Cavalry had been ordered to guard the flank and did not participate in the charge.[80] Although the Third Virginia Cavalry did advance, there is some debate whether it was actually involved in the ensuing melee or whether it remained in reserve.[81]

Hampton's men were hampered by the same fence that had stymied the First Virginia's magnificent charge. But the Confederate horsemen were now aware of the problem and initially confined their advance to the left (east) fork of Rummel's Lane. Once past the obstacle, Hampton was free to deploy his men, who quickened their gait to a trot. One of Hampton's men would recall how their chief encouraged them forward, "Charge them, my brave boys, charge them."[82] Unlike some earlier engagements, the Southern cavalrymen were now instructed to rely on their sabres and eschew the pistol. By this point in the war, Hampton himself had become a proponent of the sabre charge and his standard instructions were now "Sabre! Trot! Gallop! And Charge!" His men were to draw their pistols and fire at the enemy's backs only as they fled.[83] It seems that the men in his command complied. Some of the Union cavalrymen awaiting the charge could hear the opposing officers telling their men to "Keep to your sabres, keep to your sabres!"[84]

Union observers could never agree upon the exact direction of the charge. To Lieutenant James Chester and those positioned near the Lott House, it seemed that the Confederate cavalry was headed directly toward Chester's and Kinney's guns between the Lott House and the intersection of the Hanover and Low Dutch Roads.[85] Captain William E. Miller, who would play a pivotal role in this action, later claimed that the charge was pointed more toward the Spangler House.[86] The scale of the operation far exceeded anything the Union troopers had ever witnessed and they were momentarily awestruck by the "spectacle." The demeanor of the advancing troopers augured a hard fight. Captain David M. Gilmore of the Third Pennsylvania, positioned along the orchard near the Lott House, realized that "their erect bodies and deliberate movements indicated their determination to march through our [Union] lines and complete their purpose of creating havoc and panic in the rear of our army."[87] Apart from the perfect order and alignment, the Union cavalrymen were impressed with the brightness of the uplifted swords, which struck Lieutenant Brooke-Rawle as "glistening like silver" in the bright afternoon sun."[88] This was a common reaction to the sight of so many glistening blades: "the *fannade,* the glitter of the keen blades in the air in the event of a charge, produce in themselves a most terrifying effect."[89]

The Union artillerists were the first to respond. Most of the descriptions penned after the war by Union veterans talk about the storm of shell, shrapnel, and canister that tore huge gaps in the advancing Confederate formation. Chester's account corroborates this. Exhausting his supply of shrapnel shell while firing at Griffin's Battery and then the Rummel barn, he was forced to withhold fire until the oncoming horsemen had approached to within about three hundred yards, whereupon he opened first with canister and then double canister (i.e., two canister charges were fired at the same time).[90] Lieutenants Woodruff and Hamilton, on the other hand, using shell, were able to open at a much greater range by elevating their guns to five degrees. Though decreasing this elevation as the enemy neared, they never switched to canister, shell proving effective.[91] Regardless of which type of missile was employed, initially Hampton's horsemen seemed unaffected and closed and redressed their ranks "as though nothing had happened." Union mounted skirmishers in their path were forced to retire quickly. Dismounted Union cavalrymen in the area were forced back to their mounts.[92]

There was but one Union cavalry regiment that as yet remained uncommitted, the First Michigan Cavalry, then formed in a close column of squadrons near Pennington's battery about one thousand feet from Spangler's House. General Gregg ordered its commander, Colonel Town, to have his command move forward to meet the approaching threat. Town was in the last stages of tuberculosis, and it was with great physical difficulty that he implemented Gregg's orders. His men moved forward at the trot, the first stage of the countercharge,[93] when the oncoming Confederate riders were about five hundred yards away.[94] General Custer, at the rear, instantly galloped forward and placed himself at the head of the formation. The First Michigan then set off with Custer riding bareheaded four horses' lengths in the lead, his sabre gleaming and his hair blowing in the breeze like a "battle flag."[95] Captain Miller's account of what happened next is probably the most oft-quoted, and to a large extent molded how this engagement would be viewed for decades to come:

> As the two columns approached each other the pace of each increased, when suddenly a crash, like the falling of timber, betokened the crisis. So sudden and violent was the collision that many of the horses were turned over and crushed their riders beneath them. The clashing of sabers, the firing of pistols, the demands for surrender, and the cries of combatants now filled the air.[96]

Although Miller and several other witnesses would claim that the two sides raced into each other at speed—that is, where the horses literally ran into and knocked each other down during a frontal assault over clear, open ground—there is good reason to believe that this was pure hyperbole. To anyone who has investigated cavalry-versus-cavalry actions throughout the eighteenth century and Napoleonic Wars, Miller and Brooke-Rawle's claim that the opposing cavalry formations contacted each other at speed and that horses were knocked over by the shock is suspicious. During the entire era that the musket reigned over the battlefield, there are no known instances of cavalry contacting opposing cavalry at speed. True, there were cases of individual horses that crashed into one another at the end of a charge, but invariably this occurred because the horse's view was obstructed by small patches of broken terrain, a horse stumbled at the last moment, etc. The Turks came closest to being able to burst through a line of prepared infantry without stretched bayonets. The bravest of their warriors, only a handful during any battle, would ride up to the line, turn their horses around, and try to get them to rear so high that they would fall backwards onto the waiting enemy infantry.[97] In any situation where cavalry charge was met with countercharge, there were four possible outcomes. One side or the other could waiver and then flee before they came to contact. Alternatively, the riders along each of the opposing lines could spread out so that they passed through the oncoming enemy formation (a process known as threading). Occasionally, one of the horses in the lead turned to the left or the right and all the others followed. The last possibility was that both sides pulled up as they approached each other. The officers or bravest men approached their counterparts and individual sabre duels occurred. Usually, this quickly devolved into a general melle. This is what probably led to the grand cavalry melee that day at Gettysburg.

In his memoirs a member of the Third Virginia Cavalry provides a compelling clue of how the two cavalry forces really closed together. According to Sergeant Robert S. Hudgins II, as soon as both sides made contact the fight devolved into "individual encounters," which in some cases were settled by "weight and the strength" of the horse.[98] In other words, the pushing and shoving, then the toppling of men and horses occurred only after the melee started. This, in turn, suggests that the two sides came together at the final moment more slowly, probably at a walk, and fits in with our understanding of how horses conducted themselves in a charge and melee.

It seemed to be a stalemate as both dished out as much as they took. Many of the combatants heeded their officers' orders and kept to the sabre.

For a few minutes the dense mass of men and horses writhe in the agony of a death struggle; the quick pistol shot, the harsh grating of the sabre falling upon human bones, the groans of the wounded, formed a scene beyond the power of description.[99]

Desperateness of the Cavalry Melee at Gettysburg: Drawn to depict the hand-to-hand fighting that took place at Kelly's Ford. Nevertheless, it illustrates equally well the desperateness of the close action between the remaining Union cavalry and Wade Hampton's command at the close of the great cavalry-versus-cavalry fight on July 3. *Courtesy of Library of Congress, Prints & Photographs Online Catalog (PPOC). LC-USZ62–62758.*

All the way down the animated line there was a furious and frenetic clashing of sabres as alternately one man and then his opponent tried to end the duel with a mortal thrust or a debilitating slash. Private Cassius Norton would remember how nimble some of the Rebel cavalrymen were, able to cling to the horse's neck to minimize their exposure to Union sabres.[100] Captain Amasa E. Mathews's squadron formed the rear of the First Michigan column. It was with the greatest difficulty that he prevented his men from resorting to their revolvers or disordering the ranks.[101] Despite the efforts and exhortations of the officers, some dropped their swords, eager to rely on their pistols instead. The "rattle of the small arms, the frenzied imprecations, the demands to surrender, the undaunted replies, and the appeals for mercy" created a veritable din.[102] Here and there a trooper would fall grievously wounded, only to be crushed by the

ever-moving horses as their riders jockeyed for position in a deadly
dance of death. The lines like a living snake moved backward and
forward, first as one side then the other gained a momentary advantage.[103] Custer, almost maniacal in these situations, was in the thick of
the fighting. He was forced to mount a riderless horse quickly after
his own, "Roanoke," tripped and fell.[104]

However, a short while earlier, before the opposing sides had
come to contact, several Union officers took measures that would
deny victory to Hampton's and Fitz Lee's men. General McIntosh
dispatched his adjutant general, Captain Walter S. Newhall, to
the left with orders to Captains Treichel and Rogers, who had
previously been involved with the spirited and prolonged duel
with Jenkins's men around Little's Run, to collect whatever of the
First New Jersey Cavalry was available and take the advancing
Confederate column in flank.[105] Treichel and Rogers were all too
willing to comply, and joined by Captains Rogers and Wetherill,
Lieutenant Edmonds, and eleven troopers, they immediately
rushed in on the right of the Confederate column, making contact
near the latter's color guard. A fierce fight ensued, the effect of
which was out of all proportion to the small number of Union attackers. Sergeant Joel G. Rammel, Company B, with a few others
forced their way into the Rebel column. Rammel was confronted
by a "long-haired, swarthy rebel" who immediately delivered a
"front cut." Rammel deftly parried the blow with the regulation
"head parry." Though the third finger of his right hand was
crushed as the enemy's blade slid down his weapon, Rammel had
the presence of mind to strike his opponent with one of his knees.
The Confederate trooper, having raised himself in the stirrups to
deliver the blow, was exposed and knocked off his horse. Captain
Newhall meanwhile rushed directly toward a standard-bearer,
who lowered the point staff, in effect a spear, catching McIntosh's
adjutant in the jaw.

Determined to be personally involved, McIntosh meanwhile
gathered up whatever mounted troopers were available around
him, and with his "headquarters men" charged the enemy, who by

this point were engaged in a confused, but nevertheless desperate, sabre fight with the First Michigan Cavalry. A third and possibly the most important body of reinforcements that would tip the balance and hand victory to the Union was spread out along the fringe of the orchard just north of the Lott House. Lieutenant Miller and his brother officer Lieutenant William Brooke-Rawle were standing on a slight rise during the final moments of the initial charge/countercharge. Miller had been suffering from a severe leg cramp and Captain Gilmore was rubbing down the affected leg with whisky. Miller announced his intention to lead his men in a charge, provided that Brooke-Rawle would back him if he were court-martialed for leaving the position he was expressly ordered to hold. Without hesitation, Brooke-Rawle assented. Miller instructed Sergeant Gregg and Corporal Weakley to rally the skirmishers to the right, while Brooke-Rawle did the same with the troopers to the left. The company line reformed, the Pennsylvania cavalry fired a volley, and then drew their sabres. According to Miller, the men were "restive to get their fists in," and without orders they set off at a gallop with a yell.[106] Within moments they sliced into the enemy column about one-third the way from its rear. Captain James Hart's squadron of the First New Jersey, positioned to the left of Miller's squadron, had also charged, its commander directing it toward the front of Hampton's column.[107]

A few of Hart's men were able to fight their way into the Hampton mass and accost the general himself. Hampton, a large and extraordinarily strong man, one of whose favorite pastimes was to hunt bear armed with only a bowie knife, at first easily defended himself against superior odds. A pistol shot and a sabre stroke cut down his first two assailants. He was now surrounded and greatly outnumbered, however. Privates More and Dunlap, Mississippians from the Jeff Davis Legion, came to his assistance but soon fell. Next it was the turn of Sergeant Nat Price, First North Carolina, and Private Jackson, Cobb's Legion, to try to rescue their leader.[108] One Union cavalryman finally managed to strike Hampton on the scalp, and a few moments later another shot him in the side from the rear. His men were able to help the general to the rear, and he would survive his wounds.[109]

In the accounts of this engagement penned by Union veterans during the closing decades of the century, the great melee ended suddenly in a Confederate defeat. Major Trowbridge, for example, told his readers that Hampton's and Fitz Lee's formation "staggered, broke and fled, leaving the Union troops in possession of the hotly contested field."[110] Lieutenants Miller and Brooke-Rawle provided similar accounts. "These flank attacks demoralized the Confederate column. . . . Their column was swept back to its starting point, and the field was ours,"[111] and "the enemy turned, then there was a pell mell rush, our men followed in close pursuit."[112] This version of events has found its way into many modern histories and undoubtedly has become the received wisdom for most modern Civil War enthusiasts.

However, in his poignantly written study, *"Come on, You Wolverines!" Custer at Gettysburg,* Michael Phipps suggests that the melee yielded a far less one-sided outcome, and ended instead by a mutual, but unspoken, agreement to disengage: "In assessing the fight, no one could say that Stuart's cavalry had broken. Rather, in the words of one participant, the opponents drifted apart 'as if satiated.'"[113] Phipps, although still acknowledging that the engagement had been a substantial Union victory—not only bolstering the cavalrymen's morale but thwarting Stuart's attempt to work his way to the Federal rear and wreak havoc—went one step farther and acknowledged that "both sides ended up more or less where they began."

There are several considerations that suggest that the traditional view of the closing moments of the engagement not only contain some inaccuracies but are overly simplistic and in need of revision. Most accounts, for example, claim that Chester's artillery fire, and to a lesser extent that of the other Union gun sections, battered the onrushing Confederate cavalry and just about stopped the charge by their fire alone. There is one compelling account that disputes this. After the war, Chester would write several letters to Colonel John Bachelder.

According to Chester, the Confederate horsemen managed to approach the slope near his guns. There, for some inexplicable reason, they stopped. They were close enough, about one hundred yards distant, that the Union artillerists could hear the officers talking to their men. They stayed in this position "as if paralyzed" for several minutes and then wheeled by fours and withdrew.[114] Chester could not figure out why they had retired seemingly on the brink of success. While drinking beer in a saloon in Columbus, South Carolina, in 1868, Chester overheard several men who had been in Hampton's command that day. Talking about that affair he heard them say that when they pulled up, they saw heads peeping up just over the rise behind Chester's guns. They thought this was a line of infantry and that, had they driven the charge home, they would have been crushed.

This is extraordinary testimony to the apparent success of Hampton's charge, since Chester had no personal motive to lie or aggrandize his opponents' accomplishments. Chester's version of events is indirectly corroborated by another Union artillery officer's letter to Bachelder during the 1880s. Lieutenant Hamilton, whose own section had been positioned some distance from the Spangler House, in at least two letters would derisively claim that at some point "Randol's battery"—which presumably was Kenney's section where Randol was positioned—limbered and galloped to the rear at "full tilt."[115] If true, this would, in turn, substantiate Colonel Thomas T. Munford's claims that they had driven back a "battery"—a section in reality—during the charge.[116]

Now, whether Chester had materially contributed to the Confederate withdrawal or not probably appears to be academic, of little practical consequence. Nevertheless, if Chester's account is indeed accurate, it does impact on another aspect of the popular accounts that have been handed down. Custer's and McIntosh's final charges would have been directed toward a body of cavalry already retiring, albeit in a very controlled way, and there could not have been the gallop-versus-gallop confrontation that has so frequently been portrayed. This version of events is supported by a second memoirist, Samuel Harris, who served with the Fifth Michigan Cavalry.

By this time the rebs in the front had got within less than ten rods of the guns. The lieutenant in charge of the two right guns thought it was about time to be getting out of the way, and ordered the caissons to limber up.

At this moment Lieutenant Pennington, turning his head, saw what was being done and ordered them to unlimber and to give them a double charge of canister. This order was given in very forcible language, and it was obeyed instantly; all four of the guns were fired point-blank with a double charge of canister into the face of the Rebs. This iron hailstorm was more than they could stand. They wheeled to the right to retreat, but found that they were cut off by the First Michigan. They made a wide detour to the right, and the most of them got back to their lines.[117]

Although less dramatic and heroic, the dynamics of the charge and the resulting melee would be much consonant with our understanding of how men and horses are known to react under such circumstances.

The Bachelder letters, recently published, point to another possible anomaly. The voluminous correspondence to the self-appointed "Gettysburg military historian" included a number of letters from veterans of the First and Second Virginia. To a man, these adamantly claim that their force had not been defeated and that they remained master of their part of the field after the fighting had subsided. Colonel Carey Breckenridge of the Second Virginia Cavalry, for example, would write, "The enemy could not fairly claim a victory there as our men were not driven from the field but held their position until withdrawn," and this is fairly representative of these men's claims.[118] Naturally enough, these letters have largely been ignored; it can be argued that they were written by men with an agenda—that of protecting the pride of their regiments and brothers in arms. But one suspects there may be another unconscious, less laudable reason why these letters have been so easily dismissed: they don't easily gel with the account of the cavalry-versus-cavalry fight as it has been passed down to posterity.

There is some evidence that the cavalry fight on the Union left was less successful than the First Michigan's Cavalry charge that had been assisted by McIntosh's party and Miller's and Hart's squadrons. Although Major Charles Irving of the First Virginia Cavalry admitted that his men slowly pulled back, the Union cavalry that followed them "kept at a respectful distance."[119] Veterans of the Second Virginia Cavalry, too, would adamantly claim that at the end of the day they maintained control of their positions. Over the years, Colonel Witcher, who commanded Jenkins's Brigade that day, would send out a number of letters that made claims similar to those of Breckenridge and other Confederate veterans who wrote to Bachelder. Writing to General L. L. Lomax in 1908, for example, Witcher emphatically averred that Union forces at no point took Rummel's farm, which was held by his command throughout the day and all evening.

> Now, I know this narrative is not in accordance with the maps and diagrams that have been gotten up of the battlefield. I know that Alger claims his regiment was at the Rummel barn at 2 P.M. He never got closer than the woods at the stake and rider fence. My wounded were put in the Rummel barn and another to the left and rear of that, and I personally visited both that night. I held the Rummel all day, was never driven from it, and no Federals ever got closer than the 3rd stone fence, which was the second one in front of the barn.[120]

In his own letter to Colonel Bachelder, Dr. Talcott Eliason, chief surgeon of Stuart's Cavalry Corps, corroborates this claim. He and his staff attended to wounded Union soldiers brought into the barn from the hotly contested adjoining fields.[121]

In the last two decades, several highly detailed, well-written works have appeared that have greatly furthered our understanding of the great cavalry battle at Gettysburg. Such works include Eric J. Wittenberg's *Protecting the Flank: The Battles for Brinkerhoff's Ridge and East Cavalry Field, Battle of Gettysburg,* Edward G. Longacre's *The Cavalry at Gettysburg,* and Michael Phipps's *"Come on, You Wolverines!" Custer at Gettysburg.* The present work is not intended as a definitive treatment, but more as an introductory essay to introduce readers to one of the largest and most significant Civil War cavalry engagements. It is hoped that others will continue to explore this interesting and highly complex engagement and resolve some of the remaining anomalies and mysteries.

8

ATTACK AND DEFENSE
OF FORT SANDERS

A native Georgian, after graduating from West Point in 1841, Lafayete McLaws served as a captain of infantry throughout the 1850s. When war broke out, he quickly advanced through the Confederate ranks, and on November 10, 1861, he assumed command of Paul J. Semmes's and J. B. Kershaw's Brigades to form the Second Division of the Army of the Peninsula. On April 12, the next year, his command became the Second Division in the Right Wing, an organization that would become Longstreet's First Corps of the Army of Northern Virginia. McLaws's men saw frequent action and took part in the Seven Days Battles, the Second Battle of Bull Run, and Gettysburg. McLaws's Division was part of the contingent sent to reinforce General Braxton Bragg in September 1863, and much of the fighting against General Burnside's Army of the Ohio at Knoxville would fall on the shoulders of McLaws's regiments.

THE STRATEGIC SITUATION

The capture of Vicksburg and the almost simultaneous victory at Gettysburg had not only boosted the morale of Union soldiers and citizenry, it also opened the eyes of Union military planners to the possibilities of future military gains. With the elimination of the last major Confederate stronghold on the mighty Mississippi, Winfield Scott's goal of severing the trans-Mississippi lands from the main body of the Confederacy was now largely achieved. However, before moving more into the Deep South, a few preliminary measures were necessary. In the months following Vicksburg, Union military authorities decided to establish a permanent presence in East Tennessee. This was as much to protect the pro-Union population as it was to interdict Confederate communications. To this end, Major General William S. Rosecrans, then at Murfreesboro, was to advance his Army of the Cumberland against General Braxton Bragg's Army of Tennessee, while the Union Army of the Ohio under Major General Ambrose E. Burnside was to move out of Kentucky and capture Knoxville. At first Burnside's side of the intended operations unfolded as planned, and the Army of the Ohio took possession of Knoxville on September 2. Although this city was regarded as a stepping-stone along the path to even more important operational objectives, its importance was nevertheless appreciated. Before pushing on with his main force south along the Valley of the Tennessee, Burnside took appropriate steps to protect his prize. Accordingly, a six-hundred-man Union garrison was stationed in Knoxville to prevent a Confederate cavalry dash to seize the coveted city as Burnside moved south. The garrison included some engineers who were charged to improve the defensive works that had been begun by the Rebels but not completed.

Meanwhile, during the first weeks of September, Burnside's main force pushed on, and a little more than two weeks later (September 18), advance elements reached Cleveland, Tennessee. The unfavorable conclusion of the Battle of Chickamauga (September 19–20), however, put an end to any realistic hopes Burnside had of joining up with the Army of the Cumberland, and the offensive impetus now swung to the Confederates. First, Union forces in and around Bull's Gap were momentarily threatened during the second week of October by General John S. Williams's command, before the latter was counterattacked by Burnside. Renewed attacks later in October forced Burnside to give up hope of controlling the Valley of the Tennessee south of Loudon.[1] The tenability of the Army of the Ohio's isolated position, miles from the nearest functioning railroad, further deteriorated after November 4, when Bragg detached Lieutenant General James Longstreet's fifteen thousand men and Major General Joseph Wheeler's cavalry to retake Knoxville and, if possible, destroy all nearby Union forces.[2] The situation came to a head a week later (November 13) when some of Longstreet's forces constructed a pontoon bridge to the northern bank of the Tennessee River and Wheeler's four brigades of cavalry rapidly crossed the Little Tennessee River. The two Confederate forces were now poised to advance to Knoxville before the main Union force and its supply train could retreat back into the city and reinforce its garrison.

WORK ON THE DEFENSES

Burnside was forced to react quickly or give up Knoxville. The next day he assumed personal command of the Army of the Ohio, which immediately began falling back toward the city. Captain Orlando M. Poe, Burnside's chief engineer, had been ordered to return to Knoxville to work on the defenses in preparation for the main force that would arrive several days later. Although Captain Poe and his engineers had been ordered to extend the existing defenses, little work had been done because of lack of tools and materials. There were three small creeks that flowed from the northwest more or less parallel to the Holston River. One of these, Third Creek, crossed Loudon Road about a half mile west of Knoxville. Near the point where this road entered the city, there was a noticeable ridge between Second and Third Creeks, known as White's Hill. The ascent continued for one to two hundred yards north of the road, where it crested. Union engineers found a partially constructed star fort on the hill and crude earthen parapets along the bluff overlooking the railway station, erected during the Confederates' occupation of the city.[3] The defenses near Loudon Road and nearest the southeastern part of the city and the river were the most advanced.[4] The northern defenses amounted to little more than a breastwork,[5] and the remainder of the fortifications were nothing more than a series of intermittent small rifle pits, four feet wide, two and a half feet deep, protected by a two-foot parapet.[6] The engineers decided to construct more elaborate defenses upon the existing works, as well as another fortification on the opposite side of the city on Temperance Hill. General Burnside approved the plan, and the engineer battalion of the Twenty-third Corps assisted by some former slaves began construction. However, there was still a dearth of building materials and the work only progressed slowly.[7]

Burnside's forces managed to win the race to Knoxville and reached the outskirts of town at Third Creek at daylight on November 17. Here, the battle-weary soldiers were met by the engineers, who led each regiment to its assigned position along the intended fortifications. Thoroughly "played out," many of the men were allowed to fall on the ground and sleep for two hours. The much-needed respite over, the men were ordered to get up and "dig with all their might," and by the middle of the afternoon the entire force was hard at work strengthening the entrenchments.[8] It was a makeshift operation; the quartermaster was able to provide a few captured picks, but there were no spades or shovels to be found.[9]

Time was of the essence, and work continued around the clock, with many male civilians pressed into service. Unfortunately for the defenders, many of these civilians had Southern sympathies and "worked with a very poor grace, which blistered hands did not tend to improve." Nevertheless, by the end of the next day (November 18), the defenders could boast that they were "tolerably

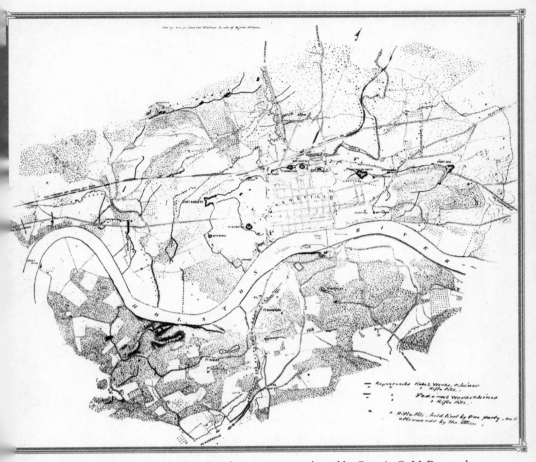

The Assault Against Fort Sanders: Based on a survey conducted by Captain O. M. Poe, under whose direction the Union defenses were built, this map shows the positions of the defenders (Union) and besiegers (Confederates) during the days leading up to the attack. *Courtesy of Library of Congress, Online Map Collection (Civil War Maps), Call No.: G3964.K7S5 1864 .R6 Vault : CW 427.1.*

well under cover." Unfortunately, satisfaction was tempered by loss that day. Through constant vigilance and untiring efforts, recently promoted Brigadier General William P. Sanders had slowed down the Confederate advance, giving time for the Union infantrymen to complete their defensive preparations. That day Sanders fell mortally wounded in front of a redoubt near Third

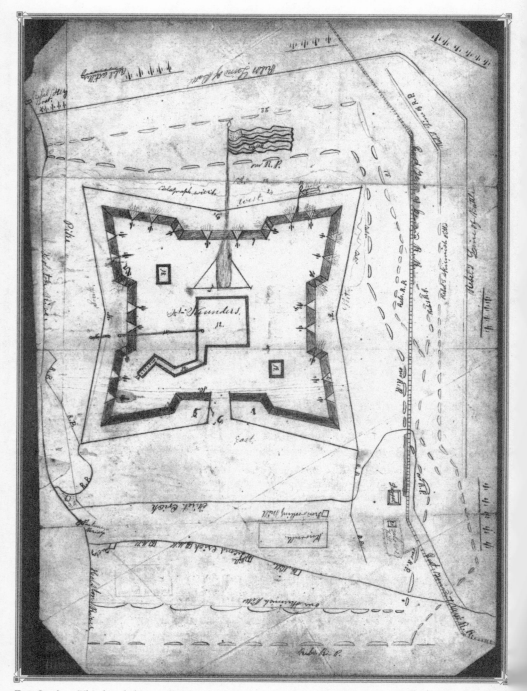

Fort Sanders: This hand-drawn sketch was made by one of the Union defenders, probably immediately following the Confederate assault of this bastion. Its detail allows us to determine the density and location of the defending artillery. *Courtesy of Library of Congress, Online Map Collection (Civil War Maps), Call No.: G3964.K7:2F6S5 1863 .O7 Vault : CW 426.4.*

Creek, and the officers recommended to Burnside that this bastion be named after the fallen cavalry hero. Burnside agreed and this part of the defense works, originally called Fort Loudon by the Confederates, was now renamed Fort Sanders.[10] Captain Poe would provide a description of Fort Sanders in a report submitted after the attack:

> It is a bastioned earth-work, built upon an irregular quadrilateral, the sides of which are, respectively, 125 yards southern front, 95 yards western front, 125 yards northern front, and 85 yards eastern front. The eastern front was entirely open, and is to be closed with a stockade; the southern front was about half done; the western front was finished, except cutting the embrasures, and the northern front was nearly finished. Each bastion was intended to have a *pan coupé*.[11] The bastion attacked was the only one that was completely finished. A light 12-pounder was mounted at the *pan coupé,* and did good service. The ditch of the fort was 12 feet in width, and in many places as much as 8 feet in depth. The irregularity of the site was such that the bastion angles were very heavy, the relief of the lightest one being 12 feet. The relief of the one attacked was about 13 feet, and, together with the depth of the ditch, say 11 feet, made a height of 20 feet from the bottom of the ditch to the interior crest.[12]

First Lieutenant Samuel N. Benjamin of the Second U.S. Artillery, Burnside's chief of artillery, immediately set to work improving the defenses in and around Fort Sanders, as well as positioning all the artillery in the general area. The ordnance collected could be characterized as "motley" by any standard. Though a majority of the guns were rifled, all the batteries employed ordnance of different calibers. Lieutenant Erskine Gittings's Battery L & M, Third U.S. Artillery, consisted of four 10-pounder Parrotts; Captain Jacob Roemer's Battery L, Second New York Light Artillery, had four 3-inch rifle guns; and Lieutenant Samuel N. Benjamin's Battery E, Second U.S. Artillery, had four 20-pounder Parrotts. Captain William W. Buckley's Battery D, First Rhode Island Light Artillery, was the only battery in the area with smoothbore weapons, six of the ever-popular light 12-pounders (Napoleons).[13]

Lieutenant Gittings's battery was stationed near the depot and Captain Roemer's rifle guns on Seminary Hill. Buckley's six Napoleons and Benjamin's four Parrotts moved up to the ridge on the northwest hill. Benjamin found Fort Sanders only about 25 percent completed. Lacking sufficient time and labor, the defenders had managed to construct only three sides to the fort. Benjamin decided to leave the rear of the fort open. It took two hundred black laborers four hours just to drag the artillery pieces into the bastion and then dig out the embrasures and sunken trenches to hold the artillery. As soon as this was done, Benjamin's and Buckley's batteries, supplemented by two additional 3-inch guns, were placed along the fort's walls. The artillery was carefully positioned to sweep the approaches to the breastworks and rifle pits thoroughly on either side of the bastion. Benjamin's battery was positioned on the south and west angle of the fort, Buckley's on the east front, while Roemer's guns were placed in lunettes along the breastwork just north of the fort. The portion of the line in front of the northwest salient of the bastion was purposely denuded of fire, in order to induce the Confederates to direct their assault to this point in the defenses. Fort Sanders's garrison consisted of 100–125 men from the Seventy-ninth New York, four companies (about eighty men) from the Twenty-ninth Massachusetts, four companies (about sixty men) from the Second Michigan, and three companies (about eighty men) from the Twentieth Michigan.[14] Four companies of the Seventeenth Michigan were placed in reserve, to reinforce the fort in the event of an attack.

Benjamin also ordered the construction of two lines of rifle pits about eighty and thirty yards in front of the fort, respectively. The one farther out was used to station skirmishers, the closer one to rally in if the men were driven from the first. The bastion was connected to the remainder of the line by a series of breastworks and rifle pits. These had been thrown up by the infantrymen and ran south from the ends of the gorge to the river and on the east side up to the town. The ground eighty yards in front of the fort had been completely cleared.

Here, there was a sudden descent. The slope itself was sprinkled with a thin growth of pines, the outcropping of a large thick wood below.[15]

Although it was expected that the main brunt of the Confederate assault would strike the northwest salient that protruded out slightly in front of the line, Burnside's chief of artillery recognized that a small hill south of the fort and on the other side of the road to Campbell's station was the key to the position. Occupying this position, the attackers would then be able to take the defensive lines in reverse. After some heated discussion, Lieutenant Benjamin managed to convince Brigadier General Edward Ferrero, commander of the First Division, to occupy the hill, supported by two of Buckley's 12-pounder Napoleons.

Another defensive precaution had only been recently introduced to warfare, the use of wire entanglements. Telegraph wire was stretched from tree stump to tree stump to trip or otherwise embarrass the enemy soldiers as they advanced. In the years following the return to peace, a controversy gradually flared up over who was responsible for implementing these defensive measures. In a paper read on December 7, 1898, Captain Robert Armour claimed this was done on direct orders from Lieutenant Benjamin.[16] In a submission to *The National Tribune* on May 23, 1918, the Fourth Sergeant of Company F, 100th Pennsylvania, claimed that the idea spontaneously occurred when several members of his company "the evening preceding the assault" (the twenty-eighth) were strolling outside the fort in an area thickly strewn with tree stumps. While the men speculated about the likelihood of an assault and the chances of their success, a soldier named John Smith observed that their chances would improve if they strung wires between the tree stumps. The sergeant averred that the men immediately took off their coats and proceeded to stretch out the wire.[17] There is probably more reason to believe Captain Armour's explanation. Confederate cavalry in the eastern theatre had used telegraph wires to protect themselves from Union cavalry on at least two occasions earlier in the war (December 4, 1861, and April 6, 1862),[18] and Major Samuel H. Lockett, chief engineer of Confederate forces at Vicksburg, had ordered his engineers on May 25, 1863, to strengthen the various defensive works with "entanglements of pickets and telegraph wire."[19] Clearly, the precedent had been set, and given the importance of the operations at Vicksburg, these practices would have been known to almost all engineer and artillery officers.

LONGSTREET'S ARRIVAL

CONFEDERATE FORCES ATTACKING FORT SANDERS[20]
LONGSTREET'S CORPS
McLAWS'S DIVISION

MAJOR GENERAL LAFAYETTE McLAWS

KERSHAW'S BRIGADE
Second South Carolina, Colonel John D. Kennedy
Third South Carolina, Colonel James D. Nance
Seventh South Carolina, Colonel D. Wyatt Aiken
Eighth South Carolina, Colonel John W. Henaga
Fifteenth South Carolina, Colonel Joseph F. Gist
Third South Carolina Battalion, Lieutenant Colonel William G. Rice

HUMPHREYS'S BRIGADE
Thirteenth Mississippi, Colonel Kennon McElroy
Seventeenth Mississippi, Colonel William D. Holder
Eighteenth Mississippi, Colonel Thomas M. Griffin
Twenty-first Mississippi, Colonel William L. Brandon

WOFFORD'S BRIGADE
Sixteenth Georgia, Colonel Henry P. Thomas
Eighteenth Georgia, Colonel S. Z. Ruff
Twenty-fourth Georgia, Colonel Robert McMillan
Cobb's Legion, Lieutenant Colonel Luther J. Glenn
Phillips Legion, Lieutenant Colonel E. S. Barclay
Third Georgia Battalion Sharpshooters, Lieutenant Colonel
N. L. Hutchins, Jr.

BRYAN'S BRIGADE
Tenth Georgia, Colonel John B. Weems
Fiftieth Georgia, Colonel Peter McGlashan
Fifty-first Georgia, Colonel Edward Ball
Fifty-third Georgia, Colonel James P. Simms

FROM HOOD'S DIVISION—ANDERSON'S BRIGADE
Seventh Georgia, Colonel W. W. White
Eighth Georgia, Colonel John R. Towers
Ninth Georgia, Colonel Benjamin Beck
Eleventh Georgia, Colonel F. H. Little
Fifty-ninth Georgia, Colonel Jack Brown

Burnside's men had managed to arrive in Knoxville only hours before their pursuers. The leading components of Longstreet's command appeared along Loudon Road that same evening (November 17). The defenders braced themselves for an immediate attack, which fortunately for them did not materialize. Instead, the Southerners chose to conduct what might be termed a lazy form of circumvallation. On the nineteenth, Longstreet's men drove the outlying pickets back upon the defensive works and then occupied a wood in front of Fort Sanders that later served as the staging area for the attack against the fort.[21] During the next several days, as Union forces were feverishly attempting to shore up the perimeter, the Confederates slowly began to cut off the city and its defenders from the outside world, a task that would largely be accomplished a week later (November 24). The Confederates did not neglect the virtues of pickax and shovel, and like the defenders extended a series of rifle pits from the woods in front of Fort Sanders to strategically important positions closer to the fort. From these relatively safe positions, Confederate sharpshooters started to make life difficult for those manning the defenses.[22]

Despite Longstreet's cautious approach that seemed to portend a long, drawn-out, formal siege, there were other forces at work, which would ultimately trigger a much more violent resolution of the standoff. As Longstreet's Corps cautiously closed around Knoxville, Brigadier General Micah Jenkins was the first to report a possible weak spot in the defenses. On November 20, Jenkins's Brigade had faced resistance from Union skirmishers. Ordered that night to push these as far back as practicable, his men ended up about seven hundred yards from the defensive fortifications around Knoxville, and the brigade commander thought this portion of the defenses could be successfully stormed. However, after reconnoitering the entire length of the enemy works, Longstreet believed that the "key" to the enemy's position was near the heights south of Holston, and the next twenty-four hours were spent maneuvering Major General Lafayette McLaws's Division into position for the proposed assault.[23]

The need to penetrate the Union defenses and take Knoxville quickly was underscored the next day by a telegram from General Bragg, commander of the Army of Tennessee. Complaining that his left was threatened by General U. S. Grant's forces near Chattanooga, Bragg requested that Longstreet swiftly engage the opposing Union forces. Longstreet turned to General McLaws and proposed that he attack Fort Sanders with three brigades "in the moonlight." In testimony later submitted during McLaws's court-martial, the corps commander conceded that he was reluctant to order this attack without the approval of his subordinate officers. The escalade of any fortification was necessarily a bloody affair and the officers' buy-in to the plan not only would raise morale, but also ensure every effort was made to accomplish the mission. The last thing that a commander wanted was to send men and officers reluctantly into a desperate fight where complete cooperation and esprit de corps were essential for success. McLaws, therefore, was asked to prepare a plan of attack and consult with his officers as to its feasibility.

McLaws's Division, meanwhile, continued to push slowly forward, and by November 22, the division commander felt he was close enough to attack Fort Sanders successfully. Of course, the Confederate forces, positioned seven to eight hundred yards away, did not possess a detailed picture of the fortifications they were about to attack. They were able to see the walls of the redoubt and knew its dimensions; they were also able to gauge the lay of the land they would have to cross during the approach. However, they could only speculate about the extent and depth of the ditch meandering immediately in front of the defensive works. It could be surveyed only by approaching its very edge, an act of friendly cooperation that for some unfathomable reason the Union forces adamantly refused to allow.

During his court-martial, General McLaws claimed that while discussing the feasibility of an attack against Fort Sanders on November 22, he suspected that there was a ditch, and he proposed that his infantry carry bundles of straw to fill up any declivity should one be encountered. At first, some among the Confederate command doubted whether the ditch even existed, and if it did, almost everyone agreed it would pose little difficulty to the attackers. Local residents explained that the earth used to construct the fort's parapet had been excavated from inside the redoubt. Fort Sanders was situated on top of a hill and this essentially smoothed off the top of this promontory. The citizenry went on to add that if the Union troops had indeed dug holes, these were only sporadic pits for outlying skirmishers and marksmen; they were dispersed and certainly not a continuous trench.[24] Further reconnaissance partially dispelled this misconception, and it became evident that there was indeed a ditch in front of the redoubt. However, it was believed that this was a relatively shallow trench and did not pose an insurmountable obstacle. E. P. Alexander, at that point chief of Longstreet's artillery, made several reconnaissance trips himself and at one point managed to work his way to within four hundred yards of Fort Sanders. He reported back to Longstreet that the ditch was of such a shape and dimensions that it was "no obstacle to an assault." This issue was considered to be critical to the success of the proposed assault, and Alexander personally led Longstreet to a spot where the Confederate commander could see for himself. As they stood looking at the redoubt, they espied a Union soldier leaving the fort and crossing the ditch on the northwest side, the point of the proposed attack. As he traversed the ditch, he disappeared up to his waist and at no point was lost to view. Longstreet and

Alexander concluded that the ditch on this side was very shallow and used only as a source of dirt for the earthworks.[25] There appeared to be no reason to modify the planned attack.

Longstreet ordered the escalade to be carried out that night. However, later that day McLaws reported to Longstreet that most of his officers felt the proposed assault would fail, especially if conducted at night. They argued that they must be able to see the men they were to direct. Lieutenant Colonel John C. Fiser of the Seventeenth Mississippi, and Lieutenant Colonel W. C. Holt of the Tenth Georgia, however, were more optimistic, and McLaws decided that should an attack occur these two regiments would be prominently positioned in the assault column.[26]

Longstreet reluctantly delayed the attack to November 25 and acceded to the request by McLaws's officers that it should be conducted in daylight. Like its predecessors, however, this plan was doomed to postponement. Before the attack could be launched, news came that Longstreet's forces were about to be reinforced by two brigades under Brigadier General Bushrod R. Johnson. Accordingly, the offensive was delayed an additional day to allow these troops to arrive and take up their assigned positions. However, there remained sufficient concern about the proposed assault that when General Danville Leadbetter, the chief engineer of the Army of Tennessee, arrived at Longstreet's headquarters the night before the attack, it was decided to solicit this experienced officer's opinion about the proposed plan. Leadbetter initially favored an assault against Mabry's Hill rather than Fort Sanders. As a result, all of November 26 was spent re-reconnoitering the Union defenses and the intervening ground the Confederate offense would have to traverse.[27] In instructions to General McLaws, Longstreet explained the essentials of the new plan. The assault was to be conducted by Hood's Division augmented by part of Buckner's. McLaws's men were now to play only a supporting role. Other than Bryan's Brigade, which was to be thrown out as a picket line along the front occupied by General Jenkins's command, McLaws's Division was to remain in its present position and "make a diversion" by a heavy cannonade, or any other means McLaws could devise. He was to advance, supported by a cavalry brigade, only after the fort was taken.[28]

In the end, all of this effort had no effect on Longstreet's strategy, other than delaying the attack yet another day, for Generals Jenkins, Leadbetter, and Longstreet, along with Colonel Alexander, all came to the conclusion that if the new plan were implemented, the attacking troops would have to traverse a lengthy and highly exposed stretch of ground. The plan was cancelled and all the troops who had been shuffled around returned to their original positions. Once again, Fort Sanders was deemed the most promising point to attack, and the assault was yet again rescheduled, this time for November 28.[29]

The latest plan called for the attack to be launched that Saturday morning, as soon as there was enough daylight for the artillery to come into action. It seemed like Fate itself was determined to thwart Longstreet's plans. The night was stormy and visibility extremely poor. Before dawn, his subordinates were notified that the operation was suspended until two in the afternoon, when it was expected that the heavy fog and rain that completely obscured the fort from sight would have cleared.[30] Though by the early afternoon the weather had cleared enough to permit large-scale activity, some officers complained that the troops were still not in position and Longstreet decided to postpone the attack to early the next morning. In his unpublished memoirs, Colonel E. P. Alexander attributed another motive for Longstreet's decision to delay the attack yet again. Several days earlier, Major Fairfax, one of Longstreet's staff officers, had discovered a large hill on the other side of the Holston River, and after closer inspection, Longstreet and most of his advisors were convinced that from this lofty position Confederate artillery could enfilade large stretches of the defenders' lines. Alexander, certainly the most proficient artilleryman present, secretly did not think much of this plan. Years later he would explain in an unpublished memoir, intended only for his immediate family, that such long-range fire would be useless in the case of Confederate artillery. The marked inferiority of the Confederate projectiles caused most of the shells and solid shot to tumble at longer ranges, making precise fire impossible. Nevertheless, Longstreet's optimism remained unchecked, and after a number of false starts, Captain William W. Parker was dispatched with his Virginia Battery, consisting of four 10-pound Parrotts, to a forward position on the night of the twenty-seventh. Though Parker and his guns would certainly have been in position by the morning of the twenty-eighth, it is possible that Longstreet worried that the continued drizzle would hamper Parker's ability to sight his guns accurately at long range.[31]

Earlier that morning, Longstreet had issued orders outlining the overall plan of attack. McLaws's Division was to deliver the assault. During the first phase, skirmishers were to conceal themselves as near the fort as possible so that their fire would pin the defenders down during the assault. An artillery bombardment would signal the start of the engagement and serve as a signal for the infantry first to prepare itself, then advance. Brigadier Generals William T. Wofford's, Benjamin G. Humphreys's, and Goode Bryan's Brigades were to form a strong column that would be directed against the northwest salient of the fort, while the fourth brigade was to be kept in reserve along with two brigades of Major General S. B. Buckner's Division under Brigadier General B. R. Johnson, which had arrived the day before. A little later, General Jenkins was to advance a brigade and strike the enemy's lines east of the fort, and then proceed along the enemy's rear and flank.[32] General McLaws remained skeptical about the feasibility of the proposed assault, however. He knew that Longstreet was being prodded by General Bragg to take Knoxville as quickly as possible. He wrote to Longstreet arguing that the overall situation in Tennessee now actually demanded extreme caution. If, as the rumors had it, Grant had defeated the Army of Tennessee at Chattanooga, it would be impossible to recombine with Bragg's command, and Longstreet's forces had to open a line of communication with Virginia instead of going on the offensive. It would now also be impossible for Bragg to reinforce Longstreet. If, on the other hand, it was Grant who had suffered a reverse, McLaws reasoned that delaying the attack only

only worked to the Confederates' advantage.[33] Replying almost immediately, Longstreet acknowledged hearing the rumor that Bragg had been defeated and had fallen back to Tunnel Hill. Now thoroughly exasperated by McLaws's continued reticence and lack of enthusiasm, Longstreet peremptorily issued the command to attack the following morning. He further emphasized:

> it is the more important that I should have the entire support and cooperation of the officers in this connection, and I do hope and trust that I may have your entire support and all of the force you may be possessed of in the execution of my views. It is a great mistake to suppose that there is any safety for us in going to Virginia if General Bragg has been defeated, for we leave him at the mercy of his victors, and with his army destroyed our own had better be also, for we will be not only destroyed, but disgraced. There is neither safety nor honor in any other course than the one I have chosen and ordered.[34]

That evening there was a series of meetings between the principal Confederate officers whose forces would participate in the action to coordinate their efforts and work out an effective plan. To minimize casualties, Confederate sharpshooters had to pin down the defenders and thus suppress any defensive fire. Unfortunately, Union forces still held outlying rifle pits to house their own skirmishers and sharpshooters. That night Confederate skirmishers and sharpshooters would have to capture these outworks and secure their own protected positions close to the intended point of attack. So that accurate sharpshooter fire could be brought to bear against the entire front, before daylight they would have to dig rifle pits where these did not exist.

As soon as the sharpshooters accomplished their objectives and were in position to support the final phases of the assault, the infantry was to form behind them. Noticing that much of the area where the infantry was to form was closely wooded, had rough terrain with only a few narrow clearings, McLaws decided to arrange his division into two columns of regiments, i.e., each tier in the column consisted of a series of regiments deployed in line, one behind the other. McLaws also hoped this arrangement would exploit the natural rivalry that existed between the Mississippi men in Humphreys's Brigade and Wofford's Georgia regiments and would "urge them to their work with accelerating dash and vigor." Humphreys's Brigade was to be formed in the open ground on the right, with Colonel McElroy's Thirteenth Mississippi Regiment in the lead, followed by Lieutenant Colonel Fiser's Seventeenth Mississippi.[35] In a manuscript penned after the war, Humphreys would admit that when the attack finally went in, he did not strictly follow the troop dispositions called for in the above orders. Instead, the Thirteenth and Seventeenth Mississippi Regiments in line formed the first wave of attack, preceded by the Eighteenth in skirmish order with the Twenty-first Mississippi in reserve in the second line.[36]

After Humphreys's men would come Bryan's Brigade, under Colonel Edward Ball, with the Fifty-third, Fifty-first, and Fiftieth Georgia Volunteers in column in that order.[37] On the left, the Phillips' Legion was to be placed at the front of Wofford's Brigade (also formed in columns of regiments), followed by the Eighteenth and Sixteenth Georgia Regiments, with Cobb's Legion bringing up the rear.[38] As soon as the fort was taken, General J. B. Kershaw was to advance with his troops and attack the fortifications immediately to its right. The Confederate planners considered this an important precondition for success. Once the sun rose and the action began, the Rebel columns would have to advance only two hundred yards to the Union fort. McLaws's instructions to his brigade commanders also required that the assault be made with fixed bayonets and without firing a gun. The men were to advance slowly with deliberation and remain absolutely silent until they entered the fort. Then, raising a shout, they were to fall instantly upon the defenders and capture the works. The artillery, meanwhile, was to support the infantry. Anticipating that the latter would quickly pass over the two hundred yards or so to the fort, the artillery was to direct its fire against this target for only a few minutes, then switch its attention to the ground over which any Union reinforcements must come, as long as the defenders continued to resist. This was to both mini-mize friendly casualties and prevent Union reinforcements from easily entering the beleaguered position.[39]

The success of the plan depended upon a quickly delivered assault with seamless coordination between advancing infantry and sup-porting artillery. Any delay caused by the inevitable fog of war would mean certain failure. Colonel Alexander and General McLaws met together that evening and worked out the role of each command and the signals that would be used to communicate between the two. Several mortars were to fire first to signal the pick-ets to gather together and ready themselves for the advance. After a few moments, the batteries along the Rebel line were to join in and deliver a slow deliberate fire. The skirmishers, meanwhile, were to capture any Union rifle pits as soon as the batteries began to fire, and the columns of attack were to be formed. After firing slowly for twenty minutes, the batteries were ordered to begin a rapid fire. This would be the signal for the general assault to begin.[40]

THE ASSAULT

A strong wave of Confederate skirmishers from the Tenth Georgia Volunteers (Bryan's Brigade) and the Eighteenth and Twenty-first Mississippi Regiments (Humphreys's Brigade) began its advance against the defending pickets about "moonrise," apparently around 10:00 P.M.[41] Despite the darkness, this first phase of the operation went off without a hitch, and by midnight the Confederate skir-mishers had advanced to within close range of the fort and the adjoining defensive works on either side. According to Longstreet, they succeeded in capturing many of the outlying Union rifle pits, along with sixty to seventy prisoners (at least according to Longstreet) without loss on their side.[42] There was then an ebb in skirmishing for a few hours as both sides prepared for the inevitable bloodbath. The Confederates continued to improve upon their posi-tions, so that by daylight, they had completed a number of their own dugouts, wherever these had not been thoughtfully provided by the Union defenders. On their side, the defenders were not totally inactive and a number of small detachments were sent out. Some of these were to serve as sentries close to the fort; others were sent out a little farther to occupy rifle pits still unoccupied by the Confederates.[43]

The weather had turned nasty again; it was bitter cold and drizzling. A correspondent for a local Tennessee newspaper noticed the effect of the severe conditions on the men's disposition:

> Four o'clock in the morning found them chilled to the bone, their fingers almost frozen to the firelocks, and in the opposite of that buoyant condition which should ever attend an undertaking of desperate nature like that in which they were about to engage.[44]

Lieutenant Benjamin, in command of the troops in Fort Sanders, noted that it was 6:30 in the morning when the Rebels began firing, either just before the break of day or as the first rays of light were making their way over the horizon. During these first few moments the Confederate artillery, positioned between seven hundred and fifteen hundred yards from the fort, had to aim at "flashes of the enemy's guns in the darkness."[45] This fire was kept up until the flashes from the attackers' muskets were observed under the fort's parapet, at which time the Confederate artillery directed a "slow random" fire behind the defensive works until the day had fully broken.[46] Incidentally, the term "random" had a technical meaning to artillery officers. In the days of smoothbore artillery with round shot projectiles, there were four different methods of fire: *point-blank, direct, ricochet,* and *random.* Both point-blank and direct fire were intended as accurate fire where the round shot was aimed directly at the intended target. In ricochet fire the artillerymen purposely aimed short so that the round shot would skip along the ground in front of the target. Occasionally, accuracy was not an issue when the artillery was required to fire at extreme ranges, as would occur when bombarding a large area such as a town or fortification. This was known as random fire.[47]

When the shelling started, those Union sentries and skirmishers still outside the fort knew that they had to retire to the safety of the defensive works quickly. Major Charles Chipman sent orders to four companies of the Twenty-ninth Massachusetts Infantry that were still in some rifle pits near the river to return immediately. Company B of the "Seventy-ninth Highlanders" (the Seventy-ninth New York Volunteers) had just gotten into position as pickets when the Confederate artillery opened. Realizing that the enemy infantry could not advance as long as this long-range fire continued, the men decided to stay until the last possible moment and took cover among the tree stumps. Though most of the shot and shell flew harmlessly overhead, reminding them of "sky rockets," occasionally one would fall short and explode among the stumps behind them. William Todd later recalled waiting for the orders to retire:

> The shrieks of the murderous shells were well calculated to shake the morale of men less accustomed than the Highlanders to such music. Now a shell strikes a stump between us and the fort, shivers it to atoms and sends the end of a log behind which some of us are lying, and just as we think that the plaguy things are getting too familiar the fire ceases.[48]

They knew it was time to get out of there. They ran for their lives back to the fort. Some planks had been left across the ditch. As the last detachments hurried over, these were removed. The skirmishers and pickets had made it back just in time.[49]

As soon as they heard the artillery signal, the Confederate skirmishers unleashed a hail of carefully aimed fire at the Union parapets and gun emplacements. The main body of the attacking infantry meanwhile began to form behind the skirmishers. But it was here that an important error occurred. The brigade commanders had been specifically instructed to form their men immediately behind the captured Union rifle pits, a mere two hundred yards from the fort. Whether because they misconstrued these orders or because of the general confusion always part of operating in the dark, the attacking formations were instead staged several hundred yards behind the intended starting point.

Unaware of the breach of orders, the columns of regiments were ordered to advance toward the southwest salient of the fort.

Although the rain had finally stopped, the morning was cold and foggy and a thick, white mist extended almost up to the defenders' earthworks. As a result, the initial portion of the Confederate advance was hidden from the defending infantrymen, who had to withhold their fire until the attackers emerged out of the mist.[50] The fog also dampened the sound of the small arms fire, and the usual "crack-crack-crack" of the discharging rifle muskets was transformed into a diminutive "pip-pip-pip."[51]

Brigadier General Edward Ferrero, commander of the defending forces, would report that the Rebels "poured out of the woods in front of the northwest salient of the fort, and with wild cheers advanced at a run for that salient." Ferrero's allusion to the Rebels' wild cheers and advance at the run probably was more an evocation of the Rebel stereotype and the result of the braggadocio that inevitably arises after a victorious engagement than it was an accurate account of the enemy's actual demeanor.[52] In his own report, Lieutenant Benjamin suggests that Ferrero, firmly ensconced within the defensive works during the attack, had hardly been in a position to observe the enemy's motions. A very different description is found in the Confederate reports. Brigadier General Humphreys, who commanded a brigade in McLaws's Division, would boast that his men advanced "slowly, but with zeal, hope, and enthusiasm." Though in the rear at the start of the assault, Longstreet was also able to observe McLaws's advance. From his vantage point, everything appeared to be unfolding as planned. The men marched in a "gallant style" and had been able to maintain good order until they reached the side of the ditch.[53] Colonel Byron Cutcheon of the Twentieth Michigan, who awaited their advance on the Union parapets, collaborates Longstreet's assessment of the initial stage of the attack:

> They came on in column of battalions, battalion front, arms at trail, heads down, no yelling, no cheering; just a sullen, heavy tread, and a low "hep-hep-hep," as they came on at the double quick.[54]

Obviously, the men in the first wave of the attack were following Longstreet's orders to advance slowly and silently to the letter.

Unfortunately, the attacking columns came into full view just as they encountered their first obstacle: the outlying abattis and wire entanglements that had to be passed through before they could approach the fort. Lieutenant Benjamin later reported that these impediments not only slowed down the advance, but disordered the formations. The toppled trees and sharpened branches occasionally forced the men in the advancing formations to split up and seek channels through the obstacles. Of course, it was exactly in these seemingly clear spaces that the "invisible" wire had been strung, low to the ground. The first rank marched up and, as if by magic, toppled over, tripped by the "tangle," as it was called. A few moments later the second line reached the same spot with the same ignominious result; all order was lost.[55] In a paper read to the Military Order of the Loyal Legion decades after the war, a veteran would paint a vivid picture of men stumbling over the wires, as they struggled to make their way through the labyrinth of sharpened branches. A Union artillery piece placed en barbette on the parapet quickly delivered several canister shots.[56]

Despite the momentary delay, the advancing columns were still able to burst quickly through these obstacles by sheer weight of numbers. Clear of these impediments, the attackers once more came upon clear ground, and it was here that they broke into a run toward the fort. Benjamin estimated that the entire advance took less than two minutes.[57]

The defenders inside the small fort, meanwhile, tensely awaited their turn to spring into action. Realizing that the Confederates would most likely unleash a formidable assault at dawn, Lieutenant Benjamin had awoken an hour or so before. Walking around the confined area, he roused the men and stationed everyone at their assigned positions. Though he cautioned his men to be ready to fire at any moment, he also ordered them to keep down and maintain the strictest silence. All spare rifle muskets were loaded and stacked in convenient spots along the parapet. Most of the artillery was double-shotted, and the 12-pounder howitzers were loaded with canister. One artillery piece in a bastion to the right of the fort had been carefully triple shot with canister and intentionally withheld from the artillery duel until the attackers had entered the ditch.[58] The No. 4 artilleryman at each piece stood ready to fire with a lanyard in his hand. As a further precaution, the lieutenant ordered several rows of 20-pounder Parrott shells with five-second fuses placed on the "banquette tread" at several strategically important positions along the north and west fronts of the fort. This wasn't a popular measure, however. These ersatz grenades had an evil reputation, and the nearby soldiers always wished they had been placed somewhere else.[59]

As the attackers neared the fort, the Confederate artillery bombardment ceased, but was replaced by a withering small arms fire aimed at the embrasures along the parapet. Given their exposed position, the gunners of the artillery piece en barbette were forced to take shelter and could no longer man the gun. However, whether because of the fog or the protective qualities of the defensive works, despite the intensity of the attackers' fire, casualties were limited to a single artilleryman.[60] Lieutenant Colonel N. L. Hutchins, Jr., who commanded the Third Battalion Georgia Sharpshooters, reported that his men advancing to "easy rifle range" poured such a rapid fire into the embrasures and loopholes that the defenders were deprived of both defensive artillery and small arms fire.[61] Of course, from Union accounts we know that this was as much the result of a deliberate defensive tactic as it was the result of a withering, suppressive fire.

The defenders' forbearance was about to end abruptly, however. The leading elements in Humphreys's attack formation approached to within a few yards of the walls of the fort. Here they were in for a final surprise. They had been told that the ditch was only about four feet deep, and they expected to be able to get a footing on the berm—an eighteen-inch ledge between the wall of the ditch and the parapet—and scale the parapet in one or two strides.[62] However, not only was the ditch deeper than they had been led to expect, the defenders had carefully placed one final trip wire near the edge of the ditch. A Memphis correspondent would recount to his readers its effect:

> But now, what a scene of confusion! A wire stretched along the edge of the chasm caught the leg of every man who did not suspect its presence, and tripped him headlong into the yawning trap—those behind rolling like a wave on those before, until the abyss was filled with a seething, boiling mass of men and guns, out of which issued intermingled groans, shouts, yells, and orders with the discordance of a Pandemonium.[63]

Matters were swiftly made worse. The triple-shot artillery piece was fired, creating a swath of death and destruction. At this close range the carnage was terrible, and the attackers "left their track marked by writhing forms of their wounded and dying comrades."[64]

The attackers had been stymied by the ditch, which the Confederate command had greatly underestimated. There had been no lack of trying on the attackers' part. The onrushing Confederate infantrymen hesitated at the brink for but a moment, and then wave after wave of the men jumped into the ditch directly in front of the batteries along the parapet. Two or three enterprising men carried a plank, which they laid across the ditch. A few of the attackers managed to reach a ledge midway up the defensive works that way, but just as many fell off.[65] The crowds in the ditch were now confronted with a sloped, earthen eight-foot wall on top of which was a twelve-foot parapet. During the night the Union defenders had poured buckets of water down the slope, and the water had frozen, making the surface even slipperier.

The Union infantrymen defending the fort started to ply their deadly trade, delivering a murderous close-range fire, some from behind cotton bales placed at the top of the parapet, others momentarily appearing in the embrasures beside the artillery pieces, then disappearing to reload their shoulder arms in safety. Some officers cajoled their men to aim at the enemy officers. This practice certainly wasn't new to the military art—the Austrians and Russians were known frequently to employ this tactic against their French foes at the height of the Napoleonic Wars.[66]

The attackers quickly responded to this threat. Many got down behind the tree stumps that littered the ground in front of the fort and, aiming just above the cotton bales, waited for the next Union infantryman to pop up. A number of defenders thus fell hors de combat, picked off by Confederate shooters.[67] William Todd remembered seeing a number of his comrades peering over the top of the parapet to take a shot before quickly ducking down to reload their weapons. The senior sergeant, who was just returning with his detachment from picket duty, asked an orderly sergeant to stop the men from thus exposing themselves. The other sergeant nonchalantly replied that he had been doing this himself and said he would do it one last time before getting the other men to stop. However, just as he looked over the parapet, he was shot through the head, his blood and brains bespattering those near him. The senior sergeant's point had been made. From that point on, the men fired from the embrasures, and then they only held out their guns without looking, exposing just their right arms and shoulders. When it was his turn to step up, the sergeant dropped his (rifle) musket and clasped his chest. Fortunately, the ball was spent and its only effect was a painful bruise that took several weeks to disappear.[68]

The Union artillery had been carefully positioned to enfilade most of the ditch outside the walls of the fort. However, there was a dead spot at the base of the ditch under the northeast bastion that was safe from the deadly missiles, large and small. Here, masses of the attackers huddled, momentarily seeking refuge from the murderous close-range fire from above. Nevertheless, most of the attackers, despite the danger, bravely attempted to mount the ditch and parapet. A number were able to scramble onto the berm, where they now turned their attention to scaling the parapet. Many men climbed on top of their comrades' shoulders, and digging their fingers into the hardened earth struggled to work their way up the sloped defenses. It proved a gargantuan task: in places the berm had been cut away and the attackers were unable to get a toehold.

Several embrasures for defending artillery had been cut midway up the parapet, and these were therefore easier to reach. One Confederate officer managed to raise himself up into one of these and ordered the nearby defenders to surrender. He was followed by a handful of his men, but this tiny group was immediately captured. Captain Tom Cumming, an adjutant in one of Wofford's Regiments, did manage to break through and jumped into the "parade ground" below. He immediately started to attack the cannoneers, sword in hand, but was almost instantly overpowered and taken captive. When ordered to cease struggling, he coolly responded, "It is a satisfaction, sir, that I give up my sword in the interior of this Fort."[69]

Most of the attackers on the berm and in the ditch were sitting ducks to those overhead, but against all odds, many attackers did manage to reach the top of the defenses. One Union infantryman grabbed an axe and clove the skulls of three Confederates before he was hauled back to a less exposed position by his comrades.[70] A huge roar from the attackers signaled the crisis of the engagement as the first Rebel managed to reach the top of the parapet. He had planted his regiment's flag on the parapet before pulling himself over the defensive work. Almost instantly a number of muskets were trained on him and he was shot dead, his body, riddled with bullets, falling limply onto the crowd below.[71] Inspired by the man's personal bravery and devotion to his cause, other attackers quickly followed his example. Next, it was the turn of Colonel Thomas, a gray-haired officer from Georgia, to lead his men over the parapet.[72] One Union officer at the fort estimated that about one hundred Rebels reached the top of the fort's walls, and the standard-bearers of the Sixteenth Georgia and Thirteenth and Seventeenth Mississippi Regiments in turn attempted to plant their standards on the parapet. Almost to a man these brave soldiers were killed or wounded, however.[73] One Confederate officer who managed to get up near the top noticed that only three sides of the fort were fortified, and the rear face was open. In vain, he begged the men who were trying to move forward that they should work their way to the rear of the fort. His efforts proved in vain.

One of the Union artillery pieces, a 12-pounder howitzer near Todd and his band of Seventy-ninth Highlanders, had ceased firing because it had exhausted its ammunition. Believing it now to be harmless, a number of McLaws's men had climbed through the embrasure and demanded that its gunners surrender. However, the artillerists had taken the precaution of leaving the last charge unfired in the gun. The No. 4 artilleryman calmly pulled the lanyard and the threat was instantly eliminated. The artillerymen now pushed the howitzer forward into the embrasure to serve as a protective barrier against enemy small arms fire, and armed themselves with rifle muskets.[74]

It was difficult, if not impossible, for the nearby Union soldiers to depress their muskets sufficiently to be able to hit those standing on the ledge immediately below. Lieutenant Benjamin had foreseen this problem and this was one of the positions where he had placed 20-pounder Parrott shells with five-second fuses.[75] When the moment came, Captain Baird held a portfire, while Benjamin lit the first shell and rolled this ad hoc "grenade" onto the enemy below.[76] Working in tandem they were thus able to throw a series of these shells in quick order.[77] The swift succession of violent explosions in the ditch added monumentally to the carnage and confusion. At first the cause of these explosions was not apparent to the attackers, who assumed they were the result of friendly artillery fire. The Confederate artillery was ordered to stop firing, and, of course, the true source of the problem became apparent. One of the shells landed at the feet of an attacker, and he attempted to extinguish the sparkling fuse by shoving two handfuls of mud into the fuse hole. The desperate action came too late, and a moment later the unfortunate was blown "into atoms."[78] At least one Confederate, Robert Thompson of the Ninth Georgia, did manage to throw one of these shells back to its original owners, however.[79]

Those in the attacking party who refrained from jumping into the ditch did not just passively mill around, waiting for a breakthrough. Feverishly they loaded and reloaded their weapons, firing shot after shot at the embrasures and upper parapet. But it was to no avail.

Humphreys's Brigade had won the race and was the first to reach the ditch. Humphreys wanted Wofford's command to attack the bastion on the left, whose artillery was proving particularly annoying, and he sent a courier with this request. This advice went unheeded and Wofford's Brigade led by Colonel S. Z. Ruff rushed up, adding to the pandemonium along the ditch. A "fierce altercation" erupted between Ruff and Colonel McElroy of the Thirteenth Mississippi, but the artillery on the bastions "soon relieved them both of all earthly worry." McElroy had managed to reach the top of the parapet but was shot dead, his body falling into the ditch. Colonel Ruff and Colonel Thomas were mortally wounded soon after. Colonel John C. Fiser of the Seventeenth Mississippi was badly wounded in the arm and had to be helped to the rear. Hearing the familiar Rebel yell to his rear, Humphreys turned and saw Anderson's Brigade rushing up.[80] Anderson's command, stationed to the left and the rear, was supposed to advance only if the preceding waves were successful. However, feeling compelled to do their share, they surged forward in two lines: the Seventh, Eighth, and Eleventh Georgia Regiments, commanded by Colonel Little, in the First, and the Ninth and Fifty-ninth Georgia commanded by Major William B. Jones of the Ninth Georgia in the second.[81]

Humphreys sent messages asking them to stop sending any more reinforcements. Realistically, the battle was lost and more men would only needlessly add to the confusion and carnage, without the chance of producing any positive effect.

Longstreet meanwhile continued to move toward the front, confident that his men would storm the defensive works and carry the day. His optimism was shattered as he approached to within five hundred yards of the fort, however:

> I saw some of the men straggling back, and heard that the troops could not pass the ditch for want of ladders or other means. Almost at the same moment I saw that the men were beginning to retire in considerable numbers, and very soon the column broke up entirely and fell back in confusion. I ordered Buckner's brigade halted and

Fort Sanders: This illustration most probably depicts the mortal wounding of Colonel Rust, who led Wofford's Brigade toward Fort Sanders during the later stages of the Confederate assault. *Courtesy of Library of Congress, Prints & Photographs Online Catalog (PPOC). LC-USZC4-1730.*

retired, and sent the order for Anderson's brigade, of Hood's division, to be halted and retired, but the troops of the latter brigade had become excited and rushed up to the same point from which the others had been repulsed, and were soon driven back. Officers were set to work to rally the men, and good order was soon restored.[82]

Union reinforcements that had been stationed along the defensive works near the fort began to arrive. Advancing at a run, Companies A, C, D, and K of the Twenty-ninth Massachusetts and Company C of the Twentieth Michigan deployed. After several minutes, it was clear to Lieutenant Benjamin that the attacking impulse was spent, and he ordered one company from each of the Second Michigan and Twenty-ninth Pennsylvania regiments to sally out into the ditch. Eagerly complying, these men ran out and demanded the surrender of any Confederate troops still standing. Scores of men gave themselves up immediately and were funneled through the embrasures back into the security of the fort where they were taken prisoner. But a majority of the attackers did not stay to be captured. Retiring quickly, they suffered surprisingly few casualties during this phase of the engagement. Probably the defenders, although victorious, were equally played out and were glad that the deadly threat had passed. General Humphreys noticed that the Union infantrymen were no longer firing, but had started to help those who but a few moments earlier had been their mortal enemies. So as not to discourage or impede this task, Humphreys ordered his men to cease firing.[83]

A sense of normality returning, the Union defenders start to mill around and look curiously at the carnage in the ditch. They were confronted with an appalling scene. There were heaps of the dead and dying where the attackers had rolled down from the parapet. The battle over, General Burnside agreed upon a brief truce to allow the Confederates to recover their wounded.[84] McLaws's forces had lost three battle flags and five hundred stands of arms. They suffered 129 killed and 458 wounded, as well as 225 men taken prisoner.[85]

As with every other intensely fought struggle, in the days, months, and years following the engagement many participants would reflect upon the factors that led to the result. This was especially true among the proud Southern warriors who had followed their leaders to so many glorious victories. In the debate that followed the debacle, a number of reasons were offered to explain the humiliating defeat. There had been an ongoing rivalry between Wofford's and Humphreys's Brigades, and not surprisingly there was some mutual finger pointing. After the war, in an unpublished memoir, Humphreys, for example, would claim that Wofford had failed to advance his skirmishers against a nearby bastion, thus permitting its artillery to fire freely at the main attacking body with coolness and deliberation.[86] The correspondent for the *Memphis Appeal* felt that some of the blame fell on the rank and file, who obstinately continued to try to mount the defenses to their front, even after some of their officers ordered them to work their way around the flanks of the position.[87]

Others argued that the skirmishing the previous night had tipped off the defenders as to the true point of the main attack, as well as when it was most likely occur, i.e., at daybreak. Others felt that there had been an inadequate preliminary artillery bombardment, while still others blamed poor coordination between the two main attacking columns adding to the confusion that occurs during any engagement.

In his paper delivered decades after the war, Poe rejected these speculations that minimized the role of the defenders in the Union victory. Instead, he emphasized the importance of the overall defensive plan, the use of wire entanglements, and, most importantly, the courage and fighting ability of the Union soldiers who bore the brunt of the determined Confederate assault columns.[88] Though, of course, it was natural that Poe should stress the importance of the fighting mettle of the men, it was probably the nature of the fortifications and the various defensive measures employed that had the greatest impact on the outcome of the fighting that day. This was not lost on the general public, who would read these heroics in vivid accounts of the fighting in such magazines as *Harper's Weekly*.[89]

Of much greater consequence, the defensive capabilities of wire entanglements and the effectiveness of prepared defensive works to protect a strategically important position also appear to have caught the imagination of military planners on both sides of the conflict, and it is no coincidence that extensive field fortifications became part of the daily modus operandi during the Mine Run affair in November 1863 and Grant's campaign in the spring of 1864. Of course, this fighting would be horrifically bloody, and generally, like the Confederate attack at Knoxville, entirely futile in a tactical sense, as witness the sanguinary attacks against hastily built entrenchments at Spotsylvania and Cold Harbor and the assaults against even sturdier defenses in front of Petersburg.

This shift in fighting style toward a type of "trench warfare" has generally been seen as the result of the participants' belated awareness of the new lethality of warfare spawned by the rifle musket and the futility of relying upon "old-fashioned" European close order tactics. After three years of carnage and meaningless self-sacrifice, all remaining vestiges of a heroic, idealized mode of warfare finally are set aside, and the battle-worn veteran is seen as giving in to his instinct for survival and adopting a much more pragmatic approach as he begins to take advantage of all available protection.

However, there is a mounting body of evidence that suggests that this trend toward ubiquitous defensive works was more a reflection of a change in military scientific thinking among high-level officers than it was a democratic and spontaneous tendency among the rank and file. Numerous examples can be found of high-level commanders ordering their subordinates to fortify their position at the end of the day's march. At the very onset of the Overland Campaign, Hancock ordered his divisional commanders to construct breastworks as soon as they completed their advance on May 5.[90] Similar precautions had already been taken by part of the Second Division of Getty's Sixth Corps.[91] On May 6, General Benjamin Butler took exactly the same steps after his forces crossed the James River and landed at Bermuda Hundred. Probably an even more telling example is provided by Warren's Federal Fifth Corps, on May 8. Forced back by Rodes's Division that evening, his men took refuge in some entrenchments that they had constructed earlier that day. Fortifying one's nighttime resting position had become so commonplace that Lieutenant Favill on May 7 would record in his diary:

> We immediately went into position, relieving Gregg's division of cavalry, and commenced at once, *as is usual now-a-days* [italics mine], to throw up a breastwork of logs and rails, and dug a ditch behind them . . . the enemy was discovered to be entrenched on the opposite shore and opened fire as soon as our party showed themselves.[92]

Clearly, one can easily list enough examples of temporary end-of-day fortifications from the beginning of Grant's Overland Campaign to establish the existence of a trend or pattern. Moreover, after reflection it becomes obvious that these defensive precautions were the result of orders, suggestions from, or at least the opinions of the highest military circles, rather than the desires of individual regimental or division commanders. At the start of these operations, Hancock, for example, issued orders for fortifications to be erected after each stage of the advance. Even more significantly, Butler had halted his offensive four full days to erect defensive works constructed from the James River at Trent's Reach to the Appomattox River at Port Walthall. It is safe to conclude that these precautions, if not the result of explicit orders, were at least blessed by an implicit understanding from above.

It is arguable that the spontaneous efforts of the rank and file to protect themselves by digging shallow trenches with drinking cups was the direct result of the more highly organized defensive efforts, rather than the other way around. First, there is the issue of chronology. The hasty "entrenchments" that have been so frequently commented upon by military historians were first employed only after several weeks of methodical entrenching.

There is also the issue of what might be termed "psychological causality." The traditional set piece battle had called for the soldiers to master their instinct for self-preservation and be willing to make whatever sacrifice was necessary to win. Massed in tight formations they had to advance into withering defensive fire without flinching or making any evasive efforts, regardless of the potential consequences. Defensive works, by their very nature, promoted a very different psychological stance. They quickly introduced a pragmatism at odds with the traditional concept of the soldier as hero. Those behind defensive works were enjoined to take every precaution to avoid being hit. In fact, a careless defender would be rebuked for unnecessary carelessness. However, this opened a type of "Pandora's box." Once the soldier became used to doing everything to promote survival behind defenses, a new psychological model had been created that was instinctively carried over onto the battlefield. "What was done, could not be undone," and the face of battle had been irreversibly changed.

9

THE SECOND MINNESOTA INFANTRY
AT MISSIONARY RIDGE

Formed and mustered into Federal service over the summer of 1861, the Second Minnesota Volunteer Infantry Regiment had marched in the Mill Springs Campaign, reinforced Grant's army after Shiloh, and fought at Corinth, Perryville, Tullahoma, and Chickamauga—after which it was besieged at Chattanooga, in the autumn of 1863, with the rest of the Army of the Cumberland, at the end of a tenuous line of supply. Succor came with the arrival of Sherman's Army of the Tennessee and elements from the Army of the Potomac. Yet, destiny assigned to the Second Minnesota and a number of other regiments in Granger's Fourth Corps a fateful, if accidental, role in the final breakout of the besieged armies and the redemption of the Army of the Cumberland's reputation.

THE STRATEGIC SITUATION

After the crushing defeat at Chickamauga (September 19–20, 1863), Major General William Starke Rosecrans and his Army of the Cumberland fell back to Chattanooga to lick their wounds. General Bragg's victorious Confederate army was still able to take possession of Missionary Ridge, overlooking Chattanooga, and Lookout Mountain slightly to the south and west. Confederate control of these two strong points denied the Union force of both rail and river transport, and it was with extreme difficulty that a meager trickle of food and supplies was slowly and painstakingly dragged overland by wagon into the beleaguered town. The situation quickly became desperate and the defenders were faced with imminent starvation. Their ability to fight had also been greatly compromised. It was estimated that the Union infantry had ammunition enough for only a single day's combat. If that were not bad enough, his telegrams make it clear that Rosecrans had lost the will to lead a determined resistance, and hinted that he and his men would soon attempt to retreat from their isolated position.

The Union Assault up Missionary Ridge: With Lookout Mountain as a poignant backdrop, this panorama shows the full extent and depth of the Union assault. *Courtesy of Library of Congress, Prints & Photographs Online Catalog (PPOC). LC-DIG-pga–00539.*

The situation clearly critical, military authorities in Washington were quickly forced to take decisive steps. The Military Division of the Mississippi was created and placed under the command of Ulysses S. Grant, giving him authority over Rosecrans's Department of the Cumberland. In mid-October, Rosecrans was relieved and Major General George H. Thomas was ordered to take command of the Army of the Cumberland. Major General William Farrar "Baldy" Smith, chief engineer of that army, had several log bridges built over the Tennessee River increasing the trickle of desperately needed food and armament into the town. General Halleck ordered Oliver O. Howard's Eleventh Corps and Henry Slocum's Twelfth Corps from the Army of the Potomac to be placed under Joe Hooker's command and transported by rail into southern Tennessee to be available to General Thomas. The capture and subsequent fortification of Brown's Ferry further eased the logistical position, and by October 27 the Tennessee River was open to Union operations up to Lookout Valley. Bragg's stranglehold on Chattanooga and the surrounding countryside was further weakened the next day as elements of Hooker's Eleventh and Twelfth Corps gained a foothold in Lookout Valley, thus opening the river from Bridgeport to Lookout Valley. A counterattack by Longstreet's Corps against Major General John White Geary's command in that valley at Wauhatchie was repulsed that night, and the "cracker" [supply] line into Chattanooga was never again threatened.

On November 4, in a bid to defeat the gathering Union forces in detail, Longstreet's fifteen thousand men and Major General Joseph Wheeler's cavalry were sent to attack General Burnside's small Army of the Ohio, which had taken Knoxville and its environs. Grant responded by ordering Thomas to attack the right of Bragg's line along Missionary Ridge. It was hoped this would force Longstreet to abort his mission and return in order to support Bragg. But Thomas demurred, arguing that the forces available were insufficient and his horses were in no condition to move the artillery.[1] The start of Union offensive operations was delayed several weeks as Grant awaited the arrival of Major General William T. Sherman's

Army of the Tennessee from the vicinity of Corinth and Iuka in northeastern Mississippi. Sherman's leading elements managed to reach Brown's Ferry only on November 20.

The Confederate defenses surrounding Chattanooga on the south side of the Tennessee River were considered to be strong, and a frontal assault was considered inadvisable. Grant devised an ingenious plan of attack, which he revealed to his top generals when Sherman and a small party of officers first rode into Chattanooga on November 16. Although the Tennessee follows a truly serpentine course, constantly twisting and occasionally switching back and forth, the stretch in front of the town runs almost due west. Behind the town a valley with a depth of five or six miles at points stretches away in a north by north-easterly direction and is surrounded by crests and hills. This valley starts to the south and west of Chattanooga at the foot of Lookout Mountain, with its 2,200-foot elevation, and is bounded in the east by Missionary Ridge, which gradually angles toward the Tennessee River and crosses the South Chickamauga River three or four miles to the east. Opposite Chattanooga, on the other side of the Tennessee River, there are also a number of hills. At that time, several roads wended their way around Crane's Hill and swung back toward the river above the town and led to the North Chickamauga River. This stream empties into the Tennessee seven or eight miles above Chattanooga.[2]

The largest contingent of relatively fresh troops, the two corps under Hooker's command, was west of Chattanooga near Lookout Mountain. Sherman's forces would also be coming from the west. Grant's plan was to make it appear that Sherman would advance into Chattanooga and be poised to attack the left of the Confederate line, somewhere around Chattanooga Creek. In reality, Sherman's divisions would take the back roads behind the hills on the northern bank and swing all the way over to where the North Chickamauga meets the Tennessee. Then, under the cover of darkness, a brigade or two would cross over and establish a bridgehead at the point where the South Chickamauga River flows into the Tennessee. The remainder of Sherman's Fourteenth Corps would cross over a hastily constructed pontoon bridge and then attack the rightmost part of

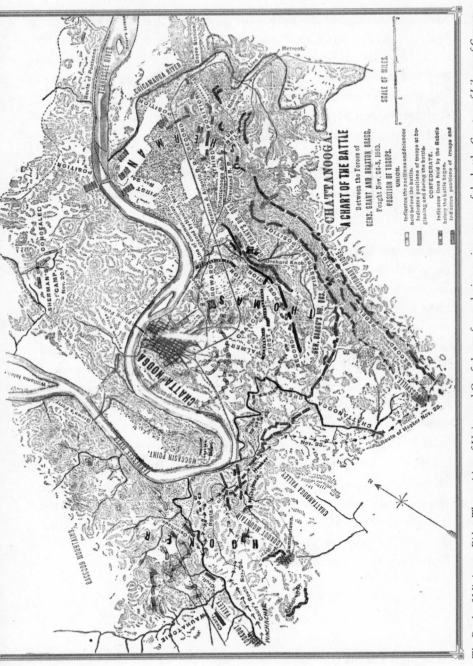

The Battle of Missionary Ridge: The position of Union and Confederate forces during various stages of the battle. Courtesy of Library of Congress, Online Map Collection (Civil War Maps), Reproduction No.: Mss5:7 Sn237:1 p. 422.

Missionary Ridge at daylight. The hope was that the Confederates, fooled into thinking that the attack was to be against their left, would not have time to reinforce their right adequately. If Sherman could seize the railway lines in front of this position, Bragg's line of supplies and communications would be cut, and the Missionary Ridge/Lookout Mountain line of defenses would no longer be viable and Bragg's army would be forced to retire.

There was one unavoidable problem. Sherman's divisions would cross the Tennessee at Brown's Ferry in full view of Confederate observers atop Lookout Mountain, aptly named as it turns out. If his men simply disappeared behind the hills to the north, their destination would be obvious, Grant's true plan would be become transparent, and any chance to surprise the Confederates would be lost. Grant hit upon a clever solution. Oliver O. Howard's Eleventh Corps, under Joe Hooker's command, was positioned behind the northern hills. After Sherman's divisions crossed over at Brown's Ferry, Howard's men would advance along the road out of the hills and cross over into Chattanooga, while Sherman's men surreptitiously continued along the back roads over Crane's Hill. The Confederate observers would see Union troops in the distance crossing at Brown's Ferry and then a little later over the bridge into the town. They would assume those troops were Sherman's.[3]

Sherman's lead troops managed to reach Brown's Ferry by November 20, but most of his force was stretched for miles on the roads behind. At this point, the weather colluded to further stymie Grant's intended offensive. The first two divisions were able to make their way across the river, but the heavy rains and rising floodwaters made it impossible for the last of Sherman's reinforcements to cross the Tennessee River for several more days.

PRELIMINARY ACTIVITY

Although forced to wait for the remainder of Sherman's forces to arrive, Grant refused to remain totally inactive. The next several days saw a number of chesslike moves as the Union command sought to expand gradually beyond the original defensive perimeter. The existing Union defensive line was about a mile in front of the Chattanooga and extended from Citico Creek on the left to Chattanooga Creek on the right. There were a number of minor hills and elevations along and behind the Union line and these, of course, had been fortified. Fort Wood, on the eastern side of the line, was one of the more important of these. During the morning of November 23, Philip H. Sheridan's Second Division and Thomas J. Wood's Third Division of Major General Gordon Granger's Fourth Corps (Army of the Cumberland) were moved up and deployed at the foot of Fort Wood; Johnson's First Division of the Fourteenth Corps supported the right, while Howard's corps was formed en masse as a reserve to the rear. Low-hanging clouds prevented the Confederates from detecting these preparations for attack. The offensive began at 2:00 P.M. and quickly pushed back the Confederate skirmishers who had been holding a series of minor elevations. By the end of the operation, two hundred prisoners of war had been taken and the Union line had been pushed forward nearly a mile and the advanced line of Confederate rifle pits taken. Granger was ordered to strengthen the captured fortifications quickly and throw out a strong line of skirmishers.

The next day witnessed another Union success. General Hooker had been ordered to take a little more than two divisions from Thomas's and Sherman's armies and make a "strong demonstration" up the western slope of Lookout Mountain to draw the enemy's attention to that section of the front in order to allow Sherman to cross the Tennessee River at the mouth of South Chickamauga Creek unnoticed. Both parts of the operation were completely successful. Hooker's men started their advance very early that morning and by 2:00 P.M. had taken possession of the slope from the road to the Chattanooga Valley to the White House.[4]

Sherman and his men, meanwhile, had also been busy. Although General John E. Smith's division of the Seventeenth Corps had managed to get behind the northern hills on November 20, Brigadier General Morgan L. Smith's Second Division was able to cross at Brown's Ferry only the next day. Despite laboring day and night, Hugh Ewing's Fourth Division was able to get over only on the twenty-third. By nightfall, Sherman finally had three of his divisions ensconced in the hills behind the mouth of the North Chickamauga River. The moment to unleash Grant's plan had finally arrived! Two regiments of Giles A. Smith's brigade (Second Division) surreptitiously crossed the river by boat and snuck up on the Confederate pickets guarding the river's edge. These were easily overpowered and captured. The boats plied their way back and forth across the river, and by daybreak of November 24, two divisions, about eight thousand effectives, were across and ready for action. The steamer *Dunbar* finally arrived and helped ferry the men over the Tennessee, and by noon a pontoon bridge finally had been completed and all three of Sherman's divisions, complete with horses and artillery, were finally ready for offensive operations. General Howard, meanwhile, had advanced with three regiments along the riverbank. These he left in Sherman's charge to help establish contact with Thomas's forces in front of Chattanooga. Sherman's men advanced in columns protected by clouds of skirmishers and by 3:30 P.M. had taken some foothills. Realizing the importance of the ground just gained, Sherman, ordered that it be fortified that evening.[5]

THE SECOND MINNESOTA'S ASSAULT UP MISSIONARY RIDGE

At midnight, orders came for Sherman to attack the next series of hills in front of him at dawn's first light. On the other extremity of the battlefield, after being pushed off the summit the Confederates had evacuated the remainder of Lookout Mountain during the night. Hooker was to push forward to Rossville, east of the mountain, in order to apply pressure to the rear and extreme Confederate left, while Sherman's attack on the other side of the battlefield did the same to the enemy's right. When the time was right, that is, when the defending line had been sufficiently thinned, Thomas's forces would advance straight up the main section of Missionary Ridge, almost due east of the town.

But events did not unfold exactly as Grant had envisioned. Although Hooker's men had set off early, they encountered a four-hour delay crossing Chattanooga Creek. Sherman, meanwhile, met with much stiffer resistance than had been expected. During the night, the enemy had fortified the hills in front of his position. Although at first Sherman's assault made progress, capturing the ends of some Confederate works, Bragg ordered as many reinforcements into the area as could be spared. Now subjected to overwhelming artillery fire and hammered by numerous columns, after two hours Sherman's brigades were forced to fall back. Brigadier General John E. Smith counterattacked with two brigades from the Seventeenth Corps, but, despite coming to very close quarters with the defenders, was also repulsed. Observing this unfortunate turn of events from his command post on Orchard Knob near the center of the Union position, Grant realized that he could not wait until Hooker's command reached Rossville. Something had to be done immediately to help alleviate the situation facing Sherman. He ordered Thomas to send a division to support Sherman's stalling offensive. Thomas, in turn, directed Brigadier General Absalom Baird's Third Division of the Fourteenth Corps to move to the left and join Sherman's forces.

Baird was then in the process of reconnoitering the ground in front of his position. Earlier that morning it had been discovered that the Confederates had abandoned their position along Missionary Ridge around Chattanooga Creek. Several small parties had been sent out to determine the extent of the withdrawal. It was at that point that Baird received Grant's instructions. He complied immediately and his division started to maneuver toward the far northern edge of the battlefield. Grant, however, had second thoughts about the wisdom of expending valuable resources in what might be a lost cause and decided that the best succor was a strong attack on the Confederate center. Just as the lead elements of Baird's force were reaching Sherman, the divisional commander received a second set of instructions, requiring him to return to his

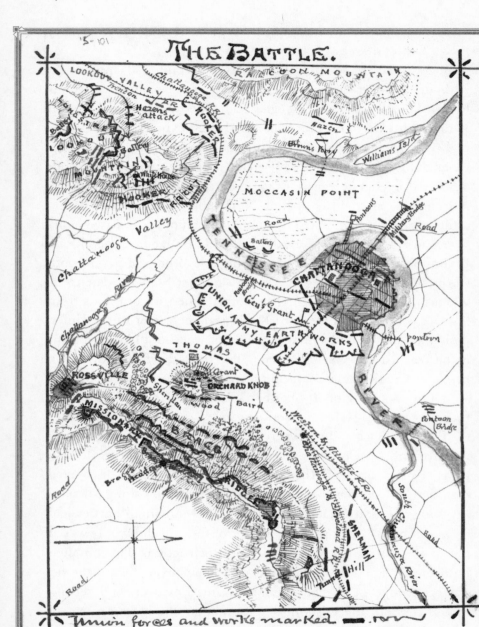

The Battle of Missionary Ridge: This rougher hand-drawn map provides a little more detail regarding the position of Baird's division during the assault up Missionary Ridge. *Courtesy of Library of Congress, Online Map Collection (Civil War Maps).*

original position, where he was to deploy his force to the left of General Granger's First Division. The main portion of Thomas's force was to consist from left to right of Baird's, Wood's, Sheridan's, and Johnson's divisions; no fewer than twenty-three thousand men stretched out over two miles

The ground was intersected with marshes, streams, and thickets, and it took Baird several hours for his men to comply with his second set of instructions. His force was now to the north of Orchard Knob, immediately to the left of General Samuel Beatty's brigade of Granger's corps. Baird followed traditional protocol and positioned his three brigades according to seniority. General John B. Turchin's First Brigade was on the right, Colonel Van Derveer's Second in the center, and Colonel Phelps's Third on the left.[6] Colonel Ferdinand Van Derveer ordered his brigade to deploy along two lines. The Eighty-seventh Indiana, the Thirty-fifth Ohio, and the 101st Indiana were positioned from right to left along the first line, while the Seventy-fifth and 105th Indiana and the Ninth Ohio were relegated to the second line. Two of Baird's Minnesota regiments were on detached duty,[7] but acting as the advance guard the Second Minnesota was positioned about three hundred yards in front of the first line. Two companies of the Minnesota regiment led by a Captain Calvin S. Uline were deployed as skirmishers an additional 150 yards out along the brigade front. Six other companies functioned as a skirmisher reserve and so were stationed between the skirmishers and the brigade formation.[8] Baird's division, with slight variation, was now deployed in a formation similar to those found among the other divisions along the vast Union line. Those in Granger's Fourth Corps, for example, were shielded by a double line of skirmishers; most of his command was deployed in a single line, followed by a reserve "in mass," i.e., in columns.[9]

Just as his men had taken up their positions, Baird, then on the left of his division, was approached by one of General Thomas's staff officers and given instructions for the upcoming assault. In the light of later events, Thomas's instructions to his various subcommanders would become matters of some controversy. In the reports written after the battle, some like Colonel John Martin of the Eighth Kansas Infantry admitted they were instructed to take only the rifle pits and then await further orders. Others, such as Major John McClenahan in charge of the skirmishers in front of General August Willich's brigade, had the impression that they were to continue on up Missionary Ridge after seizing the rifle pits and take the main Confederate line of defense. In his own report, Baird maintained that Thomas's staff officer verbally instructed Baird, upon the sounding of six signal guns, to advance his men and take the rifle pits on the slope to their front. He added pointedly that he was also informed that "this was intended as preparatory to a general assault on the mountain, and that it was doubtless designed by the major-general commanding that I should take part in this movement, so that I would be following his wishes were I to push on to the summit."[10] General "Baldy" Smith provides a different story; according to his account he personally brought Thomas's orders to Baird. Baird was incredulous, asking, "And when I have captured the rifle-pits, what then?" Smith shrugged his shoulders and rode away.[11]

In any case, Baird passed on the orders as he understood them, first to Phelps's Third Brigade and then to Van Derveer's Second. Now finally in position and having received their orders, there was nothing to do but await the signal to attack. The Confederate artillery opened fire from time to time, but most of the Union forces gathered before them remained under cover of woods at the base of the hill.[12] There were a few casualties, and as a result Baird's men were ordered to stack arms and lie down.[13] Immediately in front of Baird's division lay an open field that descended gradually to a small creek. The ground on the far side of the creek then rose about a quarter mile to a low ridge that ran parallel to Missionary Ridge, which was another quarter mile distant. Originally, most of the slope had been forested, but during the previous months the Confederates had cut down all of the trees for firewood and so that their artillery would have free play. All that was left were a few stumps and logs.[14] Atop the first ridge were log breastworks and rifle pits, the Confederates' first line of defense. Observing the objective with their field glasses, Union officers spotted two Rebel colors floating among the rifle pits and concluded that this advanced Confederate position was held by two battalion-size Confederate units.[15] On the other side of the rifle pits there was a narrow plateau, about one hundred yards wide. Here and there on this level ground the Confederates had built a few huts. The ground beyond sloped gradually for three or four hundred yards to the foot of Missionary Ridge. The approach up the latter was gradual at first but became much steeper as one neared the top. The main Confederate line ran along Missionary Ridge, at this point five or six hundred yards in height. The defenses directly in front of Van Derveer's brigade were manned by two brigades from Hardee's Corps—Vaughan's Brigade from Hindman's Division and Jackson's Brigade from Cheatham's. These works were further protected by "entanglements," in a number of strategically important parts of the line.[16] The abundance of forest made these wooden field fortifications, or abatis as they were known in military science, very popular. At first they were made by simply placing one log on top of another to form a type of wall. It was quickly found that these did not provide adequate protection against artillery, so a deep embankment of earth was placed in front. Eventually, Civil War infantrymen discovered that further protection could be derived simply by chopping down trees, stripping the leaves off, and sharpening the branches to jagged points. These were placed with the branches facing the enemy so that they presented a formidable obstacle to anyone trying to get over them.[17] Such were the measures taken by the Confederates along Missionary Ridge.

Van Derveer's Second Brigade had been in position for about an hour when at around four o'clock in the afternoon the signal guns sounded the call for the four divisions from the Army of the Cumberland (Baird's, Wood's, Sheridan's, and Johnson's) to advance simultaneously out into the open and take the rifle pits roughly halfway between the edge of the woods on the Union side and Missionary Ridge held by the main Confederate force.[18]

Before committing the main body of his brigade, Van Derveer decided to let the advance guard attempt to take the position. He ordered the Second Minnesota under Lieutenant Colonel Judson

W. Bishop to advance in skirmish order and if possible to seize and occupy the advanced breastworks. We know from a letter that the colonel sent to his mother in the weeks following the battle that each skirmisher was about five feet from his neighbor as they advanced.[19] The men were to withhold their fire and move directly toward their goal. If unsuccessful, Bishop and his men were to retire back upon the brigade; however, if they managed to take the breastworks, they had to defend the captured outpost at all costs. The tactic that Van Derveer had selected for his infantry, that is, the quick advance without firing, was an accepted practice throughout the war. In tactical instructions issued several days before Bull Run, General Beauregard cautioned his men to hold their fire until directed, and then to fire only when they had "a distinct object in full view";[20] the next year McClellan issued similar directives: "aim carefully and low, and above all things rely upon the bayonet."[21] These injunctions had been hammered home by General Rosecrans in a number of his own missives.[22]

There was but a momentary delay, more a pause, as Bishop briefed his men regarding the seriousness of their mission. The six companies that had been kept in reserve quickly extended out into a skirmish line, and with fixed bayonets the Second Minnesota began its advance into the open field. So as to remain within supporting distance, Van Derveer ordered the remainder of his brigade into the position just vacated by the Second Minnesota at the edge of the woods.

The attackers did not have to wait long for the Rebels' response. Both the infantry in the rifle pits and the artillery along the top of Missionary Ridge redoubled their fire almost as soon as the attackers emerged from the woods.[23] The Confederate artillery was particularly intimidating. Bright flames flashed along the ridge and thick clouds of smoke were thrown upward into the sky. Two gun sections were placed every one or two hundred yards along the ridge and thus a concentric fire converging upon the advancing forces was achieved. Given the relatively short range, most of the defending artillery opted to fire spherical case.[24] The roar of the enemy artillery, extremely loud under any circumstances, was further amplified by the hilly terrain. Some of the individual reports echoed as much as five or six times. There seemed, as a result, to be continuous artillery fire, the rapidity of which reminded one soldier of "the rattle of musketry." But despite the overwhelming cacophony of artillery, the attackers suffered few casualties from these long-range missiles,[25] for the Union lines—advancing at the double-quick, in some cases even at the run—did not allow the Confederate gunners to establish the proper range.[26] Even a competent artillerist usually required one or two preliminary shots to establish the range of a target. However, this was not possible with quickly moving troops, since by the time a range had been established they were no longer there. As a result, most of the shot and shell flew harmlessly overhead or landed in front of them.

Seemingly unfazed, the Minnesotans continued their advance "silently and steadily," first across the small creek and then up the gentle slope in front of the rifle pits. In a report submitted after the engagement, Van Derveer noted that the Rebels were shaken by the attackers' calm resolve. As the attacking line approached to within one hundred and fifty yards, the uneasiness of the defenders in the rifle pits became noticeable to the Union officers.[27] The reason for the defenders' sudden trepidation is known from letters written home shortly after the battle and from personal narratives published after the war. Although the attacking Union soldiers did not have a clear view of those they were attacking, those defending on the ridge above were able to see the entire Union army on the plain before them, as it turns out a most intimidating sight. Confederate Brigadier General Arthur M. Manigault would later remember the sight as "grand and imposing in the extreme." He and his men were impressed with the "order" and "precision" with which the advancing Union lines seemed to move; but it was also the sheer number of adversaries coming toward them. To those standing and waiting, it seemed that they were outnumbered many times to one.[28]

As the Union skirmishers advanced to within one hundred yards of the enemy emplacements, they broke into double-quick pace. It seemed to the attackers that the defenders, faced with this silent determination, lost their will to stand and unceremoniously and precipitously deserted their breastworks. This may have been a contributing factor. However, we now know that both Bragg and Breckinridge had issued instructions that the troops in the rifle pits were not to offer a determined resistance. They were to fire a volley and then fall back to the main line of defense. A majority of the defenders complied; however, a few units, for example, the Seventh Florida, attempted to hold on to their position and dished out continuous small arms fire as long as they could.[29]

Regardless of what motivated the Confederate advance guard to retire, in Van Derveer's part of the front they did not retreat far. Running down the gentle slope directly behind the rifle pits many of the Rebels sought shelter behind the tree stumps and huts in the area at the foot of Missionary Ridge. Here, they rallied and once again began to fire quickly on the Union skirmishers who were trying to shelter behind the far side of the breastworks. Not all defenders managed to escape, however, and the Minnesotans took fourteen prisoners at this point.[30]

Thanks to his precaution of placing a strong line of skirmishers in front of his first line, Van Derveer's brigade appears to have suffered fewer casualties during this initial stage of the attack than many of the other brigades that had deployed in close order formations.[31] Bishop and his officers were quickly able to restore order to the Second Minnesota and dress its ranks, and about five minutes after taking the rifle pits, Van Derveer's first line could be seen emerging from the woods at the bottom of the hill. These latter, though not subjected to any "musketry," had to endure a redoubled effort on the part of the Confederate artillery on the ridge, who concentrated all their efforts on these formed lines advancing up the gentle slope. The second line was also ordered out of the woods, but this halted as it reached the midway point to the rifle pits and was ordered to throw itself on the ground.[32] Bishop calculated that about twenty minutes elapsed from the time his men captured the rifle pits to the time the first line of the brigade reached his regiment. A few more minutes went by as the latter caught their breath, redressed, and reformed.

The exact details of what happened next have never been unraveled to the satisfaction of modern historians. Grant, the original author of the attack against the Confederate rifle pits, had never intended this small force to throw itself against the lofty Missionary Ridge. Remember, by this point he was awaiting the arrival of Hooker's forces on the Confederate left flank. It is probable that he ordered the taking of the rifle pits so that Thomas's men would be in a much better position to exploit the Confederates' confusion once they perceived that their left flank was threatened.

The Union men along the long line of rifle pits, now very much in harm's way, thought otherwise. Although they had driven off the Confederate infantrymen from the rifle pits, the Second Brigade, like the other formations along the lengthy Union line, found itself in a trying situation. The artillery in the heights above now focused its attention on the rifle pits and rained canister on the Union soldiers below, while the Rebel riflemen along the ridge did their best to wreak whatever havoc they could.

Unfortunately for Bishop's men, the breastworks they had just captured offered the Minnesotans less protection than they had to the previous occupants. The Confederates standing in a prepared ditch on the near side had been protected up to the shoulders and head. There was no ditch on the outside and Bishop would later claim that his men were sheltered only up to their knees.[33] This was the same situation that confronted the men in Turchin's First Brigade and also in Wood's division, who had managed to take the rifle pits in front of their portions of the field several minutes earlier. Brigadier General August Willich's observations about the men in his command were therefore equally applicable to the situation facing the Minnesotans:

It was evident to every one that to stay in this position would be certain destruction and final defeat; every soldier felt the necessity of saving the day and the campaign by conquering, and every one saw instinctively that the only place of safety was in the enemy's works on the crest of the ridge.[34]

Despite their exposed position, the Union infantrymen returned the Confederate fire with determination, and the original occupants of the rifle pits were soon induced to continue their retreat, this time up to the top of Missionary Ridge in order to get out of effective range. In their report after the battle, Lieutenant Colonel Bishop and Brigadier General Van Derveer would both vouch that what happened next, if not directly ordered, was at least condoned by General Baird, the commander of the Third Division, Fourteenth Corps. Discovering their position to be untenable, the Union soldiers all along the advancing line instinctively began to fan out, moving slightly forward to shelter themselves behind the stumps and huts, just as their enemy had a few moments before. And some of the more adventurous ran a little farther to the foot of the slope leading up to the main ridge. Here, the concave nature of the slope offered a dead space where they were safe from the artillery fire from directly above, though still somewhat subject to cross fire from the ridge on either side.

According to Bishop's history of the Second Minnesota, in which he had an opportunity to expound upon his original report, General Baird was heard to say, "Let the men go on up the ridge," and as Bishop would express it, "off they went."[35] Their horses unable to climb the steep and uneven incline, the field officers dismounted. It must be added that this was not a localized event, confined to the Second Minnesota or even Van Derveer's brigade. The same scenario was being played out in almost identical fashion along the entire length of the Union line.

In Van Derveer's section of the advance, the Second Minnesota was placed in the first line, and the other regiments from the brigade as they arrived attempted to redress and reform formation around the colors during the advance. However, once they reached the steeper gradient, the broken terrain meant that any formation, even regular skirmish order, could not be maintained and all semblance of order quickly disappeared. Bishop would long remember the confusion of that moment:

My regiment moved forward with the others of the brigade, assembling on the colors as far as it was possible to do on the way, until, in ascending the steepest part of the slope, where every man had to find or clear his own way through the entanglement, and in the face of a terrible fire of musketry and artillery, the men of the different regiments of the brigade became generally intermingled; and when the brigade finally crowned the enemy's work on the crest of the ridge, the regimental and even the company organizations had become completely merged in a crowd of gallant and enthusiastic men, who swarmed over the breastwork and charged the defenders with such promptness and vigor that the enemy broke and fled. . . .[36]

The brigade's second line, still lying on the ground on the Union side of the rifle pits, was finally ordered to stand and then run forward in order to support the first line now trudging up the steep slope. Reaching the rifle pits, the men of this supporting line stopped to regain their breath; however, after only a few minutes they resumed their quickened pace, trying to catch up to the leaders now nearing the crest.

The Confederate infantry and artillery shifted much of their fire to this second Union advance. But though rapid, their fire became increasingly wild and inaccurate and inflicted few casualties on the assailants.

Unchecked by the errant defensive fire, the Union infantrymen finally managed to reach the top of the ridge and sprang over the crowning breastworks that ran along its length. There were six artillery pieces along the front attacked by Van Derveer's Second Brigade. Incredibly all of these were caught in the act of loading at this critical moment. Here and there, a brief but desperate hand-to-hand encounter took place, especially around the guns as the enemy artillerymen were bayoneted or chased away before they could reload their pieces. But most of the Rebels, aware of Hooker's and Sherman's threats on either flank, and disheartened by the loss of the rifle pits and the Union's unstoppable climb up the slope, fled almost at the first moment, most running along the ridge to the left and being pursued about half a mile.

How long the crest was physically contested by the combatants is uncertain. Estimates range between five and fifteen minutes.[37] What is not debatable is the result. The attackers succeeded in taking about two to three hundred prisoners during the melee. The Ninth Ohio and the Seventy-fifth Indiana, part of the second line, probably advancing at a more controlled pace, and comforted by the events taking place up the slope ahead of them, managed to retain their closed order formation. Consequently, upon reaching the crest they were ordered to form line perpendicular to the ridge in either direction thus securing the newly captured position against a potential counterattack.

The defenders barely managed to save most of the caissons attached to the artillery battery; they had no such luck with the guns themselves. All had to be left behind, the Second Minnesota capturing two pieces, the Thirty-fifth Ohio three. These guns were quickly manned by the Union infantrymen and turned against their former owners as they retired. A sixth artillery piece was later discovered by the Seventy-fifth Indiana after all the fighting had ceased.

It was now late in the autumn day, and night began to fall. With this, most of the fighting ceased and the victorious Union troops began to bivouac on the position just conquered.[38]

One of the most notable characteristics of this engagement was the relatively light number of casualties suffered by Van Derveer's attacking force, even though it had to break through two sets of fieldworks. The main crisis had been resolved within about an hour of marching and fighting, and the entire engagement including the pursuit at the end was over in less than an hour and a half. In his after-battle report, Van Derveer stated that the Second Brigade, which had started the action with an effective force of 102 commissioned officers and 1,577 enlisted men, suffered 161 casualties; two officers and eighteen men were killed, and fifteen officers wounded.[39] The rest of the casualties came from the rank and file. The seven noncommissioned officers in the color guard were particularly hard hit, only one coming out of the battle unscathed. Most other brigades along the Union line were not as fortunate. August Willich's brigade, for example, lost 338 officers and men, while George D. Wagner's brigade, which had been ordered to retire before taking the hillcrest, only to be ordered to advance a second time, suffered a staggering 730 casualties.[40]

Not surprisingly, the Second Minnesota, the only regiment in the brigade involved in the fight for the rifle pits, suffered the highest percentage of losses. Among its 170 men and fifteen officers, there were thirty-nine casualties: one officer and four men killed and three officers and thirty-one men wounded. Three of the latter would later die of their wounds. A little over 21 percent of the regiment became casualties during the action, compared to slightly more than 8 percent for the entire brigade.

One other statistic of note: the ammunition expended during the battle averaged fifty-two rounds per man. A hundred rounds had been distributed to each infantryman that morning, so they were supplied with more than twice the amount normally carried.

Lieutenant Colonel Bishop, who played a prominent role in this action, later advanced three reasons for the Union forces' success. The first two were purely tactical in nature, the third more grand tactical in scope.

First, Bishop felt that Van Derveer's dispositions for the attack were the most suitable under the circumstances. The initial assault of the rifle pits had been made by a Union line that essentially advanced in skirmish order. Though subjected to a concentric artillery fire, deliberately aimed fire by sharpshooters on the ridge, and the more common variety of musketry from those manning the first breastworks, the attackers suffered only a fraction of the casualties that would have occurred had they advanced in a close order formation. Had Bishop's men been repulsed, most of the Second Brigade would have been available for a second, more threatening assault by greater numbers. Of course, as it turned out this did not prove necessary. Bishop attributed the skirmishers' success to these soldiers' ability to follow their orders and advance determinedly all the way to the objective without returning fire, "reserving all for the final rush and contest."[41]

These two arguments were offered to explain the light casualties and the relative ease of taking the rifle pits. Bishop was convinced that, despite the initial successes, had the Confederates along the ridge remained confident and fired at the Union soldiers climbing up the slope carefully, "every man of us would have been shot on the slope or driven back to the foot of it."[42]

Bishop attributed the breakdown of Confederate morale during the last critical moments partially to the easy defeat of the advanced parties in the rifle pits, but much more to the overall grand tactical situation that had been evolving throughout the day. According to Bishop, the Confederate rank and file realized that their position was threatened by Hooker's army on their left and Sherman's forces on their right. Their courage sufficiently dampened by these factors, they quickly lost their will to stay and fight, and the Union force was victorious.

All of these are legitimate arguments that help explain why the Union attackers were successful at certain stages. There is one further factor hitherto unmentioned that must be considered, since it significantly diminished the Confederates' ability to resist the Union advance at virtually every stage of this contest.

If Van Derveer, his staff, and chief subordinate officers had chosen a wise tactical solution to the task at hand, that is, attacking the rifle pits with the least number of men necessary for success in a formation that minimized casualties, the Confederates conversely had chosen to defend themselves from a position that guaranteed that the least number of casualties would be inflicted on the attacking force.

To the untrained eye looking at the defenses way up on Missionary Ridge the afternoon of November 25, 1863, the Confederate position must have appeared impressive, possibly impregnable, and if not impregnable, then capturable only after the expenditure of many lives. This was the opinion of the Confederate commanders who had chosen to defend the position. After all, the Union army's appearance was not so sudden that the bulk of the defenders were caught up on the ridge, unable to deploy anywhere else. Had they chosen, the Confederates had ample opportunity to deploy the bulk of their army near the rifle pits below. This, of course, was never seriously entertained, as the lofty position along the ridge was deemed a far superior defensive position.

Unfortunately for the Confederates, the military reality was quite the opposite. A high ridge immediately above a steep gradient is one of the worst imaginable defensive positions, about equivalent to placing one's forces in a line with their back to a river and no avenue of retreat.

The liabilities of the high position probably had first been observed with respect to the placement of artillery. In the mid-eighteenth century, Frederick the Great in his many tactical writings enjoined his artillery officers to eschew lofty positions with steep gradients. Writing roughly about the same time, the Austrian artilleryman Johann Gottlieb Von Tielke issued the same series of cautions.[43] There were a number of problems inherent to this situation. Given the type of carriages then in use, artillery pieces, for one thing, simply could not be depressed to the same extent as a rifle or musket barrel. If the hillside were too steep, the artillery could not be directed so as to fire down its course. And convex slopes posed even more serious problems: at the initial stages of the ascent, the line of sight to the attackers at the foot of the hill was obstructed by intervening terrain, making them at least temporarily immune from artillery fire. Concave slopes were hardly an improvement, almost always involving the steepness problems just discussed.[44] And artillery placed atop a straight gradient did not necessarily avoid all the problems associated with this type of terrain; it might have a clear and effective shot at troops actually advancing up the slope, but its ability to injure troops on the plain below was usually lessened—the trajectory was simply too plunging. The shell's or ball's career ended when it hit the ground and there could be no ricochet effect. Musket fire from elevated positions also tended to be less effective than that delivered on level ground. The troops almost always failed to lower their barrels sufficiently, and the resulting fire often sailed harmlessly over the attackers' heads. During the Battle of Belgrade (August 16, 1717), Maurice de Saxe witnessed the total destruction of two battalions of Imperial infantry perched on a large hill, though they had reserved fire until the Turkish horsemen had advanced to within thirty paces.[45]

So, what appeared to be a strong, almost impregnable position actually was quite vulnerable, provided, of course, the offensive force was sufficiently strong, well led, and had the courage and resolution to try and take the position. All three prerequisites were present that November day in the Chattanooga Valley.

10

A LAST HURRAH! THE SEVENTH SOUTH CAROLINA CAVALRY AT THE BATTLE OF DARBYTOWN ROAD

*T*he Seventh South Carolina was raised late in the war, being formed in March 1864, from the amalgamation of five independent companies and some cavalry from Holcombe's South Carolina Legion. Taking part in operations around Petersburg, it saw almost continuous action and participated in the Battle of New Market Heights (September 29, 1864) as well as another action around Roper's Farm the next day. Its colonel, Alexander C. Haskell, a dauntless, bold youth—he was but twenty-two years old when he assumed command—seeking glory, and completely dedicated to the cause for which he was fighting, repeatedly put himself in harm's way. Possibly his most glorious moment came about a week later when he found that he and his men would be a lead element in a flanking maneuver designed to retake Fort Harrison and ground lost during the previous week's fighting.

The succession of sanguinary engagements during Grant's 1864 Overland Campaign signaled to the Southern population a new-found Northern determination to achieve victory at any cost, and the prospect of winning the war by a decisive Confederate battle-field victory was shown to be correspondingly unrealistic. Prospects only grew bleaker as the months passed and Union forces gradually, but ineluctably, closed in around the Confederate capital. Not that hope was completely lost. Periodically, the citizenry's morale would be lifted by some tactical victory, such as when Southern troops entrenched in the lines of fortifications beat back a stubborn assault. One such "success" that was touted in Southern newspapers at the time occurred near the start of an engagement that would become known as the "Battle of Darbytown Road," or more infrequently the "Battle for Johnson's Farm," October 7, 1864. Though strategically a failure, as it did not achieve its basic goal, the recapture of Fort Harrison, it more than made up for losses in opportunity and materiel by embarrassing the Union military and showing that the ever-increasing hordes of Northern soldiers on Southern soil could still be beaten. Brigadier General Martin Witherspoon Gary and the men in his two brigades covered themselves with glory, especially Colonel Alexander C. Haskell and his Seventh South Carolina Cavalry Regiment. Jubilation was tempered with sadness, however:

> Our joy, however, is clouded by the death of brave Gen. Gregg, of the Texas brigade, and of the serious and perhaps mortal wounding of the notable and accomplished gentleman, Col. A.C. Haskell of the 7th South Carolina Cavalry. Col. Haskell behaved during the day with the most conspicuous gallantry; killed with his own hand a number of the enemy, and fell in the moment of victory.[1]

As it turned out, Colonel Alexander Haskell not only survived and recovered from his wounds, but returned to service and, as the old saying goes, went on to "fight another day." Nevertheless, his accomplishment at Darbytown Road would not be forgotten. As the decades passed after the war, Haskell's exploits would occasionally be set to print, such as in his biography written by his daughter or the published memoirs of some of the men he commanded. One of the most popular of these accounts, *The Story of American Heroism: Thrilling Narratives of Personal Adventures during the Great Civil War,* fell squarely within this genre. The chapter on the exploits of Colonel Haskell and his Seventh South Carolina Cavalry was written by no less than General E. P. Alexander, Haskell's brother-in-law. In this account, which was based almost exclusively upon information and memories provided by the protagonist himself, Colonel Haskell is portrayed as the central figure in the initial Confederate success during the early stage of the battle.

If this account of the Battle of Darbytown Road is to be believed, it was Haskell's idea to turn the Union right flank; the success of the operation was due solely to the efforts of his regiment, and the brave and daring young colonel almost single-handedly crushed Union resistance to its charge.

Now, if there was ever a brave and heroic figure, young Alexander Haskell fits the mould. Joining the Confederate forces at twenty-two years old, he was wounded in a whole series of battles. He was badly wounded at Fredericksburg (December 18, 1862) and again in the leg at Chancellorsville (May 3, 1863). He was then severely wounded in the hip at Old Church and Matadequin Creek during the Battle of Totopotomoy, May 30, 1864, the very first day that the regiment had been formed.[2] So, on the face of it E. P. Alexander's claims have the ring of truth. A number of battle reports, memoirs, and regimental histories, as well as, of course, contemporary letters to the folks back home, survive, so that it is possible to reconstruct the events that took place on the Union right flank and provide a more objective account of the experiences of Gary's Cavalry Brigade and the causes of its successes during the first part of the battle.

PRELUDE TO BATTLE

Gary's Brigade, which consisted of the Seventh South Carolina Cavalry Regiment, the Hampton Legion, and the Twenty-fourth Virginia Cavalry Regiment, had spent the last six months defending the approaches to Richmond on the north side of the James River, and had already seen action about a week earlier on September 29.[3] The engagement that day did not favor those fighting for the Confederacy, and Fort Harrison and the adjoining lines of fortifications were lost. General Lee did not accept the loss "sitting down," and during the morning of October 6 he called a council of war to plan a counteroffensive to take back all or some of the lost ground and fortifications. Major Generals Richard H. Anderson, Charles W. Field, and Robert F. Hoke, among the most senior Confederate officers on the north side of the James River, were ordered to attend a meeting that was to take place at Drewry's Bluff. James Longstreet, the commander of their corps (First Corps), had been wounded during the Battle of the Wilderness and had spent the summer convalescing; he would resume active command only on October 19.[4]

Several plans were submitted and discussed; however, the most promising was proffered by General Gary, who, called to the meeting at the last minute, was unprepared and had to improvise his ideas on the spot.[5] Union forces in the area were to be attacked by two infantry divisions and Gary's Cavalry command. Gary was to swing around the Union northern flank (the Confederate left), after which General Field, deployed in front and slightly outside of the enemy on that flank, would pivot his division toward the right and push the foe south. As soon as Field's men started to cross in front of Hoke's Division, the latter was to take over and continue to sweep Union forces southward toward the New Market Road.[6]

The plan decided upon, Field's and Hoke's Divisions were withdrawn from the trenches around Richmond that afternoon and evening and replaced by the city militia[7] so that they could move surreptitiously to the point from which they were to launch their attack

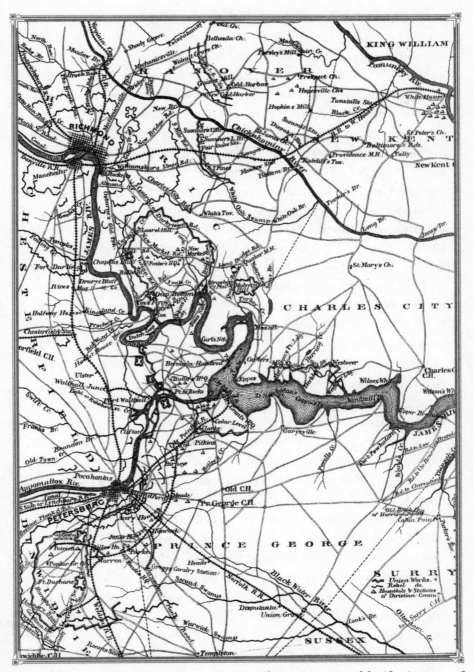

Richmond and the Darbytown Road Area: Position of opposing series of fortifications east of Richmond during late 1864. *Courtesy of Library of Congress, Online Map Collection (Civil War Maps), Call No.: G3880 1864 .C7 CW 627.*

early the next morning. As night fell, Haskell's Seventh South Carolina bivouacked just inside the fortifications. The men were issued an extra forty rounds of ammunition and two days of cooked rations per man. They also received brand-new sabres. A firm believer in the sabre, the Seventh South Carolina's colonel had appealed personally to Colonel Josiah Gorgas, chief of ordnance, several weeks previously for a supply. Serendipitously, he received the sabres the afternoon prior to the attack. As an experiment, Colonel Gorgas also sent a French LeMat revolver, a model that had originally been introduced in 1861. Radically different from the Colts and Smith and Wessons then becoming so popular, the French revolver consisted of a central smoothbore barrel for buckshot surrounded by nine rifled barrels that fired a cylindro-conical projectile, thus allowing nine shots to be fired before it became necessary to reload.[8]

That evening, the colonel and his officers appropriated some grindstones and sharpened the men's sabres as much as possible to a "razor-edge,"[9] thus suggesting that he had read Captain Nolan's views on the value of ultra-sharp-edged weapons for the cavalryman.[10] Haskell himself sported his favorite weapon, a straight Austrian blade. According to E. P. Alexander, the colonel was a tall muscular man whose extraordinary strength allowed him to wield this long stabbing weapon, which was about three inches longer than the regulation length, "better than an ordinary man would the ordinary sabre." In preparation for the upcoming fight, Haskell also armed himself with the LeMat revolver in addition to the normal revolver that he always carried.[11]

As troopers in the Seventh South Carolina Cavalry were handed their weapons and rations, they were informed that they would have "hot work" ahead of them and they must be prepared to move out very early the next morning. Accordingly, after working on their weapons, Haskell's men retired early under a canopy of stars and "slept as only soldiers can sleep." The troopers of the Seventh were awakened well before the break of day. There is no consensus about the exact time; some say between 3:00 and 4:00 A.M., while others claim as early as two o'clock. No bugle was sounded; that would have

tipped off Union forces that something was afoot.[12] The men quickly
ate breakfast and then fed their horses before forming into line
around 4:00 A.M. Colonel Haskell addressed the men to explain what
was to come, and, of course, to inspire the bravest actions. Much
would be expected of Gary's Brigade that day, for if it did not meet its
objective, that is, to turn the enemy's flank, the entire attack would
likely fail. Joseph Waring, one of those in the ranks that morning,
remembers Haskell's summation: "Officers, I expect you to lead your
men. Men, I hope you know your duty too well not to follow your
officers." Writing in his diary later that day, the trooper noted that
Haskell's words had a powerful effect, and that he and his comrades
would "have charged then against even such odds as at Balaclava."[13]

Haskell also detailed how his men were to conduct themselves
during the upcoming fight. In a letter written to E. P. Alexander
decades after the war, Haskell recalled these tactical instructions.
They were to charge and rely exclusively on the sabre, and he
warned his men "that a pistol fired before the enemy was routed
was a death offence."[14] Haskell's stance, in this regard, was in contrast to many Confederate cavalry commanders who regarded and
handled their commands, in effect, as mounted infantry. Most Confederate cavalrymen frequently fought dismounted, and even when
they remained on their horses, generally relied on their revolvers
and carbines.[15] The men in the Seventh were no strangers to the
sabre and its use, however. They had frequently been drilled by a
"Frenchman," and considered themselves quite adept in the use of
this weapon.[16]

It is possible that Colonel Haskell's choice of tactics was influenced by two recent developments. When the war had first
erupted, many of the newly appointed officers sought to hone
their military skills by consulting recently published works on
various aspects of military art and science. Although initially these
were mostly published in the North for the countless volunteer officers from those states, several notable military works were published in the Confederate states as the war dragged on. In 1863,
several pamphlets authored by Baron Jomini and Marshal

Thomas Bugeaud de la Piconnerie were published as a single work in Richmond.[17] The next year, another work, *Cavalry: Its History and Tactics,* was republished in Columbia, South Carolina. Authored by Captain Lewis E. Nolan of the British Army, this tome comprehensively analyzed the practices and needs of cavalry in the post-minié military environment, and would have been much closer to Haskell's interests and heart.

One of Nolan's concerns was what he considered to be the substandard armament of British cavalry. Although this arm had performed with honor throughout most of the Napoleonic Wars, the swords the troopers wielded were notoriously dull, something that became all too obvious during the First and Second Sikh Wars in India (1845–1846 and 1848–1849). Nolan provided several compelling descriptions of how individual British troopers were vanquished by their enemy counterparts, despite the latter's lack of coordinated tactics and the smaller size of horse and rider. The difference was simply that the Sikh horsemen were armed with sharper swords, capable of inflicting devastating, even lethal, wounds, while the dull blades of the British cavalrymen usually had little effect.[18] There is no evidence that Haskell read Nolan's seminal work, which had been recently republished in his home state. However, Captain Nolan's reputation had only been enhanced by his death during the famous Charge of the Light Brigade at Balaclava (October 25, 1854). It is possible that Haskell at least encountered a highly distilled version that, inevitably, would have been verbally passed around among many Southern officers then completely immersed in the exigencies of day-to-day campaigning. Haskell's fondness for the sabre was undoubtedly partially due to his love of the daring and a close-in physical fight. However, there may have also been another factor that stimulated his interest in the sabre charge. This was the resurgence of charge tactics, first among Union cavalry in the West and then among their comrades in arms in the East. Begrudgingly, some Southern commanders openly acknowledged the success of these tactics. However, this is a story that will be told in greater detail in the tactical observations at the end of this chapter.

ADVANCE TO BATTLE

Haskell and his Seventh South Carolina Cavalry began to move to their assigned position probably just before daybreak. First they moved south to the Charles City Road, where they joined the rest of Gary's Brigade.[19] In view of the importance of his mission—turning the Union right flank—Gary's command was augmented by Law's Brigade, consisting of the Fourth, Fifteenth, Forty-fourth, Forty-seventh, and Forty-eighth Alabama commanded by Colonel Pinckney D. Bowles,[20] and a "battalion of artillery" under Lieutenant Colonel Charles E. Lightfoot. The latter probably consisted of the Caroline, Second Nelson, and Surry Artillery, all from Virginia.[21] The men in Field's Division, meanwhile, approached the field up the Darbytown Road, while Hoke's Division, after marching laterally along the York River Turnpike,[22] was able then to advance slowly toward the enemy behind their cavalry counterparts on the Charles City Road.[23]

Apart from its general location, few details about the Union position had been known to Confederate planners prior to the start of the engagement. From after-battle reports, it now is possible to provide a more detailed picture. The Union Eighteenth Corps occupied Fort Harrison and the lines to the left that extended to the James River, at that point ten miles from Richmond. The Tenth Corps guarded the line to the right of the fort to the Charles City Road (five miles from the capital). The area slightly to the front of the Tenth Corps and in front of the Darbytown Road was garrisoned by Brigadier General August V. Kautz's cavalry division,[24] which in August had consisted of Robert M. West's First Brigade (Third New York and Fifth Pennsylvania Cavalry) and Colonel Samuel P. Spear's Second Brigade (First District of Columbia and Eleventh Pennsylvania) with the Wisconsin Light, Fourth Battery.[25] Kautz's forces were strengthened by the addition of Battery B of the First U.S. Artillery. Colonel Edwin V. Sumner's First New York Mounted Rifles were also on duty in this area, but these troops appear to have reported directly to the Tenth Corps.[26] Kautz's forces have been estimated variously as between fifteen hundred and seventeen hundred men. However, Kautz would later claim that he had only a little more than eleven hundred soldiers during the fighting, since almost four hundred men were required to tend to the horses after their riders had dismounted.[27]

Theoretically, the main defenses in General Kautz's sector consisted of a line of "well-constructed" entrenchments along a long ridge running across most of his front. All the trees outside the fortifications had been cut down and the position further strengthened by a series of abatis. Three days earlier General Kautz, still not satisfied, had ordered Lieutenant Robert M. Hall of Battery B, First U.S. Artillery, to construct two additional earthworks in Dr. Johnson's farm, about a half mile to the front between the center and right flank of his line.[28] Although by the time of the engagement these had been only partially completed, Hall's artillery was fixed in this relatively advanced position.[29] The division's other battery, the Wisconsin Light, Fourth Battery, was posted on the left of the Darbytown Road near the breastworks originally constructed by the Confederates. One of its sections (two guns) was placed on the other side of the road twenty rods farther back.[30] In order to detect any Confederate encroachments, pickets were positioned still farther forward along the Darbytown Road, about a mile from the main entrenchments and up the Charles City Road to Jordan's and White's Tavern.[31] Deserters crossing over to the Union lines the night before had tipped Kautz off to the Confederates' intention to attack the next morning. The Union general notified his superiors and made whatever preparations for the impending assault that he could.[32]

Given the fragmented nature of the accounts that survive, it is difficult to piece together an exact chronology of the events that occurred that morning. Nevertheless, one is left with the distinct impression that Gary's Cavalry first made contact with the forward elements of the Union line on Kautz's extreme right flank before Field was able to bring up his infantry and form line.

From Union reports, we learn that the engagement commenced around daybreak. Advancing along the Charles City Road, the leading elements of Gary's Brigade came in view of the enemy's videttes (mounted cavalry pickets), which they quickly captured. At this point, there was a wood on the left of the road. The attackers dismounted and advanced in skirmish order through these woods. They easily pushed back the first Union pickets they encountered, but met with stiff resistance minutes later when they ran into the reserve picket post. The commander of Kautz's Second Brigade, Colonel Spear, who had been a short distance to the rear, quickly moved to the front. The Confederate cavalrymen remained on horseback, strung out in a long column along the road. A sudden and unexpected fire from the Union reserve and reinforcements momentarily threw the column into disorder. As Union reinforcements rushed to the front, Gary responded in kind, and Colonel Haskell ordered the remainder of the Seventh to dismount and form a loose battle line. The Confederate skirmish line, now strengthened, was able to gain the far side of the woods. Here, the men could see the Union-held defensive works in the distance.[33]

On his side, Lieutenant R. M. Hall, who commanded Battery B, First U.S. Artillery, sighted the Confederates massing on the edge of the distant woods and responded immediately by methodically firing a mixture of percussion and time fuse shells at the target.[34] Before long, a Confederate battery managed to catch up with Gary's troopers and started to return the Union fire. As was by now customary, the dismounted cavalrymen along the advanced line instinctively took several measures to offer less of a target and increase their chances of survival. Everyone lay down, most staying in their assigned positions along the line. However, a few crouched down behind some nearby trees several feet behind the line. As Robert West vouched in his published memoirs after the war, these measures "did not exhibit cowardice; it was practiced by all."

An incident happened that showed how the most trivial, seemingly harmless events could have the greatest of consequences and determine whether a soldier would live or die. One of the soldiers who decided to take advantage of the available terrain was Frank

Millwood of Company C. Noticing that Millwood had crawled behind an old tree stump and was five to ten feet in back of his comrades, Lieutenant G. H. Jeter, the company commander, rose to his feet and ordered the private back into line. Frank had just managed to get back into line when an enemy shell blew the stump into smithereens. Of course, there were too many other things to preoccupy the private at that point, so that it was only later that day when the fighting had subsided that the soldier began to appreciate how close had been his brush with death. Thanking his lieutenant for, in essence, saving his life, Frank humorously reflected, "Lieutenant, I thank you very much for ordering me from behind that stump; if you had not there would not have been any of poor Frank today."[35]

The rapid exchange of small arms and artillery fire continued until about 7:00 A.M., when there was a lull in the fighting as the senior Confederate officers in the area waited for the infantry to catch up and form line to their right. The cessation of firing was necessary for another reason. Gary's main assault was to signal the infantry to wheel to the right and begin their own attack. Of course, even though the firing had stopped, undoubtedly the Confederates did not remain completely inactive, and scouts probed to find a weak point in the Union position. It was soon discovered that the right flank of the advanced Union position had not been properly anchored and ended a little ways into the woods on the left of the Charles City Road. By eight o'clock Brigadier General John Bratton's command finally had managed to get into position six to twelve hundred yards from the series of detached redoubts that had been lost to the Union at the end of September.[36] Colonel James R. Hagood's First South Carolina Infantry Regiment was left (north) of the Darbytown Road, while the remaining regiments in the brigade—the Second, Fifth, and Sixth South Carolina, plus the Palmetto Sharpshooters—were on the right side. Colonel A. Coward's Fifth South Carolina immediately deployed in skirmish line. A few minutes later, Brigadier General George T. Anderson's Brigade also came up and positioned itself to the right of the existing Confederate line.[37]

Haskell's Charge

Conditions were finally right to implement the next stage of General Gary's plan of attack. Haskell's Regiment supported by the other nearby cavalry would work its way around the Union right flank and push this end of the Union line back toward Darbytown Road. This also signaled the Confederate infantry to wheel and continue to roll up the Union forces as they were pushed, it was hoped, from left to right across their front. Despite Haskell's claims in his biography and *The Story of American Heroism,* several Union and Confederate sources maintain that the attack was supported by a simultaneous infantry attack in the same area. The next day, Jasper Davies explained in a letter to his wife that his company in the Fifteenth Alabama was detached and sent on a "flanking expedition" under General Gary's direct command.[38] In an article later published by the Southern Historical Society, General Field claimed that all of Perry's (Evander M. Law's) Brigade participated in Gary's outflanking maneuver. However, other sources suggest that Gary's force included only parts of the Fourth and Fifteenth Alabama Infantry Regiments, far less than a brigade.

Soon after the infantry advanced it bumped into a company of mounted Union cavalry and immediately delivered fire. Demoralized, the enemy broke and fled back to an old farmhouse in which they took cover. Firing through the cracks in the boards, their fire was now more deliberate. Two men from Davies's company were wounded and one man killed in this stage of the action. Gary ordered the Confederate line to lie down; he then ordered another portion of his command to work their way around to the rear of the house. Most of the Union cavalrymen in the house, realizing that they were surrounded, surrendered; however, a few managed to escape. Without delay, the attackers resumed their forward motion at the "double quick," firing as they advanced.[39]

Understandably, the mounted portion of the Confederate attack unfolded at a much faster tempo. Receiving his orders from General Gary to begin, Haskell ordered his men to mount quickly. This done, the charge was sounded. The regiment galloped forward in a column of fours with the "usual yell."[40] Captain Jeffer's Company G (Trenholm's Squadron/Rutledge Mounted Rifles Company B)[41] of the Seventh was at the front, followed immediately by Company B (Rutledge Mounted Rifles Company A) and Tucker's Company A (Marion's men of Winyah).[42] About half of the regiment was without mounts and, of course, these men were left behind to fight with the infantry line. It seems, therefore, there were only about one hundred men involved in Haskell's charge.[43]

By this point, Colonel Spear had managed to bring up several companies of Union cavalry, which naturally were spread out in front of the Seventh South Carolina Cavalry's position when it had been dismounted and in line. It seems that these advanced to meet the oncoming rush of Confederate cavalrymen. Haskell's riders had the momentum; they had initiated the attack and were at the gallop first. Moreover, advancing quickly in a column of fours, they achieved a preponderance of force at the point of impact. Unprepared, and perceiving themselves outnumbered, at the last moment the Union cavalry turned and fled.

In his published memoirs, Robert West would admit that in the hell-for-leather charges his regiment tended to make, the horses would quickly lose alignment and the faster horses would surge ahead.[44] This tendency was further exacerbated by another factor. Confederate cavalry at this point in the war found it extremely difficult to procure quality remounts, as the original horses were lost to disease, battle, and the wear and tear of campaigning. The Seventh Carolina Cavalry was no exception, and by this time most of its men were mounted on "broken down" horses. As a result, in one company, only W. G. Hinson and two others were able to keep up with Colonel Haskell as he maintained his position at the head of the charge. The remainder of the men quickly fell back about five yards to the rear.[45] It was probably the strung-out nature of the charging column that has led to such widely conflicting accounts of what happened next, and the extent of resistance put up by the opposing Union cavalrymen.

Those on the faster mounts were easily able to catch up to the flee-ing Union cavalrymen directly to their front, and within moments, riders from both sides found themselves flying at breakneck speeds literally beside one another. One of those who were able to keep up with the furious pace was Lieutenant B. A. Munnerlyn of Company F (Marion's men of Winyah, Company B), who that day was serving as acting adjutant. Noticing a Union trooper on his side, he drew his revolver and pulled the trigger three times. All to no avail, however; the handgun was jammed. He then drew his sabre and slapped the enemy across the back. Though undaunted by having a gun thrust into his face, the trooper was unnerved by the sabre. Curiously, he drew his own revolver and proffered it to Munnerlyn with the barrel pointed toward himself. He explained, "This will shoot, I think." Fortunately, he surrendered before the lieutenant felt compelled to use his newly acquired weapon.[46]

Lieutenant Munnerlyn apparently was also close behind the colonel and, though quite preoccupied with his own fight, at times was able to glimpse Haskell's exploits. In a letter written to Colonel Haskell many years after the war, Hinson mentions that after the engagement, Munnerlyn had acknowledged that he had seen the colonel unhorsing a number of men.[47] Several days after the affair, Willie Workman wrote to "Miss Jane" telling her that his colonel "with the keen edge of his saber sent three of the vandals to their long home" (i.e., succeeded in killing them).[48] Hinson noted in his diary that Munnerlyn claimed that Haskell had, in fact, cut down thirteen of the Union cavalrymen.[49] In his own description of the affair written at the behest of his brother-in-law, Colonel E. P. Alexander, Haskell admits that he was able to maintain his position at the forefront of the wild galloping charge only because of the fleetness of his horse. This large brown horse had been a last-minute replacement for his own horse, "Jeb Stuart," which proved to be too nervous and high-strung to rely on for serious fighting. He claims that by the end of the fighting, his sabre was "red to the hilt" with his enemy's blood and all the ammunition in his "pistols" expended.[50]

Although, of course, most of the events during the fast-evolving fray were a blur and would soon have been forgotten, Haskell never forgot two particular "sabre incidents" during the fighting. At one point he realized much to his chagrin that an opponent was bringing a pistol to bear against his head; he quickly dealt a "blow," that is, a slash, across the fellow's head. His head split open, the Yankee fell from the saddle. Haskell encountered a similar situation a little later as the charge proceeded through a narrow corridor in the woods. A Union trooper aimed his revolver at Haskell as the latter was passing by. The soldier was "too close for a blow and too near for a thrust." Thinking quickly, Haskell lifted his sword over the soldier's head (a right-to-left motion) and then reversed the sabre's direction and thrust the weapon into the man's ribs, a blow, that ordinarily would have proven fatal. Given the force of the blow the sabre should have passed through the cavalryman's body; instead, it penetrated but an inch or two and was stuck. In agony, the other man's face was completely distorted. Haskell demanded that he throw his revolver away. The man complied. Next, Haskell ordered him to throw himself from his horse. As his enemy fell off his horse, Haskell was able to withdraw his weapon. Only three months later did he manage to find out what had happened. This soldier, not badly injured as it turns out, was taken prisoner by one of Haskell's men and taken back to the Confederate lines. When he surrendered his sword, it was discovered that Haskell's sword had entered an iron ring on the sword belt, and thus was prevented from penetrating farther.[51]

Of course, most of the Union cavalry involved in the skirmishing prior to Haskell's charge had fought dismounted, and much of this skirmishing took place in relatively open terrain. Their horses were considered to be too much of a target and were led a considerable distance to the rear.[52] The Seventh South Carolina had managed to outflank them. Their position now completely untenable, the dismounted cavalrymen dispersed and in small groups attempted to flee into the woods behind them. Some managed to escape, but many were seen and quickly captured by those on the slower mounts not involved in the frenzied surge at the front of the column. "Willie," one of the men in Company G, had not heard the command to charge and was thus slow getting started. This didn't make him any less successful, however. As he rode along he noticed a group of five or six Union soldiers, who immediately surrendered. Unfortunately, he was not quick enough to get back to the Confederate lines, and upon the approach of Union reinforcements, his captives liberated themselves and it was Willie's turn to be made prisoner.[53]

Those Union cavalrymen who remained mounted did not fare much better. Disordered and surprised, they were easily swept aside or pushed back. All resistance gone, the rush toward their lines soon degenerated into a wild stampede. A surgeon who served with the Tenth Corps witnessed the tangled and completely disorganized mass galloping toward his position along the road from the front. In his own memoirs, he painted a vivid picture of the spectacle:

> Looking up the road toward the front could be seen a mass of disordered and tangled up cavalry in a wild stampede; some horses were riderless, with saddles turned and stirrups swinging about, which served to increase their speed. Troopers, hatless, with hair flying, rushed frantically by, whooping and cursing; scabbards and canteens swinging and clanging amid the clatter of hoofs, made up the scene of a most disgraceful rout. There seemingly was no one in command, and the horses were as frantic as the riders.[54]

Unfortunately, Kautz's positions violated one of the most fundamental precepts of military science. His force had been stationed in front of nearly impassable terrain. Though his men had been positioned mostly in open areas in the front of Johnson's farm, the rear area of the farm was heavily timbered, and the west fork of Four Mile Creek ran to the rear of and parallel to the fighting line. To further worsen matters, the creek bed was swampy and difficult for man or horse to cross. There was a road leading back through this marshy land, and it had been repaired as soon as the Union troops had moved into the area. Unfortunately, this backbreaking effort was largely undone by the series of supply trains that were necessary to supply Kautz's men; the wagons cut up the roads and made them largely unserviceable.[55] This was a serious defect, because it was an accepted axiom that although one had to plan for victory, one also had always to be prepared for defeat. When one fought in front of impassable terrain, such as along a riverbank or as in this case in front of a swamp, one risked total annihilation, if defeated. This hadn't escaped the general's attention, and in the days preceding the fight, he had verbally complained to General Butler, his superior, asking permission to move his command to a more favorable locale. Unmoved, Butler ordered Kautz to remain in his assigned position.[56]

The broken terrain and condition of the road made retreat difficult enough for the Union infantry and cavalry, but for the artillery the situation was disastrous. As the fleeing Union cavalrymen passed by Hall's Battery B and the Fourth Wisconsin Battery, the artillery officers realized that their now exposed positions were no longer tenable. The Wisconsin battery was the first to limber up and retreat. Hall's artillery continued to fire for another fifteen minutes. Hall finally gave the order to "limber to the rear" when the advancing Confederate line had approached to within thirty yards. The guns and their crews started off toward the rear at the trot. However, they had gone no more than three hundred yards into the woods when they discovered the road blocked by the guns and caissons of the Wisconsin Battery.[57] The latter, before leaving the field, had taken casualties among men and horses. While retreating down the road, the lead piece in the column became hopelessly mired. The gun crews frantically tried to drag the piece free, but Confederates were beginning to outflank the position. The artillerymen had no choice but to spike their guns and then abandon them.[58] A few minutes later the Confederate infantry under Gary's command caught up and went running, yelling, and screaming through the Union artillery. One veteran remembers "it was a regular picnic for the boys."[59]

Eventually, as all resistance ceased on the front between the Charles City and Darbytown Roads, the blood lust of the Confederate riders at the head of the charging column subsided, and the focus shifted from attacking and defending oneself to gathering up enemy prisoners and materiel. Colonel Haskell himself took one prisoner, an Irish teamster in charge of the headquarters wagon of the First

New York Mounted Rifles. Riding up to the wagon, Haskell demanded that the man surrender. Told that he wouldn't surrender to one man, Haskell explained that he would count to three and then run the Irishman through with his sabre. The wagoneer asked the colonel if he was serious, and, told that he was deadly serious, "Pat" surrendered without further remonstrance. Haskell ordered the wagoneer to take the wagon to the Confederate lines and explain to the men in the Seventh that he was a prisoner.

As Haskell watched "Pat" to make certain that he followed his orders, his attention was caught by a Union horseman riding toward him with a drawn revolver. Haskell had thrown his two revolvers at his opponents' heads after each had been emptied. All he could do was demand that the approaching cavalryman give him his pistol. Haskell remembers that the man "seemed dazed" as a result of this command. Reining in his horse, he handed over his revolver without even attempting to fire, and surrendered. Haskell ordered the man to dismount and then slap the horse's flank, which he did. Rejoining Sergeant DuBose Snowdon and several other men, Haskell then rode up a small hill to survey the situation.

On the opposing side, General Kautz had been unaware that the right end of his line had been completely outflanked. He became aware of the Confederate presence on the right only as he and his staff were moving quickly up to the right front. They suddenly espied Haskell and his small group a short distance in front of them and called upon the Confederates to surrender. The Rebels drew their revolvers and fired, and the Union officers and their staff returned the fire. Sergeant Snowdon was killed instantly. Colonel Haskell was shot in the head and fell prostrate on the ground. One of the Confederate riders managed to bolt and make good his escape. A fourth was captured. On the other side, a captain and a lieutenant fell wounded; the captain's wounds were severe and he would be paralyzed for the rest of his life. Assuming that Haskell had been killed, a Union officer stripped him of his sword, watch, and papers. Kautz and his officers knew that there could be larger groups of Confederate cavalry around and to remain where they were was needlessly perilous. Besides, the sounds of continuous musketry to their left told them that another Rebel force had begun to attack and was threatening to push the left wing of Kautz's command past the New Market Road and into the James River. The small group circled back to the left of what remained of the Union line to rally those who had fled from Gary's attack. Colonel Haskell was left for dead. However, the bullet had only creased the skull, knocking him senseless. Some Confederate soldiers would find him and bring him back within friendly lines, where he would recover. The injury, though nearly fatal, made no lasting impression upon Haskell, and he would continue to lead his men with the same abandon and bravado.

EPILOGUE

The larger attack, on the Confederate right, was now beginning to unfold. The men in Major General Hoke's Division had finally formed in line to the right of Field's Division. Field's command rushed forward, the brigade commander advancing on foot a few feet in front of the rank and file.[60] The Union forces had not been idle, and the Tenth Corps had rushed forward to the right edge of Kautz's original position and occupied a series of fieldworks that were roughly parallel and to the left of the New Market Road and perpendicular to the exterior Confederate defenses captured on September 29. Presumably, these had been constructed to provide against just such a contingency as was now occurring.[61] Hoke's Brigades were supposedly to move at the same time as Field's men, but for some inexplicable reason were delayed.

Attacking a prepared position that had been reinforced with a large number of fresh troops, and with only half the men called for by the official plan of attack, the assault was doomed to failure. An account penned after the war by J. B. Polley of Gregg's Brigade probably provides the best encapsulation of what happened next:

> Hoke's division was to have supported us by engaging the enemy on our right, but they made such a poor cut at it that the Yankees had abundant leisure and opportunity to concentrate their strength against us. The fire

from the works was terrific, and in climbing under, over, and around the trees tops [forming the abatis] our folks lost their alignment and scattered. A bullet struck my gun, and, glancing, passed between my thumb and forefinger of my left hand, barely touching the skin, but nevertheless, burning it; another bored a hole in my jacket. Catching sight of the Fifth Texas flag to my left and fifty yards or so ahead of me, and taking it for that of the Fourth [his regiment], I made for it with all possible dispatch. But before I reached it, its bearer cast a look behind him, and finding himself alone in the solitude of his impetuosity and bravery, prudently sought protection from the storm of lead behind a tree scarcely as large around as his body and within sixty yards of the breastworks. First one and then another of the Fourth and Fifth dropped behind him, until seven or eight of us were strung out in a single file, your humble servant, as last comer, standing at the tail-end. Discovering that I gained no benefit from the tree, that our little squad could not hope to capture the breastworks without aid, and that our comrades in the rear seemed loath to reinforce us, I hurriedly stated the last two conclusions to my comrades, who, without a dissenting voice, sensibly agreed that an instant and hasty retreat must be made.[62]

Despite localized successes such as Gary's, in the weeks that followed, the Union noose slowly continued to tighten. True, the Confederates would again stave off Union assaults later that month, on October 27, beating back Weitzel's corps as it tried to advance up the Darbytown Road, while stymieing Hancock and Warren's attempt to secure the crossing over Hatcher Run on the south side of the James River that same day. The cherished goal of a shining victory, with Lee's veterans breaking the Union forces in a gallant charge and sending Grant's army fleeing back to the North, proved to be but a phantasm, one that evaporated in the wooded thickets east of Richmond and south of Petersburg, to be replaced by a succession of mechanical moves to forestall a Union breakthrough for one more month, one more week, one more day. But, to someone not subjectively immersed in the dramatic struggle, the outlines of the ultimate fall of Richmond and of the Confederacy were now becoming clear.

Tactical Observation #3

*C*olonel Haskell's espousal of the sabre and traditional charge doctrine was less idiosyncratic than it might strike the modern reader. Rather, it reflected a growing trend among many Northern cavalry commanders and, to a lesser extent, their Confederate counterparts. Attitudes had been different at the start of the war, however, when many considered sabre charges as a thing of the past, made obsolete by recent advances in the range and accuracy of small arms. Several weeks after the fall of Fort Sumter, a contributor to Scientific American speculated:

> Formerly the position of an army could be approached within 300 yards without experiencing injury from enemy fire. With the modern rifles, they could not approach men nearer than 1000 yards. Cavalry must now keep at a respectable distance until they can dash in under the cover of smoke, or be preceded with riflemen and artillery.[63]

Similar attitudes were harbored by many on all levels of the Union military machine. Under Scott's leadership, Union military authorities, for example, accepted only one volunteer cavalry regiment into service until after the embarrassing defeat at Bull Run.[64] On April 7, 1862, Brigadier General J. M. Schofield would write to General James Totten that despite their clamor to be armed with edged weapons, his men had "no more use for a saber than for a columbiad—i.e., extremely heavy artillery pieces."[65]

The sabre and associated charge doctrine, however, was destined not to be permanently dismissed to the drawer of useless and obsolete practices, and in early 1862 would gradually start to regain tactical respectability among an increasing number of Union cavalry leaders. Confronting secessionist Texan cavalry that relied religiously on the revolver, Colonel James H. Carleton of the First California Volunteers ordered his men to refrain from *returning fire, but rather rush in "as quick as thought" with out-stretched sabres.*[66] *A few weeks later, Major General H. Z. Curtis issued kindred instructions to the Army of the Southwest when he advised his cavalry to keep their sabres polished, drill with them every day, and "watch the opportunity to show the heroic deeds you may accomplish."*[67] *Here and there, Union cavalry regiments started to demonstrate that this newfound confidence in traditional charge doctrine was not misplaced. On October 13, 1861, the Frémont Battalion of Cavalry conducted a successful charge at Henrytown, Missouri, as did the Seventh Pennsylvania Cavalry on March 4, 1862, while advancing toward Columbia, Tennessee. These accomplishments did not go unnoticed. In a communiqué to General Halleck, Rosecrans noted that these men had "used the saber where the carbine would delay."*[68] *On April 1 when responding to an inquiry of what he needed, besides the revolving rifles he had persistently lobbied for, Rosecrans requested three thousand sabres, tangible testimony of what he thought of their utility. Other Union commanders in the West were reporting similar successes with the sabre and charge doctrine during this same period. Colonel William B. Hazen, a brigade commander in the Twenty-first Corps, praised actions of the Third Ohio Cavalry during an expedition from Readyville to Woodbury, Tennessee, in April.*[69] *At Chalk River, the Third Missouri Cavalry successfully charged Confederate infantry and artillery on April 30.*[70]

These were but a precursor to what Union cavalry using similar methods would accomplish the next year in the eastern theatre of operations. On March 17, 1863, Brigadier William W. Averell's cavalry overthrew Brigadier General Fitz Lee's riders at Kelly's Ford. The First Rhode Island Cavalry had been taught to advance at a walk, then speed up to a trot, advancing so that each rider touched the next man's stirrups. Faced with this moving wall, Fitz Lee's troopers were forced to scatter and then regroup to the rear. Three times the opposing cavalry forces met; three times the Rhode Islanders were victorious.[71] *As we have already seen, this type of success would be repeated less than four months later at Gettysburg,* when Gregg's cavalry eventually bested that of Stuart on the third day of the battle.

More of these successes would follow the next year. In his report after an engagement near Cedarville (August 16, 1864), Sheridan would boast that Devin's and Custer's cavalry brigades had employed the sabre "freely."[72] Custer's brigade enjoyed the same type of success again during the Battle of the Opequon (September 19) when near the end of the engagement Lomax's cavalry, armed with revolvers, was unceremoniously forced back several times. Forced to rely exclusively on revolvers, they were unable to withstand the charge and each time broke before the onrushing Union cavalry entered pistol range.[73]

The "modern" cavalry charge, incidentally, had been first formulated by Frederick the Great soon after the start of the War of Austrian Succession. The situation that the Prussian military authorities faced was very similar to that confronting the Union military 120 years later. The Prussian cavalry was notoriously incompetent and was no match for the Austrian cavalry. To help rectify this deficiency, Frederick introduced in stages a tactical doctrine that gave an immense psychological advantage to the hitherto incompetent Prussian troopers. When charging, the Prussian cavalry set off first at a walk, then at a trot, then eventually a gallop, before bursting into the "hell for leather" charge. All the while, every effort was made to maintain complete order, the troopers along the line advancing knee to knee. The opposing cavalry seeing nowhere to go (they couldn't ride through— "thread"—the tight Prussian line), and faced with what appeared to be an unstoppable force, almost always turned and fled. A psychological advantage replaced a strict dependence upon horsemanship and adeptness with weapons. This was exactly why these tactics were so appealing to the Union cavalry, who—in the East—faced an enemy of superior horsemen. Of course, just as had been the case with the Prussians, this took several years to master, and this explains why Union successes with sabre charges became more frequent in 1863 and 1864.

This string of successful Union cavalry charges was not completely lost upon the Confederate military, and there were some who advocated adopting similar tactics. Attempting to explain the causes for the Confederate discomfiture, General Jubal A. Early complained that the Union cavalry was superior to its Confederate counterpart in numbers and equipment. However, most interesting was his conclusion about the relative value of Union and Confederate cavalry armament in "country . . . so favorable to the operations of cavalry":

> *Lomax's cavalry are armed entirely with rifles and have no sabers, and the consequence is that they cannot fight on horseback, and in this open country they cannot successfully fight on foot against large bodies of cavalry.[74]*

Confederate cavalry in the West had encountered the same problem roughly during the same period. Increasingly this lament would be echoed in other Confederate officers' reports after finding themselves manhandled by a Union cavalry charge. During the Atlanta Campaign, the Ninth Texas Cavalry initially found itself beaten back by waves of "better armed opponents," i.e., sabre-brandishing Union cavalry, and were saved only by reinforcements. Again, it was a case of the superiority of the sabre to the rifle once the opposing cavalry had advanced to very close range in open terrain.[75] About a week later (August 7, 1864) Confederate cavalry at Moorefield, West Virginia, was similarly overpowered because "the long Enfield musket once discharged could not be reloaded, and lay helpless before the charging saber."[76]

Of course, many Confederate cavalry regiments had been equipped with sabres, among other weapons. However, the commanders of many of these regiments preferred firing with their revolvers or, when appropriate, dismounting and indulging in carbine fire. The demonstrable and ever-increasing Union success with sabre charges succeeded in forcing at least some Confederate cavalry officers to revisit this issue. At Kelly's Ford, Brandy Station, and

Aldie, while approaching their mounted opponents the Union cavalrymen heard the Confederate officers yelling the likes of "Put up your sabres! Draw your pistols and fight like gentlemen!" In contrast, during the cavalry-versus-cavalry engagement on July 3, those in the Third Pennsylvania Cavalry could now hear these same officers enjoining their men to "Keep to your sabres, keep to your sabres!"[77]

The publication of Captain Lewis Nolan's Cavalry: Its History and Tactics, *probably further strengthened the case for aggressive cold steel tactics among the Confederate cavalry. Nolan's work had originally been published posthumously in London in 1860, but its popularity as well as the need for such works in the South caused the work to be reprinted in Columbia, South Carolina, four years later. So when Colonel Haskell appealed to Colonel Josiah Gorgas, Chief of Ordnance, for sabres, it was unlikely that he was acting purely upon a personal whim. Rather, it is much more probable that he was aware of the changing attitudes regarding the sabre and cavalry charge doctrine, which, incidentally, did fit nicely with his propensity for swashbuckling and daring antics.*

II

<figure>decorative ornament</figure>

CONCLUSION

The need for a "conclusion" to this present work became clear only near the completion of the manuscript. Unlike a study that focuses on a discrete, easily definable subject, such as the psychological dimension to Civil War combat or a prominent commander's conduct during a particular campaign, a work that seeks simply to describe a number of unrelated engagements hardly lends itself to the type of analysis and sweeping generalizations usually associated with a conclusion. Each of the different engagements that has been covered appears to be its own separate entity with little or no connection to the next, and the author is thus deprived of the intellectual fabric out of which this type of closing chapter is generally made.

Nevertheless, several phenomena encountered while preparing some of the preceding chapters deserve some commentary. These relate to trends in Civil War historiography, that is, how the great

American internecine struggle has been viewed at different times, rather than the subject matter in and of itself.

The first historical works on the Civil War were published as early as 1862. Wardner and Catlett's *Battle of Young's Branch or, Manassas Plain* became available to Southerners but a year after the event. A few even more ambitious tomes that chronicled the course of the war appeared before hostilities ceased. A stream of books quickly turned into a flood of titles as the veterans returned to civilian life and a sense of normality was eventually restored. Interest seemed to peak with the approach of the twentieth and then the twenty-fifth anniversaries of the various battles fought during the war. Monuments were erected not only in parks and town squares but also on some battlefields, particularly those fields that had been deemed notable Union victories such as Vicksburg, Shiloh, and Gettysburg. Monumentation on the latter battlefield began as early as 1867, when survivors of the First Minnesota Infantry placed a memorial urn in the National Cemetery to commemorate their fallen comrades. Monumentation expanded exponentially in the 1880s and 1890s, when numerous Northern states and regimental veterans associations provided significant funding to erect a dizzying array of sculptures, monuments, tablets, and markers to past heroism. In the South, where economics often belied the ability to match this brigade of stone warriors, monumentation was much more modest, but a large cadre of writers, both military and civilian, attempted to "spin" the results of the recent war, leading to the "Lost Cause" phenomenon.

Historical committees were set up to document the role played by various state troops during the war. Numerous articles in newspapers around the country were supplied by aging veterans only too happy to share with a wider circle what had to be the most intense and interesting part of their lives. The ever-greater abundance of works on the Great Rebellion, as it was usually called during this period, did little to satiate the American public's interest in the conflict. *Century Magazine,* the successor of the New York *Scribner's Monthly Magazine,* published numerous articles written by those who had played a significant role in various engagements. These covered a wide spectrum of major battles and events of the war and were published as a four-volume set entitled *Battles and Leaders of the Civil War* during 1887–1888. Even the federal government was caught up in the excitement, and between 1880 and 1891 it published many of the after-battle reports warehoused in its archives in a 128-volume series known as *The War of the Rebellion: A Compilation of the Official Records of the Union and Confederate Armies.*

There were two trends that, though subtle and unconscious, would soon affect how historians, and hence eventually the public, would view or interpret many aspects of the fighting that had taken place. For a few years after the war, there were some military men who sought to analyze the battles and methods of combat in order to gain a better insight into the evolution of warfare and how best to fight in the future. Colonel Francis Lippitt's *A Treatise on the Tactical Use of the Three Arms: Infantry, Artillery, and Cavalry* (1865) is an excellent example of this type of effort. Of course, the 1870s and 1880s were a period of ever-increasing technological change, and interest in the Civil War as a *modern* war soon waned. As it began to be viewed as an *historical event,* writers and historians began to filter out technical details, such as how an artilleryman loaded and fired his weapon, the various types of infantry and cavalry tactics that were used, and so forth. These were now viewed as unimportant and, in fact, impedimenta when trying to tell a compelling and interesting story.

At the same time, there were a number of attitudes that stemmed from the technologically more advanced world then emerging around them. In an age that saw the introduction of the modern machine gun, dreadnoughts, and electricity, many of the older military weapons and methods started to appear strangely archaic. This, coupled with the just noted reluctance to concern oneself with matters purely military, promoted the adoption of what can be called a "folkloric" view of many Civil War weapons and military practices. One of the clearest examples is how the rifle musket and its battlefield performance came to be regarded. Those advocating its adoption in the 1840s and 1850s were painfully aware of the weapon's low initial muzzle velocity and the resulting "rainbow" trajectory. They devoted an enormous effort to teaching the "scientific method of firing" needed for accurate long-range fire. Many tacticians were skeptical that the new small arms would have any significant effect on how combat henceforth would be conducted. However, future generations, unwilling to look through mind-numbing range tables and old out-of-date military scientific tomes, forgot that these limitations ever existed. The idea that ordinary infantrymen in close order formations were able to fire their Enfield and Springfield rifle muskets accurately up to the limits of their effective range became received wisdom. It was assumed that firefights during the Civil War took place at much longer ranges than when the combatants had been armed with smoothbores.

If these intellectual trends fostered a prejudgment of what was and what was not effective on the Civil War battlefield, a second attitudinal trend affected how future generations of historians would tend to tell the story. The veterans who decided to put pen to paper were driven by a range of motivations, from pride in one's regiment or an obligation to hand down to posterity an accurate account of events to, in some cases, unbridled ego and ambition. And the 1880s in many ways can be said to be a period of lionization or "hero-icization" of some of the war's more prominent figures, in both the North and the South. This process was not limited to those who had played the greatest roles, such as Robert E. Lee and "Stonewall" Jackson, but extended to moderately known personalities such as Russell Alger, one of the Union heroes at Gettysburg, and even to figures known only in their hometown or state, such as Alexander Haskell in South Carolina.

A tendency to glorify many of those who had been seen as heroes during the war was clearly developing. Obviously, from a purely historiographic point of view, this was not a neutral event. It affected not only how the story was told, but in many cases also its accuracy or even basic truthfulness. And it is this problem that one bumps into frequently in late-nineteenth-century Civil War literature. A number of examples were stumbled upon during the research for this present work. For example, during the 1880s, Admiral Porter's account of the storming and capture of Arkansas Post, one that emphasized the role of his river flotilla at the expense of the land-based artillery, became the popularly accepted version. So did Colonel Haskell's rendition of the Confederate activity during the early phases of the October 7 Battle of Darbytown Road and the reasons for its success, especially because it was penned by no other than E. P. Alexander, one of the most observant, perspicacious, and honest Civil War veterans. Now, it is not the intention in any way to malign the memory of Colonel Haskell; Haskell was a truly *brave* man, who repeatedly performed what can fairly be described as genuinely heroic deeds. Reveling in his memories after the war, and deservedly so, the South Carolina colonel probably genuinely believed in the account he transmitted to his even more famous brother-in-law.

Unfortunately, the same cannot be said of some other personalities and their autobiographical accounts that gained currency during this period. Having gained public recognition, after the war a number of well-known officers entered politics, the most notable of these being Ulysses S. Grant, who became the eighteenth president, and Russell Alger, who was elected governor of Michigan in 1884 and during William McKinley's term of office was appointed secretary of war in March 1897. It was inevitable that some of these military-turned-political men, in the pursuit of their own personal ambition, would leverage the emerging cult of personality that was then taking place in the study of what soon would become known as the "Civil War." One such person was Russell Alger. The quintessential political creature, Alger propagandized the story of the great cavalry fight between Stuart's and Gregg's troopers on the third day of Gettysburg much in the same way a modern political party "spins" controversial events to bolster its own credibility while undermining that of its opponents. If we are to believe his version of events, the action was almost entirely fought by the Michigan cavalry. McIntosh's brigade is relegated to a subordinate support role, contributing little to the ultimate outcome. Even worse, Alger, in letters to General Bachelder, dismissed the fighting capabilities of those he faced that day, an injustice not only to his former adversaries but to later generations seeking an accurate understanding of that part of the Civil War's greatest battle. Grant, incidentally, never succumbed to these political tactics, and his memoirs to this day continue to provide valuable insights into the Union management of the war at the highest levels.

The historian wishing to unravel the mysteries of an engagement, therefore, has to approach many of the early accounts with a great deal of caution. In fact, it has often been said that the veterans' memoirs, as a class, are a notoriously unreliable source. Most of these appeared decades after the fighting, and it is only natural that the participants' memories had dimmed over time. Then, of course, there was the already discussed problem of "aggrandizement," the tendency to attribute greater importance to the events one personally was involved in, than is warranted by a more objective approach.

However, it is this author's opinion that the veterans' memoirs to a great degree have taken a "bad rap." For one thing, *all* of the other potential sources of information are subject to the same types of errors, biases, and misrepresentations. The *Official Records* are replete with self-serving reports in which an officer has attempted either to garner more than his fair share of the credit or, alternatively, to deflect the blame for a defeat or a failure. For example, Major General George Pickett's post-Gettysburg battle report was apparently so critical of those brigades assigned to support his assault that Robert E. Lee ordered all copies destroyed, fearing that the negative backlash would destroy the morale of the Army of Northern Virginia. Newspaper accounts, especially those written immediately after a battle, can also often be incredibly misleading. The correspondent, hearing rumors on all sides, often pieced together a picture that had little to do with what actually occurred on the battlefield. Events separated by time and distances can be blended together. Or, motivated by national sentiment, the correspondent exaggerates the accomplished in the case of a victory, or the strength of the enemy's forces in the case of a defeat. The newspaper accounts that appeared in the weeks following the First Battle of Bull Run provide examples of all of these inaccuracies. Seeking to explain the unexpected Union loss, a correspondent for the *Providence Evening Daily Press* explained to his readers that the Union army had no chance, since it faced a "hundred thousand rebels" and numerous "masked batteries" totaling over ninety guns and mortars.[1] Northern papers would talk about numerous daring Union bayonet charges that took place that day, events that clearly didn't transpire. These types of problems certainly weren't limited to Northern papers. Most Georgia papers applauded the role played by its native sons and recounted the exploits of the Seventh and Eighth Georgia Infantry Regiments during the battle. Unfortunately, most inaccurately had the Seventh Georgia participate in the events in the pine woods in front of Matthews Hill, when in fact, Bartow was killed leading the regiment against Rickett's guns later in the battle.[2]

After each major engagement, many of the fortunate survivors would write to friends and family to let them know they were all right and tell them of the dramatic events they had just experienced. Although many historians have placed a greater value on this potential source of information, these letters frequently contain the same types of inaccuracies as newspaper articles. The person writing the letter has seen only a tiny portion of the engagement and frequently weaves into his narrative hearsay information about other parts of the battlefield. And, again, personal biases often color the description of what one has witnessed. One does not have to go further than the letters that were published in the Georgia and Rhode Island newspapers to find highly distorted accounts of the events that actually transpired on Matthews Hill.

This means that the conscientious historian has to evaluate every source of information scrupulously and take nothing for granted. Details gleaned from letters and newspaper accounts must be cross-checked against descriptions of events found in the official records and vice versa. The same must be done with regimental histories and modern historical studies. Of course, this is hardly a revelation, since it is axiomatic to every competent historian, regardless of the period or topic of specialization.

Nevertheless, this approach in the present work did lead to one unexpected, and rather surprising, result. Despite the tremendous volume of works that have been written, so much still remains to be discovered about the Civil War. Someone looking through the card catalogue entries for this subject in a large research library would be tempted to think that most of what should be said about this great conflict has already been written, and future books must necessarily be a regurgitation or synthesis of existing historical analysis. The ease with which a patient researcher can come up with a new but justified interpretation of an already well-documented event, or be the first to plot what is still uncharted territory, is truly counterintuitive.

The process of chronicling the events that befell Burnside's brigade at Bull Run was an eye-opener in this regard. The initial assumption was that these events would already have been well documented, and that the task was only to revisit this part of the battle in greater detail, with a redoubled focus on the soldiers' experiences during the combat. However, the closest thing to a detailed account of the fight between Burnside's brigade and Evans's and Bee's men is found in John Hennessy's excellent *The First Battle of Manassas: An End to Innocence, July 18–21, 1861*. Hennessy does provide a blow-by-blow description of how events unfolded at the beginning of this action, but then shifts to a more experiential, more subjective treatment of the later stages of the fight. One suspects Hennessy was forced to adopt this treatment because of the highly fragmentary nature of available source material and what appear to be irreconcilable differences in the participants' accounts. Multiple sources on both sides, for example, accuse their opponents of approaching with the other side's flag held high, only to raise their true colors at the last moment in order to deceive the enemy and thereby gain an advantage. Many participants would later claim that their particular regiment participated in several successful charges that repulsed the enemy. There is no eyewitness who provides a comprehensive, detailed step-by-step account of how the entire fight unfolded, explaining at what time each regiment entered the fray, where each was positioned relative to the others, etc. The firsthand accounts that do exist provide only slivers of the needed information, and these do not fit well with information provided by others.

This caused no end of frustration when working on the two chapters devoted to Burnside's fight at Bull Run. Gradually, however, it became possible to isolate some chronological "landmarks." In an account penned after the war, Captain Robbins explains that the Fourth Alabama Infantry approached the edge of the pinewoods as Sloan's Louisiana Battalion was running back down the hill. In his memoirs, John Reed tells us that when his regiment finally reached roughly the same location, he could see three enemy regimental flags evenly spaced along the hillcrest. Thus we are able to ascertain that the Alabama regiment entered the fight after the Louisianans' unsuccessful charge against the Second Rhode Island Infantry and its artillery accompaniment, while the Eighth Georgia Infantry came into play only after the Seventy-first New York finally got into the battle line. Augustus Woodbury talks of the Seventy-first taking the place of the Second Rhode Island when the latter was moving to the Union left, while in a letter to his father Hamilton Couper explains that the right of the Eighth Georgia was fired upon by Union troops that began to work their way around this flank, so we are able to identify which Union troops were involved in this effort and when during the engagement it occurred. Thus, by cross-referencing tiny "signpost" types of details, one can gradually piece together a detailed chronology of events.

This type of "bottom up" approach is certainly nothing new to the systematic study of history, and recent Civil War literature contains a number of informative and groundbreaking "microhistories" that go into much greater detail than would have been considered acceptable only a generation ago. Gordon Rhea's trilogy (*The Battle of the Wilderness, May 5–6, 1864; To the North Anna River, Grant and Lee, May 13–25, 1864; Cold Harbor: Grant and Lee, May 26–June 3, 1864*) on Grant's Overland Campaign is one of the best examples. For the Civil War enthusiast, it must appear that we have once again entered a "golden age" of the study of this, the great American conflict. More and more works are appearing that investigate and chronicle many minor engagements that, until recently, have been ignored by history. The increased "degree of magnification" that characterize these microhistories does not simply allow the exploration of hitherto ignored areas and topics; frequently it also facilitates the reevaluation of the most well-known, most thoroughly studied events, such as the most dramatic crises in the most well known of battles.

It is natural that some of the most cherished traditional accounts will be relegated to folklore and replaced by more detailed and multi-layered interpretations that benefit from bringing together a number and diversity of primary source material that was literally impossible before the age of the Internet, electronic distribution of books, period magazines and journals, and electronic linguistic searches permitted by relational databases. Although it is natural that some Civil War enthusiasts will find this process unsettling, it should actually be a source of satisfaction, demonstrating that the study of the great American conflict continues within an intellectually healthy framework. Rather than being dependent upon a slavish and uncritical acceptance of what is religiously regarded as "fact," our understanding continues to grow and change as new information and approaches become available. Not only does this ensure that, through constant iteration, our appreciation of this conflict by painful degrees becomes ever more accurate, it also simultaneously ensures that interesting, and sometimes even surprising, new insights await discovery by future generations.

Acknowledgments

$\mathcal{T}$his work was much more a group effort than any of my previous books. Dana Lombardy graciously shipped me boxes of Confederate regimental histories and memoirs from his home in California. Bryce Suderow not only repeatedly mined the vast holdings of the Library of Congress and other libraries and archives in the Washington, D.C., area, photocopying volumes of invaluable material, but introduced me to a number of subject-matter experts whose research, views, and advice greatly facilitated the research effort. Lee Sturkey and Henry Persons, for example, have spent a lifetime collecting detailed information on their favorite Civil War military organizations, and they generously turned over folders and folders of information that would have been impossible for me to collect during the time frame available to write the present work. Mr. Sturkey essentially provided all the research required for the chapter on Darbytown Road, while Mr. Persons's research made it possible to synchronize the activity of Burnside's brigade with the Confederate regiments opposing them during the First Battle of Bull Run. Bill Adams succeeded in interesting me in the massive cavalry battle on July 3 at Gettysburg, and Scott Mingus coauthored that chapter.

Joseph Bilby, Dean West, Howie Muir, and Bill Proal all provided critical insight and valuable advice while vetting the manuscript. As always, Bruce Trinque made himself available to answer what must have seemed a countless number of queries throughout the life of the project. John Horn and Steve Newton helped resolve some loose ends with the Fair Oaks chapter. Thanks to Keith Wollman at Carroll & Graf Publishers and Lara Heimert and Sandra Beris, Linda Harper, and Robert Swanson at Basic Books for their efforts in the editorial and production processes, respectively. Keith Poulter went "above and beyond" while conscientiously editing the *Roll Call to Destiny* manuscript.

Special thanks also go out to all of the curators and librarians at the staff of the New York Public Library, Boston Library, Harvard College Libraries, Rhode Island Historical Society, McClellan Library at McGill University, and the Providence Public Library, at which I am especially indebted to Phil Weimerskirch, curator of Special Collections. I am also indebted to Peter Harrington, curator of the Ann S. K. Brown Collection, as well as James Andrew Moul, Patricia Sirois, and Jean Rainwater of the Hay Library at Brown University. Stacy Humphreys and Donald Pfanz of the Fredericksburg Park Service provided important source material.

As with my previous work, *The Bloody Crucible of Courage,* all the reenactment and living history groups were genuinely helpful; for the present work, I especially appreciated the support of the Twelfth Georgia Volunteer Infantry Regiment.

Finally, I must acknowledge my debt to my literary agent, Bob Roistacher, for his encouragement over the years and sound advice, so necessary to authors, as well as the patrons of the Pontiac Tap for their ongoing support.

Notes

INTRODUCTION

1. Favill, *The Diary of a Young Officer: Serving with the Armies of the United States During the War of the Rebellion*.

2. Bishop, *The Story of a Regiment, Being a Narrative of the Service of the Second Regiment, Minnesota Veteran Volunteer Infantry*.

3. Robertson, *The Battle of Old Men and Young Boys, June 9th, 1864*.

CHAPTER 1

1. "Suggestions from an Old Soldier," *New York Times,* vol. 10, no. 2993, Apr. 24, 1861, p. 2.

2. "Counsel to Volunteers," *Manufacturers' and Farmers' Journal,* vol. 40, no. 33, Apr. 25, 1861, pp. 1, 4.

3. "Practical Warfare," *Scientific American,* n.s., vol. 4, no. 19, May 11, 1861, p. 292; "Disabling Canon," vol. 4, no. 22, June 1, 1861, p. 340.

4. Garavaglia and Worman, *Firearms of the American West,* pp. 141–146; Herbert G. Houze, *Colt Rifles and Muskets from 1847 to 1870,* pp. 11–19.

5. "Colt's Pistols," *Scientific American,* o.s., vol. 7, no. 23, Feb. 21, 1852, p. 184.

6. Busk, *The Rifle: And How to Use it,* pp. 44, 47.

7. "Colt's Revolving Rifle," *Military Gazette,* vol. 3, no. 18, Sept. 15, 1860, p. 276.

8. "Iron Clad Ships of War: Part 1," *Blackwood's Edinburgh Magazine,* vol. 88, no. 541, Nov.–Dec. 1860, pp. 616–632, 633–649; Mar. 1861, pp. 304–317.

9. "The 'Merrimac' Patented Forty-eight Years Ago," *Scientific American,* n.s., vol. 7, no. 21, May 24, 1862, p. 328.

10. "Iron Clad Ships of War: Part 2," *Blackwood's Edinburgh Magazine,* vol. 88, no. 542, Nov. 1860, p. 626.

11. Tyrrell, *History of the War with Russia,* p. 311; Greenhill and Gifford, *British Assault on Finland: 1854–1855,* p. 305.

12. Chesneau and Kolesnik, *Conway's All the World's Fighting Ships, 1860–1905,* p. 286.

13. "War Frigates and Gunboats," *Scientific American,* n.s., vol. 4, no. 3, Jan. 19, 1861, p. 37.

14. "The Stevens Battery," *Scientific American,* n.s., vol. 5, no. 9, Aug. 31, 1861, p. 131.

15. Taylor, *Rifled Field Pieces: A Short History of What Is Known,* note A, p. 29.

16. Delafield, *Report on the Art of War in Europe in 1854, 1855, and 1856,* pp. 8–9.

17. Taylor, *Rifled Field Pieces,* pp. 16, citing *Canon raye Prussien,* pp. 48, 78.

18. "Breech-Loading Guns and Projectiles," *Scientific American,* n.s., vol. 4, no. 5, Feb. 2, 1861, p. 73.

19. "Correspondence," *Military Gazette,* vol. 2, no. 14, Jul. 15, 1859, p. 214, writing from Paris, Jun. 28, 1859.

20. "The Bayonet," *Military Gazette,* vol. 2, no. 16, Aug. 15, 1859, p. 243.

21. Chesney, *Observations on the Past and the Present State of Fire-arms,* pp. 286–293; citing Captain Wittlich, *Das Fahnlein oder die Compagnie als die wahre tactische Einheit,* pp. 16–63, 74–80.

22. Dixon, "The Rifle: Its Probable Influence on Modern Warfare," *Journal of the Royal United Service Institution,* p. 115, citing Captain Gilluim, *Belgian Artillery,* p. 331.

23. Blanche, *Century of Guns,* p. 66.

24. Upton, "The Prussian Company Column," *International Review,* vol. 2, Jan. 1875, p. 304.

25. Mosely, "Evolution of the American Civil War Infantry Tactics" (Ph.D. diss., University of North Carolina), p. 297.

26. Armstrong, *United States Tactical Doctrine: 1855–1861,* pp. 89–91.

27. Delafield, *Report on the Art of War,* pp. 2–3.

28. Treadwell, *On the Construction of Improved Ordnance,* pp. 10–12.

29. Mordecai, *Military Commission to Europe in 1855 and 1856,* pp. 5–10.

30. Warner, *Generals in Gray,* pp. 58–59.

31. R. E. C., "Modern Tactics," *Southern Literary Messenger,* vol. 26, no. 1, January 1858, p. 18.

32. *Frank Leslie's Illustrated Newspaper,* vol. 10, no. 244, Jul. 28, 1860, pp. 145–146, 152.

33. *Frank Leslie's Illustrated Newspaper,* vol. 11, no. 285, May 4, 1861, p. 385; *Military Gazette,* vol. 3, no. 14, Jul. 15, 1860, pp. 210–211.

34. Bishop, *The Story of a Regiment, Being a Narrative of the Service of the Second Regiment,* p. 17.

35. Alexander, *Military Memoirs,* p. 8.

36. Cox, "War Preparations in the North," in *Battles and Leaders,* 1:96.

37. Wright, *History of the Eighth Regiment Kentucky Volunteer Infantry,* p. 19.

38. Bishop, *Story of a Regiment,* p. 31.

39. Casey, *Infantry Tactics,* p. 6.

40. Jomini, *Art of War,* pp. 189–195.

41. Gay de Vernon, *A Treatise on the Science of War and Fortification,* 2:335–490.

42. Warner, *Generals in Blue,* p. 195.

43. Halleck, *Elements of Military Art and Science.*

44. Report of Brigadier General Winfield S. Hancock, U.S. Army, Commanding First Division, *Official Records (OR),* series I, vol. 21, p. 226.

45. Jomini, *Art of War,* figure 28, pp. 282–284.

46. Chesney, *Observations on the Past,* pp. 300–303.

47. Dixon, "The Rifle," p. 112.

48. Tyler, "The Rifle and the Spade, or the Future of Field Operations," *Journal of the Royal United Service Institute,* vol. 3, no. 10, p. 172.

49. Dixon, "The Rifle," pp. 103–104.

50. Bilby, *Small Arms at Gettysburg,* chap. 3 in the manuscript version of the work.

51. Longstaff and Atteridge, *The Book of the Machine,* pp. 2–3, cited in the manuscript version of Joseph Bilby's *Small Arms at Gettysburg* (chap. 3).

52. Scoffern, *History of the Eighth Regiment Kentucky Volunteer Infantry,* pp. 328–329.

53. Wilcox, *Rifles and Rifle Practice as an Elementary Treatise upon the Theory of Rifle Firing,* pp. 176–177.

54. "Bayonet!" *Military Gazette,* vol. 2, no. 14, Jul. 15, 1859, p. 214.

55. Citing Captain Brabazon in *Military Gazette,* vol. 3, no. 10, May 15, 1860, pp. 152, 155.

56. Wilcox, *Rifles and Rifle Practice,* pp. 242–243, 246–248.

57. Gibbon, *Artillerist's Manual,* pp. 144–145, 230–231.

58. "How the War Is to Be Decided," *Manufacturers' and Farmers' Journal,* vol. 40, no. 40, May 20, 1861, p. 1.

CHAPTER 2

1. Favill, *The Diary of a Young Officer,* p. 50.

2. McDowell at this point was still a brigadier general; report of Brigadier General Irvin McDowell, Commanding U.S. Forces, *Official Records (OR),* series I, vol. 2, p. 303.

3. Fry, "McDowell's Advance to Bull Run," in *Battles and Leaders,* 1:171–182.

4. Reichardt, *Diary of Battery A First Regiment Rhode Island Light Artillery,* p. 11; Woodbury, *A Narrative of the Campaign of the First Rhode Island Regiment,* p. 87.

5. This hymn was also called "Praise God, From Whom All Blessings Flow." The lyrics were written by Thomas Ken in 1674, while the music is that of the "The Old 100th," which is attributed to Louis Bourgeois, circa 1551.

6. Clarke, *History of Company F, 1st Regiment, R.I. Volunteers,* p. 52.

7. Rhodes, *Sprague Papers,* pp. 35–36.

8. Report of Major John G. Barnard, U.S. Corps of Engineers, *OR* I 2, p. 331.

9. General Orders I Headquarters Department of Northeastern Virginia, no. 22, *OR* I 2, p. 326.

10. McDowell, *OR* I 2, p. 315.

11. Sholes, *Personal Reminiscences of Bull Run,* p. 6.

12. Clarke, *History,* pp. 52–53.

13. Cook, *Cook's War Journal,* p. 24.

14. Letter from a member of Company C, First Rhode Island, *Providence Daily Journal,* vol. 32, no. 178, Jul. 26, 1861, p. 2, col. 2.

15. Rhodes claims these were from the Seventy-first New York. "The First Campaign of the Second Rhode Island Infantry," *Personal Narratives of Events in the War,* series 1, no. 1, p. 10; *Providence Daily Journal,* vol. 32, no. 182, July 31, 1861, p. 2, col. 2, extract of a letter from someone in the battery attached to the Second Rhode Island says they were twenty-five "axemen" from the Second New Hampshire Regiment.

16. Woodbury, *First Regiment,* p. 89.

17. Rhodes, "The First Campaign," p. 10.

18. Woodbury, *First Regiment*, p. 87.

19. Clarke, *History*, p. 53.

20. Aldrich, *The History of Battery A*, p. 18.

21. Report of Colonel Samuel P. Heintzelman, Seventeenth U.S. Infantry, Commanding Third Division, *OR* I 2, p. 402.

22. Woodbury, *First Regiment*, pp. 87, 89.

23. Woodbury, *First Regiment*, p. 88.

24. *Providence Daily Evening Press*, Jul. 31, p. 2, col. 4.

25. Clark, *History*, p. 54.

26. Reichardt, *Diary of Battery A First Regiment Rhode Island Light Artillery*, p. 11; Clarke, *History*, p. 53.

27. Woodbury, *First Regiment*, pp. 89–91.

28. Clarke, *History*, p. 55.

29. Sholes, *Personal Reminiscences*, p. 6.

30. Report of Brigadier General Daniel Tyler, Connecticut Militia, Commanding First Division, *OR* I 2, p. 338.

31. Clarke, *History*, p. 55.

32. Reports of General G. T. Beauregard, Commanding Confederate Army of the Potomac, *OR* I 2, p. 489.

33. Woodbury, *First Regiment*, pp. 89–92.

34. Aldrich, *History of Battery A*, p. 18.

35. Aldrich, *History of Battery A*, p. 18.

36. Clarke, *History*, p. 55.

37. Woodbury estimates the time at this point was 9:00 A.M., *First Regiment*, p. 91.

38. Burnside says 9:30 A.M.; report of Colonel Ambrose E. Burnside, First Rhode Island Infantry, Commanding Second Brigade, Second Division, *OR* I 2, p. 395; Reichardt says 10:00 A.M., Reichardt, *Diary of Battery A*, pp. 11–12.

39. In his report, Colonel Burnside claimed the men were ordered to halt and fill their canteens; Burnside, *OR* I 2, p. 395. However, this assertion is contradicted by several eyewitness accounts.

40. Aldrich, *History of Battery A*, p. 19.

41. McDowell, *OR* I 2, pp. 318–19.

42. Heintzelman, *OR* I 2, p. 402.

43. Warder, *Battle of Young's Branch or, Manassas Plain*, p. 18.

44. Beauregard reported that Evans was in position at 9:30 A.M.; Evans's own report says 9:00.

45. Report of Brigadier General Nathan G. Evans, Commanding Seventh Brigade, First Corps, *OR* I 2, p. 559.

46. Beauregard, *OR* I 2, pp. 488–489.

47. Reports of General Joseph E. Johnston, Commanding Confederate Armies of the Shenandoah and of the Potomac, *OR* I 2, p. 474.

48. Beauregard, "The First Battle of Bull Run," in *Battle and Leaders*, 1:207.

49. Bee had to have issued these orders at this point, since the Fourth Alabama had begun to move toward Evans before Reynolds's battery had unlimbered and began firing. Robbins, *Battles and Leaders*, 5:44.

CHAPTER 3

1. McDowell, *Official Records,* series I, vol. 2, p. 319.

2. McDowell, *OR* I 2, pp. 318–319.

3. Although Ward claims they faced three hundred Confederate skirmishers, this is unlikely given the size of Evans's total force. *Providence Daily Post,* Jul. 29, 1861, p. 1, col. 2. Extract of a letter written by Sergeant James A. Ward.

4. Rhodes, *Personal Narratives of Events of the War,* pp. 15–19.

5. Aldridge, *The History of Battery A,* p. 19.

6. Favill, *The Diary of a Young Officer,* p. 32.

7. Extract from a letter of Lieutenant Shaw, Jul. 22, 1861, quoted in *Providence Daily Journal,* Jul. 27, 1861, p. 2, col. 3.

8. Lynn, *Bayonets of the Republic,* p. 247; Ross, *From Flintlock to Rifle: Infantry Tactics 1740–1866,* p. 68.

9. Rhodes, *All for the Union,* p. 26.

10. Clarke, *History,* p. 56.

11. *Essays on the Art of War,* 1:232.

12. Woodbury, *First Regiment,* p. 93. Porter in his own report after the battle would accuse Burnside of attacking too rashly, but this might have been a polemical strike intended to deflect criticism for his own seeming pusillanimity.

13. Fry, "McDowell's Advance to Bull Run," in *Battles and Leaders,* 1:185.

14. A reporter serving in the Seventy-first New York Infantry, for example, claimed that the field extended as much as three to four hundred yards. "The Battle, As Seen by One of the N.Y., 71st," *Providence Daily Evening Press,* 2nd ed., vol. 5, no. 119, Jul. 26, 1861, p. 3, col. 4.

15. Orr, "The Eighth Georgia Regiment," *Daily Intelligencer,* Aug. 18, 1861, p. 2, cols. 2–6.

16. Reed, "The Journal of John C. Reed," pp. 19–20.

17. Lieutenant Shaw, Company F, Second Rhode Island, letter, *Providence Daily Journal,* vol. 32, no. 179, Jul. 27, 1861, p. 2, col. 3.

18. Report of Brigadier General Nathan G. Evans, *OR* I 2, p. 559.

19. In his report, Beauregard says this was the Henry House; Reports of General G. T. Beauregard, Commanding Confederate Army of the Potomac, *OR* I 2, p. 489. However, it was actually the Lewis House. Munroe, "The Rhode Island Artillery at the First Battle of Bull Run," *Personal Narratives of Events in the War of the Rebellion,* series 1, no. 2, p. 16.

20. Aldrich, who served with Reynolds's battery, estimated the range to be about two hundred yards, while a Mr. Manton in the Second Rhode Island felt it was as little as one hundred yards. Aldrich, *History of Battery A,* pp. 19–20, *Manufacturers' and Farmers' Journal,* vol. 40, no. 59, Jul. 25, 1861, p. 2, col. 2.

21. Favill, *Diary of a Young Officer,* pp. 32–34.

22. In his own published account, artilleryman Theodore Reichardt portrays Reynolds's command moving forward at a sharp trot as soon as it had passed Sudley Church, and then accelerating to a full-out gallop once infantry comrades were under fire, all at its own initiative before it had received orders. Reichardt, *Diary of Battery A,* p. 12. From other accounts and from the fact that Thomas Aldrich and Lieutenant Weeden were dismounted when the musket balls first let fly, we know Reynolds's command was initially stationary when the

action began. Its precipitous advance began only after receiving Burnside's orders to engage. Aldrich, *History of Battery A,* pp. 19–20.

23. Report of Colonel Ambrose E. Burnside, *OR* I 2, p. 395.

24. "Letter from the Second Battery," *Providence Daily Evening Press,* vol. 5, no. 119, Jul. 31, 1861, p. 2, col. 4.

25. *Providence Daily Journal,* vol. 32, no. 182, Jul. 31, 1861, p. 2, col. 2.

26. "Letter from the Second Battery," *Providence Daily Evening Press,* vol. 5, no. 119, Jul. 31, 1861, p. 2, col. 4.

27. Report of Colonel J. B. E. Sloan, Fourth South Carolina Infantry, *OR* I 2, p. 561.

28. Report of Brigadier General Nathan G. Evans, *OR* I 2, p. 559.

29. Report of Colonel J. B. E. Sloan, Fourth South Carolina Infantry, *OR* I 2, p. 561.

30. Hennessey, *First Battle of Manassas,* p. 54.

31. Report of Colonel J. B. E. Sloan, Fourth South Carolina Infantry, *OR* I 2, p. 561.

32. Robbins, "With Generals Bee and Jackson at First Manassas, " in *Battles and Leaders,* 5:44–45.

33. Monroe, "The Rhode Island Artillery at the First Battle of Bull Run," *Personal Narratives of Events in the War,* series 1, no. 2, p. 14.

34. Rhodes, *All for the Union,* p. 26.

35. Reed, "The Journal of John C. Reed," p. 20.

36. Monroe, "The Rhode Island Artillery," p. 16.

37. *Providence Daily Journal,* Jul. 31, 1861, p. 2, col. 2, from a letter written several days after the battle.

38. "Letter from the Second Battery," *Providence Daily Evening Press,* vol. 5, no. 119, Jul. 26, 1861, p. 3, col. 4.

39. Clarke, *History,* p. 57.

40. Favill, *Diary of a Young Officer,* p. 32.

41. Reed, "Journal of John C. Reed," p. 17.

42. *Providence Daily Journal,* vol. 32, no. 178, Jul. 26, 1861, p. 2, col. 2, letter written by a member of Company C, First Rhode Island.

43. "The Rhode Island Regiments in the Battle," *Providence Daily Journal,* vol. 32, no. 177, Jul. 25, p. 2, col. 4.

44. William Rhodes Arnold, Mss, 9001-A.

45. Sholes, *Personal Reminiscences of Bull Run,* p. 6; also Clarke, *History,* p. 56.

46. *Providence Daily Journal,* vol. 32, no. 177, Jul. 25, 1861, p. 2, col. 5.

47. Clarke, *History,* p. 57.

48. Rhodes, *All for the Union,* pp. 26–27.

49. *Manufacturers' and Farmers' Journal,* vol. 40, no. 59, Jul. 25, 1861, p. 2, col. 2.

50. "Incidents Gathered Along the Way," *Providence Daily Evening Press,* Jul. 29, 1861, vol. 5, no. 117, p. 2, col. 4.

51. "How They Fire in Battle," *Scientific American,* n.s., vol. 7, no. 18, Nov. 1, 1862, p. 279.

52. "Don't Bite the Cartridges," *Scientific American,* n.s., vol. 4, no. 5, Jul. 27, 1861, p. 56.

53. Reports of Colonel Henry P. Martin, *OR* I 2, p. 23.

54. *Manufacturers' and Farmers' Journal,* Jul. 25, 1861, p. 2, col. 2.

55. "The Eighth Georgia Regiment," *Daily Intelligencer,* Aug. 18, 1861, p. 2, cols. 2–6.

56. *Rome Tri-weekly Courier* (Georgia), Aug. 1, 1861, p. 2, cols. 5–6. A letter to the newspaper, July 23, from "M.D," Second Lieutenant Melvin Dwinell, Company A,

Rome Light Infantry, Eighth Georgia. He was the owner of the *Rome Tri-weekly Courier*. As an experienced newspaper man, he wrote accounts that were quite good. He would try to write a letter to his paper three times a week and provided a very detailed account of the history of his company, regiment, and brigade. Except for when sick or wounded (at Gettysburg), he continued his prolific accounts of the daily mundane as well as the battles until the late fall of 1863 when he left the army, having been elected to the Georgia legislature. This was a great loss to Anderson's Brigade, as he chronicled much of its history.

57. Reed, "Journal of John C. Reed," p. 20.

58. "The Eighth Georgia Regiment," *Daily Intelligencer,* Aug. 18, 1861, p. 2, cols. 2–6.

59. Haynes, *History of the Second Regiment New Hampshire Volunteers,* pp. 20–21.

60. Reed, "Journal of John C. Reed," p. 20.

61. Boatner, *Civil War Dictionary,* p. 94.

62. Woodbury, *First Regiment,* p. 94.

63. Letter from Hamilton Couper, Second Lieutenant, Company B, dated Jul. 25, 1861, in the John Couper Family Papers, Coastal Georgia Historical Society, Saint Simons Island Lighthouse Museum, St. Simons Island, Georgia.

64. "Incidents Gathered Along the Way," *Providence Daily Evening Press,* Jul. 29, 1861, p. 2, col. 3.

65. From a letter written by a member of Company C, First Rhode Island, *Providence Daily Journal*, Jul. 26, p. 2, col. 2.

66. Woodbury, *The Memory of the First Battle,* p. 98.

67. From a letter written by a member of Company C, First Rhode Island, *Providence Daily Journal,* vol. 32, no. 178, Jul. 26, 1861, p. 2, col. 2.

68. Report of Colonel William. B. Franklin, Twelfth U. S. Infantry, Commanding First Brigade, Third Division, *OR* I 2, p. 405.

69. Companies C and G of the Second U.S. Infantry, Companies B, D, G, H, and K of the Third; and Company G of the Eighth.

70. Beauregard, "The First Battle of Bull Run," in *Battles and Leaders,* 1:207.

71. Fry, *Battles and Leaders,* 1:191.

72. Henderson, *Science of War,* pp. 135–136, quoting John G. Nicolay, *The Outbreak of the Rebellion,* pp. 195–196.

73. Scribner, *How Soldiers Were Made,* p. 259.

74. United States Government, *Reports of Experiments with Small Arms for the Military Service,* p. 108; Wilcox, *Rifles and Rifle Practice as an Elementary Treatise upon the Theory of Rifle Firing,* pp. 171, 181.

75. Wilcox, *Rifles,* pp. 171, 177.

76. Wilcox, *Rifles,* p. 67.

77. Tyler, "The Rifle and the Spade, or the Future of Field Operations," *Journal of the Royal United Service Institute,* vol. 3, no. 10 (1859), p. 172.

78. Dixon, "The Rifle—Its Probable Influence on Modern Warfare," *Journal of the Royal United Service Institute,* vol. 1, no. 2 (1857), pp. 103–104.

79. Ardant du Picq, *Battle Studies,* p. 245.

80. "The Waste of Ammunition," *Army and Navy Journal,* vol. 1, p. 11.

81. Hermann, *Memoirs of a Veteran,* pp. 55–56.

82. "The Waste of Ammunition," *Army and Navy Journal,* vol. 1, p. 12.

83. Griffith, *Battle Tactics of the Civil War,* p. 147.

CHAPTER 4

1. Robertson, *Personal Recollections of the War,* p. 14.

2. Waitt, *History of the Nineteenth Regiment Massachusetts Volunteer Infantry,* p. 71.

3. Waitt, *Nineteenth Regiment,* p. 69.

4. Goss, "Yorktown and Williamsburg: Recollections of a Private," in *Battles and Leaders,* 2:194.

5. Report of Brigadier General Edwin V. Sumner, U.S. Army, Commanding Second Corps, *Official Records,* series I, vol. 11 (1), p. 763.

6. Bruce, *The Twentieth Regiment of Massachusetts Volunteer Infantry,* p. 91.

7. Waitt, *Nineteenth Regiment,* p. 74.

8. Frederick, *Story of a Regiment,* chap. 5.

9. Report of Brigadier General Israel B. Richardson, U.S. Army, Commanding First Division, *OR* I 11 (1), p. 764.

10. Bruce, *Twentieth Regiment,* p. 96.

11. Morgan, *Personal Reminiscences of the War of 1861–5,* p. 100.

12. Waitt, *Nineteenth Regiment,* p. 68.

13. Richardson, *OR* I 11 (1), p. 764.

14. Report of Captain George W. Hazzard, Chief of Artillery, *OR* I 11 (1), p. 767.

15. Richardson, *OR* I 11 (1), p. 764.

16. Favill, *The Diary of a Young Officer,* pp. 109–111.

17. Richardson, *OR* I 11 (1), p. 764.

18. French, *OR* I 11 (1), p. 782.

19. Richardson, *OR* I 11 (1), pp. 764–765.

20. French, *OR* I 11 (1), p. 782.

21. Richardson, *OR* I 11 (1), p. 765.

22. Hazzard, *OR* I 11 (1), pp. 767–768.

23. Favill, *Diary of a Young Officer,* pp. 117–118, citing La Vallée's report.

24. Horn, *The Petersburg Regiment: The Twelfth Virginia Infantry Regiment,* forthcoming.

25. Horn, *Petersburg Regiment,* ms. p. 64.

26. Frederick, *Story of a Regiment,* chap. 5.

27. Favill, *Diary of a Young Officer,* pp. 109–111.

28. Favill, *Diary of a Young Officer,* p. 118.

29. Favill, *Diary of a Young Officer,* pp. 117–118, citing La Vallée's report.

30. Whittaker, *Volunteer Cavalry,* p. 15.

31. Horn, *Petersburg Regiment,* ms. p. 65.

32. Favill, *Diary of a Young Officer,* pp. 109–111.

33. Favill, *Diary of a Young Officer,* pp. 117–118, citing La Vallée's report.

34. "Fighting," *Scientific American,* n.s., vol. 7, no. 22, Nov. 29, 1862, p. 283.

35. Favill, *Diary of a Young Officer,* p. 116, citing Chapman.

36. Favill, *Diary of a Young Officer,* pp. 117–118, citing La Vallée's report.

37. Favill, *Diary of a Young Officer,* p. 112.

38. Favill, *Diary of a Young Officer,* pp. 109–111.

39. Anonymous [generally attributed to Savorin], *Sentimens d'un homme de guerre sur le nouveau système du chevalier de Folard,* Paris, 1733, p. 100; and plate IV opposite p. 103.

40. Wolfe, *General Wolfe's Instructions to Young Officers,* p. 52; Puységur, *Art de la guerre par principes et par règles,* p. 153.

41. Richardson, *OR* I 11 (1), p. 766; French, *OR* I 11 (1), p. 783.

42. Smith, *The Battle of Seven Pines,* p. 120.

43. Smith, *Battle of Seven Pines,* pp. 112, 114. The regiment that fell back after being jointly attacked by Rebel and Yankee alike was most likely the Fifty-third Virginia of Armistead's Brigade, which briefly exchanged fire with the Forty-first Virginia.

44. Favill, *Diary of a Young Officer,* pp. 117–118, citing La Vallée's report.

45. Smith, *Battle of Seven Pines,* p. 121.

46. Return of Casualties in the Army of the Potomac at the Battle of Fair Oaks, or Seven Pines, VA, May 31–Jun. 1, 1862, *OR* I 11 (1), p. 757.

47. De Forest, *A Volunteer's Adventures,* pp. 65–66.

48. *OR* I 36 (1), pp. 225–226, 237–238, 251–252, 261–262.

49. Davis, *Weapons of the Civil War,* pp. 6, 12.

50. Anton, *Retrospect of a Military Life,* pp. 107–108.

51. Hermann, *Memoirs of a Veteran,* p. 70; Hill, *Our Boys: The Personal Experience of a Soldier in the Army of the Potomac,* p. 384.

CHAPTER 5

1. Longstreet, "The Battle of Fredericksburg," in *Battles and Leaders,* 3:70.

2. Couch, "Sumner's 'Right Grand Division,'" in *Battles and Leaders,* 3:107.

3. Cavanagh, *Memoirs of Gen. Thomas Francis Meagher,* p. 464.

4. McLaws, "The Confederate Left at Fredericksburg," in *Battles and Leaders,* 3:90.

5. Report of Colonel John S. Mason, Fourth Ohio Infantry, Commanding First Brigade, *Official Records,* series I, vol. 21, p. 292.

6. Owen, *In Camp and Battle,* p. 175.

7. See map in Longstreet, "The Battle of Fredericksburg," in *Battles and Leaders,* 3:74.

8. Report of Lieutenant General James Longstreet, C.S. Army, Commanding First Army Corps, *OR* I 21, p. 569.

9. Report of Brigadier General William N. Pendleton, C.S. Army, Chief of Artillery, Army of Northern Virginia, *OR* I 21, p. 563.

10. Allan, *The Army of Northern Virginia in 1862,* pp. 493–494.

11. Longstreet, *OR* I 21, p. 569.

12. Allan, *Army of Northern Virginia,* pp. 493–494.

13. Owen, *In Camp and Battle,* p. 185; report of Colonel J. B. Walton, Commanding Battalion Washington Artillery of Louisiana, *OR* I 21, p. 573.

14. Owen, "A Hot Day on Marye's Heights," in *Battles and Leaders,* 3:97.

15. Pendleton, *OR* I 21, p. 563.

16. McLaws, "Confederate Left at Fredericksburg," p. 86.

17. Owen, *In Camp and Battle,* p. 177.

18. Pendleton, *OR* I 21, p. 563.

19. Owen, "Hot Day on Marye's Heights," p. 97.

20. Owen, *In Camp and Battle,* pp. 178–180.

21. Longstreet, "The Battle of Fredericksburg," in *Battles and Leaders,* 3:75.

22. Couch, "Sumner's 'Right Grand Division,'" p. 108.

23. Owen, *In Camp and Battle,* pp. 178–183.

24. Evans, *Confederate Military History,* 5:174.

25. Longstreet, *OR* I 21, p. 570.

26. McLaws, "Confederate Left at Fredericksburg," p. 90.

27. Baker, *A Reminiscent Story of the Great Civil War,* p. 46.

28. Report of General Robert E. Lee, C.S. Army, Commanding Army of Northern Virginia, *OR* I 21, p. 547.

29. Originally, in his after-battle report, Longstreet stated that his artillery began firing at 11:00 A.M., but he revised this estimate when penning his article on this battle for *Century Magazine;* Longstreet, *OR* I 31, p. 569.

30. Report of Major General Lafayette McLaws, C.S. Army, Commanding McLaws Division, *OR* I 21, p. 580.

31. Owen, *In Camp and Battle,* p. 184.

32. Report of Colonel Richard Byres, Twenty-eighth Massachusetts Infantry, *OR* I 21, p. 246.

33. Report of Brigadier General Winfield S. Hancock, U.S. Army, Commanding First Division, *OR* I 21, p. 227.

34. Owen, "Hot Day on Marye's Heights," pp. 97–98.

35. McLaws, *OR* I 21, p. 580.

36. Report of Colonel David B. McCreary, 145th Pennsylvania Infantry, *OR* I 21, p. 239.

37. Kimberly, *Forty-first Ohio,* pp. 506–507; cited in Cozzens, *The Shipwreck of Their Hopes,* p. 258.

38. Owen, *In Camp and Battle,* p. 185.

39. Report of Major Gen. Darius N. Couch, U.S. Army, Commanding Second Army Corps, *OR* I 21, p. 222.

40. Owen, "Hot Day on Marye's Heights," p. 98.

41. Owen, *In Camp and Battle,* p. 186.

42. Gibbon, *Artillerist's Manual,* p. 343.

43. The earliest cannons fired stones; then they hurled spherical iron projectiles called "round shot" or "common shot." With the advent of rifled artillery these became longer and pointed and were now called "bolts."

44. "Illustrations of the War in America," *Illustrated London News,* vol. 42, no. 1186, Jan. 31, 1861, p. 126.

45. Report of Brigadier General Thomas F. Meagher, U.S. Army, Commanding Second Brigade, *OR* I 21, p. 241.

46. Sumner, "J. Albert Monroe," *Personal Narratives of Events in the War,* series 4, no. 18, p. 16.

47. McLaws, "Confederate Left at Fredericksburg," p. 91.

48. Couch, "Sumner's 'Right Grand Division,'" p. 111.

49. McLaws, *OR* I 21, p. 580.

50. Baker, *Reminiscent Story,* p. 49.

51. Hancock, *OR* I 21, p. 227.

52. Baker, *Reminiscent Story,* p. 49.

53. Owen, "Hot Day on Marye's Heights," p. 98.

54. Walton, *OR* I 21, p. 573.

55. Baker, *Reminiscent Story,* p. 51.

56. Owen, *In Camp and Battle,* p. 189.

57. Scribner, *How Soldiers Were Made, or, the War as I Saw It,* pp. 294–295.

58. Baker, *Reminiscent Story,* p. 51.

59. Owen, *In Camp and Battle,* p. 190.

60. Baker, *Reminiscent Story,* pp. 51–52.

61. Owen, *In Camp and Battle,* p. 191.

62. Report of Lieutenant Colonel E. P. Alexander, Commanding Battalion Reserve Artillery, *OR* I 21, p. 575.

63. Sumner, "J. Albert Monroe," in *Personal Narratives of Events in the War,* series 4, no. 18, p. 16.

64. Report of Lieutenant Colonel E. P. Alexander, Commanding Battalion Reserve Artillery, *OR* I 21, p. 575.

65. Couch, "Sumner's 'Right Grand Division,'" p. 115.

66. *Illustrated London News,* vol. 42, no. 1186, Jan. 31, 1861, p. 126.

CHAPTER 6

1. Lockett, "The Defense of Vicksburg," in *Battles and Leaders,* 3:483.

2. Reports of Major General John A. McClernand, U.S. Army, Commanding Expedition, *Official Records,* series I, vol. 17 (1), p. 701.

3. Reports of Major General William T. Sherman, *OR* I 17 (1), p. 754.

4. Reports of Major General John A. McClernand, U.S. Army, Commanding Expedition, *OR* I 17 (1), pp. 701–704.

5. Rogers, *War Pictures,* p. 205.

6. Report of Colonel James Deshler, C.S. Army, Commanding Brigade, *OR* I 17 (1), p. 791.

7. Reports of Major General John A. McClernand, U.S. Army, Commanding Expedition, *OR* I 17 (1), p. 705.

8. Duyckinck, *National History of the War for the Union,* 3:139.

9. Reports of Major General William T. Sherman, Commanding Fifteenth Army Corps, *OR* I 17 (1), p. 755.

10. Reports of Major General William T. Sherman, Commanding Fifteenth Army Corps, *OR* I 17 (1), p. 755.

11. Report of Colonel Charles R. Woods, Seventy-sixth Ohio Infantry, *OR* I 17 (1), p. 768.

12. Report of Brigadier General John M. Thayer, U.S. Army, Commanding Third Brigade, *OR* I 17 (1), p. 769.

13. Report of Colonel Richard Owen, Sixtieth Indiana Infantry, *OR* I 17 (1), p. 734.

14. Report of Brigadier General David Stuart, U.S. Army, Commanding Second Division, *OR* I 17 (1), pp. 772–773.

15. Report of Colonel James Deshler, C.S. Army, Commanding Brigade, *OR* I 17 (1), p. 791.

16. Report of Brigadier General Thomas J. Churchill, C.S Army, Commanding Lower Arkansas and White Rivers, *OR* I 17 (1), p. 781.

17. Reports of Major General John A. McClernand, U.S. Army, Commanding Expedition, *OR* I 17 (1), p. 707.

18. Report of Major General William T. Sherman, U.S. Army, Commanding Fifteenth Army Corps, *OR* I 17 (1), p. 756.

19. Report of Brigadier General Thomas J. Churchill, C.S. Army, Commanding Lower Arkansas and White Rivers, *OR* I 17 (1), p. 781.

20. Report of Colonel Robert R. Garland, Sixth Texas Infantry, *OR* I 17 (1), pp. 784–785.

21. Headley, *The Great Rebellion,* 2:148–149.

22. Rogers, *War Pictures,* pp. 206–207.

23. Duyckinck, *National History,* 3:139.

24. Schmucker, *A History of the Civil War in the United States,* pp. 440–442.

25. Webster and Cameron, *History of the First Wisconsin Battery of Light Artillery,* pp. 113–114.

26. Union Correspondence, Special Orders No. 23, *OR* I 48 (1), p. 615.

27. Union Correspondence, Special Orders No. 23, *OR* I 48 (1), p. 114.

28. Union Correspondence, Special Orders No. 23, *OR* I 48 (1), p. 117.

29. Union Correspondence, Special Orders No. 23, *OR* I 48 (1), p. 116.

30. Union Correspondence, Special Orders No. 23, *OR* I 48 (1), p. 115.

31. Report of Brigadier General Peter J. Osterhaus, U.S. Army, Commanding Second Division, *OR* I 17 (1), p. 747.

32. Webster and Cameron, *First Wisconsin Battery,* p. 115.

33. Frank Mason, who served with the Forty-second Ohio Regiment, remembered the conversation, cited in Webster and Cameron, *First Wisconsin Battery,* p. 118.

34. Webster and Cameron, *First Wisconsin Battery,* p. 115.

35. Report of Major Ludlow to Colonel Abbot, Bermuda Hundred, VA, Aug. 31, 1864, cited in *1st Conn. HA,* pp. 108–109.

36. Report of H. H. Pierce, Captain, First Connecticut Heavy Artillery, to Colonel Abbot, Dutch Gap, Oct. 11, 1864, cited in *1st Conn. HA,* p. 114.

CHAPTER 7

1. York County damage claims, State Archives, Harrisburg, Pennsylvania. Scott Mingus has been researching Stuart's movements for a planned article for *Gettysburg Magazine.* A total of 686 York Countians filed claims for damages arising from the Confederate movements in that area, the vast majority of which relate to Stuart's seizure of horses and supplies.

2. Correspondence, Orders, and Returns Relating to Operations in North Carolina, Virginia, West Virginia, Maryland, Pennsylvania, and Department of the East, Jun. 3–Aug. 3, 1863, *Official Records,* series I, vol. 27 (3), p. 502.

3. Phipps, *"Come on, You Wolverines!"* p. 32.

4. New York State Monuments Commission for the Battlefields of Gettysburg and Chattanooga, *Final Report on the Battlefield of Gettysburg,* p. 84.

5. Wittenberg, *Protecting the Flank,* p. 50.

6. Letter of Lieutenant A. C. M. Pennington, Dec. 5, 1884, in Ladd, *The Bachelder Papers,* 2:1082.

7. Phipps, *Wolverines,* p. 33, map, p. 34.

8. Letter of Major Luther S. Trowbridge, Aug. 27, 1885, in Ladd, *Bachelder Papers,* 2:1218–1220.

9. Trowbridge, *The Operations of the Cavalry in the Gettysburg Campaign,* p. 10.

10. Letter of Colonel John B. McIntosh, Aug. 27, 1885, in Ladd, *Bachelder Papers,* 2:1122–1223; letter of Lieutenant A. C. M. Pennington, Dec. 5, 1884, in Ladd, *Bachelder Papers,* 2:1082.

11. Miller, "The Third Pennsylvania Cavalry at Gettysburg," in *History of the Third Pennsylvania Cavalry,* p. 297.

12. Letter of Colonel John B. McIntosh, Aug. 27, 1885, in Ladd, *Bachelder Papers,* 2:1123–1224.

13. Phipps, *Wolverines,* p. 42.

14. Longacre, *The Cavalry at Gettysburg,* p. 225.

15. Trowbridge, *Operations,* p. 10.

16. Letter from V. A. Witcher to General L. L. Lomax, Aug. 20, 1908.

17. Beale, *The History of the Ninth Virginia Cavalry,* p. 86.

18. McClellan, *I Rode with J. E. B. Stuart,* p. 337.

19. Pennsylvania Gettysburg Battlefield Commission, *Ceremonies at the Dedication of the Monuments Erected by the Commonwealth of Pennsylvania,* 2:828.

20. Report of Major General J. E. B. Stuart, C.S. Army, Commanding Cavalry, Army of Northern Virginia, *OR* I 27 (2), p. 697.

21. Letter from V. A. Witcher to General L. L. Lomax, Aug. 20, 1908, from an electronic version of this letter, archival repository unknown.

22. Beale, *Ninth Virginia Cavalry,* p. 86.

23. York County damage claims; see also Mingus's forthcoming *Flames Beyond the Susquehanna: The Gordon Expedition, June 1863,* for a discussion of this.

24. Letter from V. A. Witcher to General L. L. Lomax, Riceville, VA, Aug. 20, 1908, in Ladd, *Bachelder Papers.* See note 21.

25. Report of Major General J. E. B. Stuart, C.S. Army, Commanding Cavalry, Army of Northern Virginia, *OR* I 27 (2), p. 698.

26. Pennsylvania Gettysburg Battlefield Commission, *Ceremonies,* 2:826.

27. Longacre, *Cavalry at Gettysburg,* p. 225.

28. Letter from V. A. Witcher to General L. L. Lomax, Riceville, VA, Aug. 20, 1908.

29. *Campaigns of Wheeler and His Cavalry,* p. 408, cited in Gray, *Cavalry Tactics as Illustrated by the War of the Rebellion,* p. 13.

30. Letter from V. A. Witcher to John W. Daniels, Mar. 22, 1906, in Ladd, *Bachelder Papers.* See note 21.

31. Lieutenant James Chester to Woodruff, Fort Monroe, VA, Nov. 27, 1884 (Chester commanded a section of Battery E, First U.S. Artillery, Horse Artillery, Cavalry Corps), in Ladd, *Bachelder Papers,* 2:1078–1079; report of Captain William E. Miller, in Ladd, *Bachelder Papers,* 2:1263. McIntosh says this orchard was left of the Reever House, also on the Hanover Road; letter of Colonel John B. McIntosh, Aug. 27, 1885, in Ladd, *Bachelder Papers,* 2:1123.

32. Report of Captain William E. Miller, in Ladd, *Bachelder Papers,* 2:1263.

33. Lieutenant Carle A. Woodruff, Newport Barracks, KY, Dec. 14, 1884, to James Chester, in Ladd, *Bachelder Papers,* 2:1087–1088.

34. Guibert, *Essai général de tactique,* 1:341.

35. Lieutenant Frank B. Hamilton, Washington Barracks, Dec. 12, 1884, to Woodruff, in Ladd, *Bachelder Papers,* 2:1085–1086; Lieutenant Carle A. Woodruff, Newport Barracks, KY, Dec. 14, 1884, to James Chester, in Ladd, *Bachelder Papers,* 2:1087–1088.

36. Letter of Lieutenant A. C. M. Pennington, Dec. 5, 1884, in Ladd, *Bachelder Papers,* 2:1082–1084.

37. Phipps, *Wolverines,* p. 40.

38. McClellan, *I Rode with J. E. B. Stuart,* p. 339.

39. Lieutenant James Chester to Woodruff, Fort Monroe, VA, Nov. 27, 1884, in Ladd, *Bachelder Papers,* 2:1078–1079.

40. Lieutenant Frank B. Hamilton, Washington Barracks, Dec. 12, 1884, to Woodruff, in Ladd, *Bachelder Papers,* 2:1085–1086.

41. Pyne, *The History of the First New Jersey Cavalry,* p. 164.

42. Letter of Colonel John B. McIntosh, Aug. 27, 1885, in Ladd, *Bachelder Papers,* 2:1123–1124.

43. Trowbridge, *Operations,* p. 12.

44. Letter of Colonel John B. McIntosh, Aug. 27, 1885, in Ladd, *Bachelder Papers,* 2:1123–1124; also report of Captain William E. Miller, in Ladd, *Bachelder Papers,* 2:1265.

45. Letter of Colonel John B. McIntosh, Aug. 27, 1885, in Ladd, *Bachelder Papers,* 2:1123–1124.

46. Pyne, *History of the First New Jersey Cavalry,* p. 164.

47. Letter from Captain William W. Rogers to Colonel John B. Bachelder, Mar. 14, 1886, in Ladd, *Bachelder Papers,* 2:1223.

48. First Brigade, Second Division Cavalry Corps, in Ladd, *Bachelder Papers,* 2:1261.

49. Report of Captain William E. Miller, in Ladd, *Bachelder Papers,* 2:1262–1263.

50. Captain William E. Miller, in Ladd, *Bachelder Papers,* 2:1265.

51. Letter of Colonel John B. McIntosh, in Ladd, *Bachelder Papers,* 2:1124.

52. Notes of a conversation with Major Luther S. Trowbridge, in Ladd, *Bachelder Papers,* 2:1204–1205.

53. Miller, "The Third Pennsylvania Cavalry at Gettysburg," in *History of the Third Pennsylvania Cavalry,* p. 299.

54. Beale, *Ninth Virginia Cavalry,* p. 86.

55. Notes of a conversation with Major Luther S. Trowbridge, in Ladd, *Bachelder Papers,* 2:1204–1205.

56. Report of Captain William E. Miller, in Ladd, *Bachelder Papers,* 2:1265.

57. Miller, "Third Pennsylvania Cavalry at Gettysburg," p. 299.

58. McClellan, *I Rode with J. E. B. Stuart,* p. 340.

59. Harris, *Michigan Cavalry Brigade at the Battle of Gettysburg,* pp. 7–11.

60. Rawle, "The Second Cavalry Division in the Gettysburg Campaign," in *History of the Third Pennsylvania Cavalry,* p. 276.

61. Letter from V. A. Witcher to General L. L. Lomax, Aug. 20, 1908, in Ladd, *Bachelder Papers* (see note 21); also cited in Cole, *34th Virginia Cavalry,* p. 51.

62. Letter from Major Luther S. Trowbridge to Governor R. A. Alger, Feb. 19, 1886, in Ladd, *Bachelder Papers,* 2:1207.

63. Wittenberg, *Protecting the Flank,* p. 83.

64. Lieutenant George G. Briggs, Mar. 26, 1888, in Ladd, *Bachelder Papers,* 2:1257.

65. Phipps, *Wolverines,* pp. 43–44.

66. Notes of a conversation with Major Luther S. Trowbridge, in Ladd, *Bachelder Papers,* 2:1204–1205.

67. Longacre, *Cavalry at Gettysburg,* chap. 13, p. 308, n. 42.

68. Letter from Major Luther S. Trowbridge to Governor R. A. Alger, Detroit, Feb. 19, 1886, in Ladd, *Bachelder Papers,* 2:1207.

69. Wittenberg, *Protecting the Flank,* p. 86.

70. Trowbridge, *Operations,* p. 13.

71. Phipps, *Wolverines,* p. 44.

72. Lieutenant George G. Briggs, Mar. 26, 1888, in Ladd, *Bachelder Papers,* 2:1257.

73. Letter from Colonel Thomas T. Munford to Major Henry B. McClellan, in Ladd, *Bachelder Papers,* 2:1117.

74. Miller, "Third Pennsylvania Cavalry at Gettysburg," p. 299; letter from Colonel John B. McIntosh Aug. 27, 1885, to Colonel John B. Bachelder, in Ladd, *Bachelder Papers,* 2:1125.

75. Report of Brigadier General Wade Hampton, C.S. Army, Commanding Brigade, *OR* I 27 (2), p. 725.

76. Letter from Major Luther S. Trowbridge to Governor R. A. Alger, Detroit, Feb. 19, 1886, in Ladd, *Bachelder Papers,* 2:1204–1209.

77. Letter from Colonel John B. McIntosh, Aug. 27, 1885, to Colonel John B. Bachelder, in Ladd, *Bachelder Papers,* 2:1125.

78. Report of Brigadier General Wade Hampton, C.S. Army, Commanding Brigade, *OR* I 27 (2), p. 725.

79. Longacre, *Cavalry at Gettysburg,* p. 237.

80. Letter from Colonel William C. Wickham to Major H. B. McClellan, Jul. 28, 1885, in Ladd, *Bachelder Papers,* 2:1116.

81. Letter of Private Richard H. Ingram, in Ladd, *Bachelder Papers,* 3:1337; statement of Lieutenant John M. Jordan, in Ladd, *Bachelder Papers,* 3:1375.

82. Rea, *Sketches of Hampton's Cavalry,* p. 116.

83. Logan, "Hampton and the Sabre," *The Intelligencer,* May 22, 1895, p. 1, cols. 5–6.

84. Miller, "Third Pennsylvania Cavalry at Gettysburg," p. 278.

85. Lieutenant James Chester to Woodruff, Fort Monroe, VA, Nov. 27, 1884, in Ladd, *Bachelder Papers,* 2:1078–1079.

86. Miller, "Third Pennsylvania Cavalry at Gettysburg," p. 299.

87. Miller, "Third Pennsylvania Cavalry at Gettysburg," p. 309.

88. Pennsylvania Gettysburg Battlefield Commission, *Ceremonies,* 2:831.

89. *Campaigns of Wheeler and His Cavalry,* p. 408, cited in Gray, *Cavalry Tactics,* p. 13.

90. Lieutenant James Chester to Woodruff, Fort Monroe, VA, Nov. 27, 1884, in Ladd, *Bachelder Papers,* 2:1078–1079.

91. Lieutenant Carle A. Woodruff, Newport Barracks, KY, Dec. 14, 1884, to James Chester, in Ladd, *Bachelder Papers,* 2:1087–1088.

92. Miller, "Third Pennsylvania Cavalry at Gettysburg," p. 299.

93. Trowbridge, *Operations,* p. 14.

94. Miller in a letter to his brother: Miller, "Third Pennsylvania Cavalry at Gettysburg," p. 306.

95. Phipps, *Wolverines,* p. 47.

96. Pennsylvania Gettysburg Battlefield Commission, *Ceremonies,* 2:833.

97. Rochechouart, *Memoirs,* p. 68.

98. Hudgins and Kleese, eds., *The Civil War Experiences of Sgt. Robert S. Hudgins II,* pp. 82–84, cited in Wittenberg, *Protecting the Flank,* p. 103.

99. *Constitution and By-laws Company H, Third Pennsylvania Cavalry,* p. 39.

100. Phipps, *Wolverines,* p. 49.

101. Letter of Captain Amasa E. Mathews, Jun. 11, 1887, in Ladd, *Bachelder Papers,* 3:1492.

102. Pennsylvania Gettysburg Battlefield Commission, *Ceremonies,* 2:833.

103. Hudgins and Kleese, eds., *Civil War Experiences,* 1:82–84, cited in Wittenberg, *Protecting the Flank,* p. 103.

104. Longacre, *Cavalry at Gettysburg,* p. 238.

105. Miller, "Third Pennsylvania Cavalry at Gettysburg," p. 299.

106. Miller, "Third Pennsylvania Cavalry at Gettysburg," pp. 303–307.

107. Miller, "Third Pennsylvania Cavalry at Gettysburg," p. 299.

108. Rea, *Sketches of Hampton's Cavalry,* p. 117.

109. Wittenberg, *Protecting the Flank*, p. 114.

110. Trowbridge, *Operations*, p. 15.

111. Miller, "Third Pennsylvania Cavalry at Gettysburg," p. 299.

112. Brooke-Rawle, "The Second Cavalry Division in the Gettysburg Campaign," in *History of the Third Pennsylvania Cavalry*, p. 280.

113. Phipps, *Wolverines*, p. 50.

114. Lieutenant James Chester to Woodruff, Fort Monroe, VA, Nov. 27, 1884, in Ladd, *Bachelder Papers*, 2:1078–1079.

115. Lieutenant Frank B. Hamilton, Washington Barracks, Dec. 12, 1884, to Woodruff, in Ladd, *Bachelder Papers*, 2:1085–1086.

116. Colonel Thomas T. Munford to Major Henry B. McClellan, in Ladd, *Bachelder Papers*, 2:1117.

117. Harris, *Michigan Cavalry Brigade*, pp. 7–11.

118. Letter from Colonel Cary Breckinridge (Second Virginia Cavalry) to General T. T. Mumford, Jul. 14, 1885, in Ladd, *Bachelder Papers*, 2:1112.

119. Letter from Major Charles Irving (First Virginia Cavalry) to H. B. McClellan, Jul. 29, 1885, in Ladd, *Bachelder Papers*, 2:1109.

120. Letter from V. A. Witcher to General L. L. Lomax, Riceville, VA, Aug. 20, 1908, in Ladd, *Bachelder Papers* (see note 21).

121. Letter from Dr. Talcott Eliason to Major H. B. McClellan, Jul. 23, 1885, in Ladd, *Bachelder Papers*, 2:1114.

CHAPTER 8

1. Poe, "The Defense of Knoxville," in *Battles and Leaders*, 3:731–732.

2. Grant, "Chattanooga," in *Battles and Leaders*, 3:693.

3. Cutcheon, *Twentieth Michigan Infantry*, pp. 77–78.

4. Cutcheon, *War Papers*, pp. 293–294.

5. Cutcheon, *Twentieth Michigan*, p. 81.

6. Reports of Captain Orlando M. Poe, U.S. Corps of Engineers, Chief Engineer, Department of the Ohio, *Official Records*, series I, vol. 31 (1), p. 296.

7. Poe, "The Defense of Knoxville," in *Battles and Leaders*, 3:731–732.

8. Poe, "Defense of Knoxville," p. 737.

9. Poe, *OR* I 31 (1), p. 296.

10. Poe, *OR* I 31 (1), p. 296.

11. A barbette is the mound of earth behind a parapet upon which an artillery piece was placed. When a barbette was formed in the shape of a salient, it was common practice to fill the angle with earth to form a short face that was called a "pan coupé." Wheeler, *Elements of Field Fortifications*, p. 119.

12. Poe, *OR* I 31 (1), p. 299; also in Kniffin, *War Papers*, pp. 367–368.

13. Poe, *OR* I (31) 1, p. 295.

14. Cutcheon, *War Papers*, 294.

15. Benjamin, Second U.S. Artillery, Chief of Artillery, *OR* I 31 (1), p. 342. In his own report, Poe says that a contingent from the Second Michigan also garrisoned Fort Sanders, bringing the total to about 220 men and officers, Poe, *OR* I 31 (1), pp. 298–299.

16. Armour, *War Papers*, p. 63.

17. *National Tribune,* May 23, 1918, p. 7, cols. 6–7.

18. Report of Colonel George W. Taylor, Third New Jersey Infantry, *OR* I 51 (1), p. 49; Confederate Correspondence, Aug. 20, 1862–Jun. 3, 1863, *OR* I 18, p. 963.

19. Reports of Major Samuel H. Lockett, C.S. Engineers, Chief Engineer, *OR* I, 24 (2), p. 331.

20. Organization of the Troops in East Tennessee under Command of Lieutenant General James Longstreet, C.S. Army, Nov. 30, 1863, *OR* I 31 (1), pp. 453–454.

21. Osbourne, *The History of the Twenty-ninth Regiment of Massachusetts's Volunteer Infantry,* p. 267.

22. Cutcheon, *War Papers,* pp. 290–291.

23. Longstreet, C.S. Army, Commanding Confederate Forces in East Tennessee, C.S. Army, Commanding Division, with Charges Against Brigadier Generals E. M. Law and J. B. Robertson, and Resulting Correspondence, *OR* I 31 (1), p. 459.

24. McLaws, *OR* I 31 (1), p. 484.

25. McLaws, *OR* I 31 (1), p. 488.

26. McLaws, *OR* I 31 (1), p. 484.

27. Colonel E. Porter Alexander, C.S. Artillery, Chief of Artillery, *OR* I 31 (1), p. 479.

28. McLaws, *OR* I 31 (1), p. 485.

29. Longstreet, *OR* I 31 (1), p. 460; Alexander, *OR* I 31 (1), p. 479.

30. McLaws, *OR* I 31 (1), p. 486.

31. Alexander, *Fighting,* p. 325.

32. Longstreet, *OR* I 31 (1), pp. 460–461.

33. McLaws, *OR* I 31 (1), pp. 491–492.

34. Longstreet, *OR* I 31 (1), p. 494.

35. Report of Brigadier General Benjamin G. Humphreys, C.S. Army, Commanding Brigade, *OR* I 31 (1), pp. 520–521.

36. Humphreys, *Sunflower Guards,* J. F. Claiborne Papers, manuscript 151, p. 19.

37. Report of Colonel Edward Ball, Fifty-first Georgia Infantry, Commanding Bryan's Brigade, *OR* I 31 (1), pp. 523–524.

38. Report of Lieutenant Colonel N. L. Hutchins, Jr., Third Battalion Georgia Sharpshooters, Commanding Wofford's Brigade, *OR* I 31 (1), pp. 519–525.

39. Alexander, *OR* I 31 (1), p. 479, Nov. 4–Dec. 23, 1863.

40. McLaws, *OR* I 31 (1), p. 484.

41. Humphreys, *OR* I 31 (1), pp. 520–521; Ball, *OR* I 31 (1), pp. 523–524.

42. Longstreet, *OR* I 31 (1), pp. 460–461.

43. Report of Colonel Benjamin C. Christ, Fiftieth Pennsylvania Infantry, Commanding Second Brigade, *OR* I 31 (1), pp. 358–359; Seymour, *Divided Loyalties: Fort Sanders and the Civil War in East Tennessee,* p. 193.

44. "Our Army Correspondence," *Memphis Appeal* (Tennessee), Dec. 25, 1863, p. 1, col. 4.

45. Kniffin, *War Papers,* p. 371.

46. Alexander, *OR* I 31 (1), p. 479.

47. Lallemand, *A Treatise on Artillery,* 1:80.

48. Todd, *The Seventy-ninth Highlanders New York Volunteers in the War of Rebellion 1861–1865,* pp. 385–386.

49. Seymour, *Divided Loyalties,* p. 193.

50. Cutcheon, *War Papers,* p. 297.

51. Cutcheon, *Twentieth Michigan Infantry,* p. 82; Cutcheon, *War Papers,* p. 296.

52. Report of Brigadier General Edward Ferrero, U.S. Army, Commanding First Division, *OR* I 31 (1), pp. 353–354.

53. Report of Brigadier General Benjamin G. Humphreys, *OR* I 31 (1), pp. 520–521; Longstreet, *OR* I 31 (1), pp. 460–461.

54. Cutcheon, *War Papers,* p. 296.

55. Cutcheon, *War Papers,* p. 297.

56. Seymour, *Divided Loyalties,* p. 193.

57. Benjamin, *OR* I 31 (1), p. 344.

58. Kniffin, *War Papers,* p. 371.

59. Armour, *War Papers,* pp. 66–67.

60. Lieutenant Samuel N. Benjamin, *OR* I 31 (1), p. 344.

61. Hutchins, *OR* I 31 (1), pp. 519–520.

62. Seymour, *Divided Loyalties,* p. 193.

63. "Our Army Correspondence," *Memphis Appeal* (Tennessee), Dec. 25, 1863, p. 1, col. 4.

64. Kniffin, *War Papers,* p. 371.

65. Todd, *Seventy-ninth Highlanders,* p. 386.

66. Seymour, *Divided Loyalties,* p. 193.

67. Todd, *Seventy-ninth Highlanders,* p. 390.

68. Todd, *Seventy-ninth Highlanders,* p. 390.

69. "Our Army Correspondence," *Memphis Appeal* (Tennessee), Dec. 25, 1863, p. 1, col. 4.

70. Kniffin, *War Papers,* pp. 372–373.

71. Armour, *War Papers,* p. 69; Cutcheon, War Papers, pp. 296–297.

72. Osborne, *The History of the Twenty-ninth Regiment of Massachusetts's Volunteer Infantry,* p. 267.

73. Poe, *Personal Recollections,* p. 164.

74. Todd, *Seventy-ninth Highlanders,* p. 391.

75. Armour, *War Papers,* p. 68.

76. Port fire: "A mixture of meal powder, sulfur, and saltpeter, rammed loosely into a 99–109 case of paper which was then cut into 1-inch pieces attached to a linstock or forked stick. It was used to fire guns or mortars instead of a match (a type of fuse)," "Port Fire," in *Military Dictionary.*

77. Todd, *Seventy-ninth Highlanders,* p. 389.

78. Cutcheon, *War Papers,* pp. 372–373.

79. Seymour, *Divided Loyalties,* p. 198.

80. Humphreys, *Sunflower Guards,* p. 20.

81. *Southern Recorder* (Milledgeville, Georgia), Dec. 15, 1863, p. 3.

82. Longstreet, *OR* I 31 (1) 1, pp. 460–461.

83. Humphreys, *Sunflower Guards,* p. 20.

84. Cutcheon, *War Papers,* p. 373.

85. Cutcheon, *Twentieth Michigan Infantry,* p. 82.

86. Humphreys, *Sunflower Guards,* p. 19.

87. "Our Army Correspondence," *Memphis Appeal* (Tennessee), Dec. 25, 1863, p. 1, cols. 3–4.

88. Poe, *Personal Recollections,* p. 164.

89. *Harper's Weekly,* vol. 8, no. 367, Jan. 9, 1864.

90. Poe, *OR* I 36 (1), p. 319.

91. Correspondence, Oct. 20, 1863–Oct. 31, 1863, *OR* I 36 (1), p. 696.

92. Favill, *The Diary of a Young Officer,* p. 292.

CHAPTER 9

1. Reports of Major General Ulysses S. Grant, U.S. Army, Commanding Military Division of the Mississippi, *Official Records (OR)*, series I, vol. 31 (2), p. 30.

2. Atlas to *OR,* plates XLIX and 2.

3. Grant, "Chattanooga," in *Battle and Leaders,* 3:695–698.

4. Reports of Major General George H. Thomas, U.S. Army, Commanding Army of the Cumberland, *OR* I 31 (2), pp. 90–95.

5. Grant, "Chattanooga," in *Battle and Leaders,* 3:695–698.

6. Report of Brigadier General Absalom Baird, U.S. Army, Commanding Third Division, *OR* I 31 (2), p. 508.

7. Bishop, *Story of a Regiment,* p. 118.

8. Report of Colonel Ferdinand Van Derveer, Thirty-fifth Ohio Infantry, Commanding Second Brigade, *OR* I 31 (2), p. 527.

9. Report of Major General Gordon Granger, U.S. Army, Commanding Fourth Army Corps, *OR* I 31 (2), p. 132.

10. Baird, *OR* I 31 (2), p. 508.

11. Smith, "Operations around Chattanooga," p. 216, cited in Cozzens, *The Shipwreck of Their Hopes,* p. 260.

12. Report of Captain Edward Grosvenor, Ninety-second Ohio Infantry, p. 526; report of Colonel Ferdinand Van Derveer, Thirty-fifth Ohio Infantry, Commanding Second Brigade, *OR* I 31 (2), p. 527.

13. Report of Colonel Newell Gleason, Eighty-seventh Indiana Infantry, *OR* I 31 (2), p. 532.

14. Granger, *OR* I 31 (2), p. 131.

15. Van Derveer, *OR* I 31 (2), p. 527; report of Lieutenant Colonel Judson W. Bishop, Second Minnesota Infantry, *OR* I 31 (2), p. 238.

16. Bishop, *OR* I 31 (2), p. 534; Bishop, *Story of a Regiment,* p. 121.

17. Nesbit, *General History of Company "D," 149th Pennsylvania Volunteers,* p. 29.

18. In his regimental report after the battle, Colonel Bishop claims he received his orders to continue to advance twenty minutes after his men captured the rifle pits; Bishop, *OR* I 31 (2), p. 534; Bishop, *Story of a Regiment,* pp. 121–122.

19. Letter of Judson Bishop to mother, Dec. 3, 1863, cited in Cozzens, *Shipwreck,* p. 271.

20. Confederate Correspondence, Eastern North Carolina, Pennsylvania, Virginia, and West Virginia, *OR* I 51 (2), p. 175.

21. Report of Lieutenant Colonel Oliver T. Beard, Forty-eighth New York Infantry, Commanding Expedition, *OR* I 14, p. 192.

22. Union Correspondence, Orders and Returns in Louisiana and the Trans-Mississippi States, Sept. 1, 1864–Oct. 15, 1864, *OR* I 41 (3), pp. 412, 663.

23. Bishop, *OR* I 31 (2), p. 535; Bishop, *Story of a Regiment,* p. 122.

24. Report of Major Joseph L. Budd, Thirty-fifth Ohio Infantry, *OR* I 31 (2), p. 538.

25. Cozzens, *Shipwreck,* p. 264.

26. Report of Colonel Morton C. Hunter, Eighty-second Indiana Infantry, *OR* I 31 (2), p. 517.

27. Bishop, *OR* I 31 (2), p. 535; Bishop, *Story of a Regiment,* p. 122.

28. Manigault, *A Carolinian Goes to War,* p. 137, Hemming, "Confederate Odyssey," pp. 69–70; cited in Cozzens, *Shipwreck,* pp. 263–264.

29. Cozzens, *Shipwreck,* p. 269.

30. Report of Lieutenant Colonel Judson W. Bishop, Second Minnesota Infantry, *OR* I 31 (2), p. 535; Bishop, *Story of a Regiment,* p. 122.

31. Cozzens, *Shipwreck,* p. 270.

32. Van Derveer, *OR* I 31 (2), p. 528; Bishop, *Story of a Regiment,* p. 238.

33. Bishop, *Story of a Regiment,* p. 118.

34. Report of Brigadier General August Willich, U.S. Army, Commanding First Brigade, *OR* I 31 (2), p. 264.

35. Bishop, *Story of a Regiment*, pp. 126–127.

36. Bishop, *OR* I 31 (2), p. 535; Bishop, *Story of a Regiment,* p. 123.

37. Van Derveer stated in his report that the entire second phase of the assault, i.e., from the rifle pits to securing the crest, lasted only thirty minutes, *OR* I 31 (2), p. 528; Bishop, *Story of a Regiment,* p. 239.

38. Van Derveer, *OR* I 31 (2), p. 528; Bishop, *Story of a Regiment,* p. 239.

39. Bishop, *Story of a Regiment,* pp. 125, 237.

40. Return of Casualties in the Union Forces, *OR* I 31 (2), pp. 81–85.

41. Bishop, *Story of a Regiment,* pp. 122–125.

42. Bishop, *Story of a Regiment,* pp. 126–127.

43. Tielke, *An Account of Some of the Most Remarkable Events of the War,* 1:175.

44. Maxims, *Advice, and Instructions on the Art of War,* p. 124.

45. Saxe, *Reveries or Memoirs Concerning the Art of War,* p. 30.

CHAPTER 10

1. *Edgefield Advertiser* (South Carolina), Oct. 26, 1864, p. 2, col. 3.

2. Rhea, *Cold Harbor,* p. 134.

3. *Edgefield Advertiser* (South Carolina), Oct. 26, 1864, p. 2, col. 3.

4. Report of Lieutenant General James Longstreet, C.S. Army, First Army Corps, *Official Records,* series I, vol. 42 (1), p. 871.

5. Luella Pauline Gary, "Biography of General Martin Weatherspoon Gary." This typescript is dated May 4, 1910, and was edited and partially written by Gary's sister. However, the passage referred to was written by James W. Boyd of Gary's staff, and is the only evidence that Gary himself hatched the plan.

6. William Hankins Welch to William Godber Hinson, Sept. 16, 1894; supplement to *Official Records,* pp. 445–449; Louise Haskell Day, *Alexander Cheves Haskell,* pp. 155–158.

7. Field, *Campaign of 1864 and 1865,* pp. 557–558.

8. Alexander, "The Killing of Colonel Haskell," *Story of American Heroism,* p. 404.

9. Daly, *Alexander Cheves Haskell,* p. 144; Haskell in a letter to General Alexander.

10. Nolan, *Cavalry,* pp. 64–65.

11. Alexander, *Killing,* p. 405.

12. William Hankins Welch to William Godber Hinson, Sept. 16, 1894; supplement to *Official Records,* pp. 445–449; Daly, *Alexander Cheves Haskell,* pp. 144, 155–158.

13. Hinson, "The Diary of William G. Hinson During the War of Secession, Part II," *South Carolina Historical Magazine,* 1975, p. 112; Daly, *Alexander Cheves Haskell,* p. 155.

14. Daly, *Alexander Cheves Haskell,* p. 144.

15. Alexander, *Killing,* p. 405.

16. Strain, *Found Among the Privates: Recollections of Holcomb's Legion 1861–1865,* p. 83.

17. Bugeaud de la Piconnerie, *The Practice of War*.

18. Nolan, *Cavalry*, pp. 61–67.

19. A letter written much later to General Alexander Haskell would refer to the Forty-second Virginia Battalion Cavalry; Daly, *Alexander Cheves Haskell*, p. 144. This is a natural mistake since the Twenty-fourth had been formed on June 14 that year through the expansion of the Forty-second Regiment, *Journal of the Confederate Congress*, 4:398.

20. Gary, "Biography of General Martin Weatherspoon Gary."

21. Abstract from Monthly Return of the Army of Northern Virginia, General Robert E. Lee Commanding, for Oct. 31, 1864, *OR* I 42 (3), pp. 1186–1198.

22. Dickey, *History of the Eighty-fifth Regiment, Pennsylvania Volunteers*, pp. 394–396; Price, *History of the Ninety-seventh Regiment, Pennsylvania Volunteer Infantry*, pp. 324–326.

23. Latrobe, *Osmun Latrobe Diary*, entry for Oct. 7, 1864.

24. Price, *History of the Ninety-seventh Regiment*, pp. 324–326.

25. Return of Casualties in the Union Forces, *OR* I 40 (1), Jun. 13–Jul. 31, 1864, p. 246.

26. Report of Colonel Edwin V. Sumner, First New York Mounted Rifles, *OR* I 42 (1), p. 844.

27. Letter from Kautz to Haskell, Aug. 17, 1866, *Alexander Cheves Haskell Papers*, Southern Historical Collection, University of North Carolina; Kautz, "Memoirs," vol. 2.

28. Polly, *Hood's Texas Brigade*, p. 257.

29. Report of Lieutenant Robert M Hall, Battery B, First U.S. Artillery, *OR* I 42 (1), p. 846.

30. Report of Lieutenant Dorman L. Noggle, Fourth Wisconsin Battery, *OR* I 42 (1), p. 848.

31. Report of Brigadier General August Kautz, Cavalry Division, *OR* I 42 (1), p. 823.

32. Letter from Kautz to Haskell, Aug. 17, 1866, *Alexander Cheves Haskell Papers*, SHC, UNC.

33. Welch to Hinson; supplement to *Official Records*, pp. 445–449, and Daly, *Alexander Cheves Haskell*, pp. 155–158.

34. Hall, *OR* I 42 (1), p. 846.

35. Strain, *Found*, pp. 82–83.

36. Report of Brigadier General John Bratton, C.S. Army, *OR* I 42 (1), p. 881. Bratton says the distance was between six hundred and eight hundred yards; Lieutenant Hall of Battery B, First U.S. Artillery, maintains the distance was twelve hundred yards; *OR* I 42 (1), p. 846.

37. Hagood, *Memoirs of the First South Carolina Regiment*, p. 189. In his memoir Bratton says that his entire brigade was to the right of the road.

38. Field, *Campaign*, pp. 557–558.

39. McClendon, *Recollections of War Times*, pp. 218–221.

40. *Charleston Daily Courier*, Oct. 17, 1864, p. 1, col. 5.

41. The regiment had been formed from five independent companies (Trenholm's Squadron, Rutledge Mounted Rifles Company, Marion's men of Winyah, and two others) that had been consolidated with the cavalry of Holcombe's South Carolina Legion. The men were now organized into ten companies (A to K).

42. W. K. Steadman to William G. Hinson, Sept. 18, 1894; *Alexander Cheves Haskell Papers*, SHC, UNC.

43. William G. Hinson to A. C. Haskell. Hinson says that during the days that followed, it was widely reported that there had been 105 men in the charge.

44. Strain, *Found*, p. 82.

45. William G. Hinson to A. C. Haskell, Sept. 16, 1894; *Alexander Cheves Haskell Papers*, SHC, UNC.

46. *Columbia Daily South Carolinian,* Oct. 22, 1864, p. 2, cols. 2–3.

47. William G. Hinson to A. C. Haskell.

48. Willie Workman to Miss Jane, Oct. 12, 1864, Willie Workman Letters.

49. Hinson, *The Diary of William G. Hinson,* pp. 111–120.

50. Daly, *Alexander Cheves Haskell,* p. 148.

51. Alexander, *Killing,* p. 405.

52. Kautz, "Memoirs," 1861–1865.

53. Letter from Elliott to mother and sisters, Oct. 9, 1864; reprinted in Priest, *Stephen Elliott Welch of the Hampton Legion,* pp. 58–61.

54. Clarke, *Yates Phalanx,* pp. 180–181.

55. Report of Brigadier General August Kautz, Cavalry Division, *OR* I 42 (1), p. 824.

56. Kautz, "Memoirs," vol. 2.

57. Report of Lieutenant Robert M. Hall, Battery B, First U.S. Artillery, *OR* I 42 (1), p. 846.

58. Report of Lieutenant Dorman L. Noggle, Fourth Wisconsin Battery, *OR* I 42 (1), p. 848.

59. Stocker, *From Huntsville to Appomattox,* p. 186.

60. Field, *Campaign,* pp. 557–558.

61. Hagood, *Memoirs of the War of Succession,* pp. 307–308.

62. Polley, "Polley Lost a Foot—A Furlough," *Confederate Veteran,* vol. 5, Nov. 1897, pp. 570–571.

63. *Scientific American,* n.s., vol. 4, no. 19, May 11, 1861, p. 292.

64. Starr, *The Union Cavalry in the Civil War,* 1:65, citing James H. Stevenson, *"Boots and Saddles": A History of the First Volunteer Cavalry of the War,* pp. 37–38.

65. *OR* I 8, p. 673.

66. *OR* I 49 (3), p. 1046.

67. *OR* I 13, p. 406.

68. *OR* I 23 (1), p. 127.

69. Report of Colonel William B. Hazen, Forty-first Ohio Infantry, Commanding Second Brigade, Second Division, Twenty-first Corps, *OR* I 23 (1), p. 204.

70. Report of Major Joseph W. Caldwell, First Iowa Cavalry, Glover's Brigade, *OR* I 22 (1), p. 262.

71. Meyers, *The Sailor on Horseback,* pp. 32–33.

72. *OR* 43 (1), p. 822.

73. *OR* 43 (1), p. 457.

74. Reports of Lieutenant General Jubal A. Early, C.S. Army, Commanding Valley District, *OR* I 43 (1), p. 559.

75. Reports of Brigadier General Lawrence S. Ross, C.S. Army, Commanding Cavalry Brigade (Army of Mississippi), *OR* I 38 (3), p. 964.

76. Report of Brigadier General Bradley T. Johnson, C.S. Army, *OR* I 43 (1), p. 6.

77. Regimental History Committee of the Third Pennsylvania Cavalry, *History of the Third Pennsylvania Cavalry,* p. 278.

CHAPTER 11

1. "The Battle Described by a Volunteer," *Providence Evening Daily Press,* vol. 5, no. 116, Jul. 27, 1861, p. 2, col. 3.

2. *Daily Sun* (Columbus, Georgia), Jul. 29, 1861, p. 1, cols. 3–6; *Rome Tri-weekly Courier* (Georgia), Aug. 6, 1861, p. 2, cols. 1–3, letter to newspaper Jul. 25 from correspondent.

BIBLIOGRAPHY

Aldrich, Thomas M. *The History of Battery A: First Regiment Rhode Island Light Artillery.* Providence, RI, 1904.

Alexander, E. Porter. "Longstreet at Knoxville." In *Battles and Leaders,* vol. 3, pp. 745–752. Secaucus, NJ: Castle Publishing, 1992.

——. "The Killing of Colonel Haskell, One of the Remarkable Incidents in the War." In *The Story of American Heroism.* Chicago, 1907.

Allan, William. *The Army of Northern Virginia in 1862.* Introduction by John C. Ropes. Boston, 1892.

Anton, James. *Retrospect of a Military Life.* Edinburgh, 1841.

Ardant du Picq, Colonel Charles J. *Battle Studies: Ancient and Modern Battle.* Translated by Colonel John N. Greely and Robert C. Cotton. Harrisburg, PA: Military Service Publishing Co., 1947.

Armour, Robert. "The Attack Upon and Defense of Fort Sanders, Knoxville, Tenn., November 29, 1863." In *War Papers: Being Papers Read Before the Commandery of the District of Columbia, 30, December 7, 1898,* pp. 57–72. Wilmington, NC: Broadfoot Publishing Company, 1993.

Armstrong, Marion Vincent. "United States Tactical Doctrine: 1855–1861." M.A. thesis, Old Dominion University, 1991.

Arnold, William Rhodes. Larger of two diaries, "Battle of Bull Run" entry, ms 9001-A, Rhode Island Historical Society, box 15.

Bagwell, James Emmett. "James Hamilton Couper, Georgia Rice Planter." Ph.D. diss., University of Southern Mississippi, 1978.

Baker, Henry H. *A Reminiscent Story of the Great Civil War.* New Orleans, 1911.

Bartlett, John Russell. *Memoirs of Rhode Island Officers Who Were Engaged in the Service of Their Country During the Great Rebellion of the South.* Providence, RI, 1867.

Bartlett, Napier. *A Soldier's Story of the War: Including the Marches and Battles of the Washington Artillery, and of Other Louisiana Troops.* New Orleans, 1874.

"The Battle, as Seen by One of the N.Y., 71st." *Providence Daily Evening Press* (Rhode Island), vol. 5, no. 115, Jul. 29, 1861.

"The Bayonet." *Military Gazette,* vol. 2, no. 16, Aug. 15, 1859.

Beale, Richard T. *History of the Ninth Virginia Cavalry in the War Between the States.* Richmond, VA 1899.

Beauregard, G. T. "The First Battle of Bull Run." In *Battles and Leaders,* vol. 1, pp. 196–227. Secaucus, NJ: Castle Publishing, 1992.

Bilby, Joseph G. *A Revolution in Arms: A History of the First Repeating Rifles.* Yardley, PA: Westholme, 2006.

———. *Small Arms at Gettysburg.* Yardley, PA: Westholme Publishing, 2007.

Bishop, Colonel Judson W. *The Story of a Regiment, Being a Narrative of the Service of the Second Regiment, Minnesota Veteran Volunteer Infantry.* St. Paul, MN, 1890.

———. *The Story of a Regiment, Being a Narrative of the Service of the Second Regiment, Minnesota Veteran Volunteer Infantry . . . with History of Judson Bishop and Additional Chapters.* Edited by Newell L. Chester. St. Cloud, MN: Northstar Press, 2000.

Blanche, H. J. *A Century of Guns.* London, 1909.

Boatner, Mark Mayo. *The Civil War Dictionary.* New York: McKay Books, 1988.

"Breech-loading Guns and Projectiles." *Scientific American,* n.s., vol. 4, no. 5 (February 2, 1861): 73.

Bruce, Lieutenant Colonel George A. *The Twentieth Regiment of Massachusetts Volunteer Infantry, 1861–1865.* Boston, 1906.

Bugeaud de la Piconnerie, Thomas Robert, duc d'Isly. *The Practice of War.* Richmond, VA, 1863.

Burrage, Henry Sweetser. *Gettysburg and Lincoln: The Battle, the Cemetery, and the National Park.* New York, 1906.

Busk, Hans. *The Rifle: And How to Use It.* Fifth edition. London, 1859.

Casey, Silas. *Infantry Tactics, for the Instruction, Exercise, and Manoeuvres of Soldier, Company, Line of Skirmishers, Battalion, Brigade, or Corps d'Armee.* New York, 1862.

Cavanagh, Michael. *Memoirs of Gen. Thomas Francis Meagher: Comprising the Leading Events of His Career Chronological.* Worcester, MA, 1892.

Ceremonies at the Dedication of the Monuments Erected by the Commonwealth of Pennsylvania. 2 vols. Harrisburg, PA: Pennsylvania Gettysburg Battle-field Commission, 1914.

Charleston Daily Courier (South Carolina), Oct. 17, 1864.

Chesneau, Roger, and Eugene M. Kolesnik, eds. *Conway's All the World's Fighting Ships, 1860–1905.* London: Conway Maritime Press, 1979.

Chesney, Captain Charles. *Observations on the Past and the Present State of Fire-arms and on the Probable Effects of the new Musket.* London, 1852.

Clarke, Charles H. *History of Company F, 1st Regiment, R.I. Volunteers, During the Spring and Summer of 1861.* Newport, RI, 1861.

Clarke, Charles M. *Yates Phalanx: The History of the Thirty-ninth Regiment Illinois Volunteer Infantry in the War of the Rebellion 1861–1865.* Edited by Frederick C. Decker. Chicago, 1889.

Cole, Scott C. *34th Virginia Cavalry.* Lynchburg, VA: H. E. Howard, Inc., 1993.

"Colt's Pistols," *Scientific American,* o.s., vol. 7, no. 23 (February 21, 1852): 184.

"Colt's Revolving Rifle," *Military Gazette,* 3, no. 18, Sept. 15, 1860.

Columbia Daily South Carolinian, Oct. 22, 1864.

Constitution and By-laws Company H, Third Pennsylvania Cavalry: A Brief History. Shippensburg, PA, 1878.

"Correspondence." *Military Gazette,* vol. 2, no. 14, Jul. 15, 1859.

Couch, Darius N. "Sumner's 'Right Grand Division.'" In *Battles and Leaders,* vol. 3, pp. 105–120. Secaucus, NJ: Castle Publishing, 1992.

"Counsel to Volunteers." *Manufacturers' and Farmers' Journal,* vol. 40, no. 33 (April 25, 1861): 1, 4.

Cox, Major General Jacob D. "War Preparations in the North." In *Battles and Leaders,* vol. 1, pp. 84–98. Secaucus, NJ: Castle Publishing, 1992.

Cozzens, Peter. *The Shipwreck of Their Hopes.* Urbana and Chicago: University of Illinois Press, 1994.

Cutcheon, Byron M. "Recollections of Burnside's East Tennessee Campaign of 1863." In *War Papers: Being Papers Read Before the Commandery of the District of Columbia, 39, January 1, 1907,* pp. 283–299. Wilmington, NC: Broadfoot Publishing Company, 1993.

———. *The Story of the Twentieth Michigan Infantry July 15th, 1862, to May 30th, 1865.* Lansing, MI, 1904.

Daly, Louise Haskell. *Alexander Cheves Haskell: The Portrait of a Man.* Wilmington, NC: Broadfoot Publishing Company, 1989.

Davis, William C. *Weapons of the Civil War.* New York, BDD Promotional Books Company, 1991.

De Forest, John William. *A Volunteer's Adventures; A Union Captain's Record of the Civil War.* New Haven, CT: Yale University Press, 1946.

De Saxe, Maurice. *Reveries, or Memoirs Concerning the Art of War.* Edinburgh, 1759.

Delafield, Colonel R. *Report on the Art of War in Europe in 1854, 1855, and 1856.* Washington, DC, 1861.

Dickey, Luther S. *History of the Eighty-fifth Regiment Pennsylvania Volunteers, 1861–1865.* New York: J. C. and W. E. Powers, 1915.

Dixon, Lieutenant Colonel R. A. "The Rifle—Its Probable Influence on Modern Warfare." In *Journal of the Royal United Service Institution* 1, no. 2 (1857): 95–120.

Dodson, W. B. *Campaigns of Wheeler and His Cavalry.* Atlanta, 1899.

"Don't Bite the Cartridges," *Scientific American,* n.s., vol. 4, no. 5 (Jul. 27, 1861).

Duyckinck, Evert Augustus. *National History of the War for the Union, Civil, Military and Naval: Founded on Official and Other Authentic Documents.* 3 vols. New York, 1861–1865.

Edgefield Advertiser (South Carolina.), Oct. 26, 1864.

"The Eighth Georgia Regiment," *Daily Intelligencer* (Anderson, South Carolina), Aug. 18, 1861.

Essays on the Art of War. 3 vols. London, 1809.

Evans, Clement A. *Confederate Military History.* 10 vols. Atlanta, 1899.

Favill, Josiah Marshall. *The Diary of a Young Officer: Serving with the Armies of the United States During the War of the Rebellion.* Chicago, 1909.

Field, Charles W. "Campaign of 1864 and 1865." *Southern Historical Society Papers* 14 (1886): 542–563.

Final Report on the Battlefield of Gettysburg. Albany: New York State Monuments Commission for the Battlefields of Gettysburg and Chattanooga, 1900.

Francis, Augustus Theodore. *History of the 71st Regiment, N.G., N.Y., American Guard.* New York: The Veterans Association, 71st regiment, N.G., N.Y., circa 1919.

Frank Leslie's Illustrated Newspaper, vol. 10, no. 244, Jul. 28, 1860, p. 152; vol.11, no. 285, May 4, 1861.

Frederick, Gilbert. *The Story of a Regiment; Being a Record of the Military Service of the Fifty-seventh New York Volunteer Infantry in the War of the Rebellion, 1861–1865.* New York, 1895.

Fry, James B. "McDowell's Advance to Bull Run." In *Battles and Leaders,* vol. 1, pp. 167–193. Secaucus, NJ: Castle Publishing, 1992.

Garavaglia, Louis A., and Charles G. Worman. *Firearms of the American West, 1803–1865.* Albuquerque: University of New Mexico Press, 1984.

Gary, Luella Pauline. "Biography of General Martin Witherspoon Gary." Typescript, Old Edgefield District Genealogical Society. Edgefield (South Carolina), May 4, 1910.

Gay de Vernon, Colonel S. F. *A Treatise on the Science of War and Fortification: Composed for the Use of the Polytechnick School, and Military Schools; and Translated for the War Department, for the Use of the Military Academy of the United States: To Which Is Added a Summary of the Principles and Maxims of Grand Tactics and Operations.* Translated by John Michael. 2 vols. New York, 1817.

Goss, Warren Lee. "Yorktown and Williamsburg: Recollections of a Private." In *Battles and Leaders,* vol. 2, pp. 189–199. Secaucus, NJ: Castle Publishing, 1992.

Gibbon, Captain John. *The Artillerist's Manual, Compiled from Various Sources and Adapted to the Services of the United States.* Second and revised edition. New York, 1863.

Grant, Ulysses S. "Chattanooga." In *Battles and Leaders,* vol. 3, pp. 673–711. Secaucus, NJ: Castle Publishing, 1992.

Gray, Captain Alonzo. *Cavalry Tactics as Illustrated by the War of the Rebellion.* Fort Leavenworth, KA, 1910.

Greenhill, Basil, and Ann Gifford. *The British Assault on Finland: 1854–1855.* London, Conway Maritime Press, 1988.

Griffith, Paddy. *Battle Tactics of the Civil War.* New Haven, CT: Yale University Press, 1989.

Guibert, Jacques (Antoine Hippolyte), comte de. *Essai général de tactique, précédé d'un discours sur l'état actuel de la politique & de la science militaire en Europe.* 2 vols. London [i.e., Liege], 1773.

Hagood, James R. "Memoirs of the First South Carolina Regiment of Volunteer Infantry in the Confederate War of Independence from April 12, 1861 to April 10, 1865." Typescript memoir, South Carolina Library, University of South Carolina, circa 1870.

———. *Memoirs of the War of Succession.* Columbia, SC, 1910.

Halleck, Henry Wagner. *Elements of Military Art and Science.* New York, 1863.

Harper's Weekly, January 9, 1864.

Harrell, Roger H. *The 2nd North Carolina Cavalry.* Jefferson, NC: McFarland and Company, Inc., 2004.

Harris, Samuel. *Michigan Cavalry Brigade at the Battle of Gettysburg, July 3, 1863.* Rochester Historical Commission, Rochester, MI: Ray Russell Books, 1992.

Haskell, Alexander Cheves. *Alexander Cheves Haskell Papers.* Southern Historical Collection, University of North Carolina.

Haynes, Martin A. *History of the Second Regiment New Hampshire Volunteers.* Manchester, NH, 1865.

Headley, Joel Tyler. *The Great Rebellion: A History of the Civil War in the United States.* 2 vols. Hartford, CT, 1863–1866.

Henderson, G. F. R. *The Science of War.* London, 1905.

Hennessy, John. *The First Battle of Manassas: An End to Innocence, July 18–21, 1861.* Second edition. Lynchburg, VA: H. E. Howard Inc., 1989.

Hermann, I. *Memoirs of a Veteran.* Atlanta, 1911.

Hill, Alonzo F. *Our Boys: The Personal Experience of a Soldier in the Army of the Potomac.* Philadelphia, 1864.

Hinson, William G. "The Diary of William G. Hinson During the War of Secession, Part II." Edited by Joseph Waring. In *The South Carolina Historical Magazine,* vol. 75, no. 2, (April 1974): 111–120.

———. "Letter to A. C. Haskell September 16, 1894." *Alexander C. Haskell Papers,* Southern Historical Collection, University of North Carolina.

Houze, Herbert G. *Colt Rifles & Muskets from 1847 to 1870.* Iola, WI: Krause Publications, 1996.

"How the War Is to Be Decided." *Manufacturers' and Farmers' Journal,* vol. 40, no. 40, May 20, 1861, p. 1.

"How They Fire in Battle." *Scientific American,* n.s., vol. 7, no. 18, Nov. 1, 1862.

Humphreys, Benjamin G. *Sunflower Guards.* J. F. Claiborne Papers, manuscript 151, Southern Historical Collection, Manuscript Department, Wilson Library, University of North Carolina, Chapel Hill.

"Illustrations of the War in America." In *The Illustrated London News,* vol. 42, no. 1186, Jan. 31, 1861, p. 126.

"Incidents Gathered Along the Way." *Providence Daily Evening Press* (Rhode Island), vol. 5, no. 117, Jul. 29, 1861.

"Iron Clad Ships of War, Parts 1–3." In *Blackwood's Edinburgh Magazine,* New York, vol. 88, no. 541, November 1860, pp. 616–632; vol. 88, no. 542, December 1860, pp. 633–649; vol. 88, no. 545, March 1861, pp. 304–317.

Jomini, Antoine-Henri, Baron de. *The Art of War.* Translated by W. P. Craighill. Philadelphia, 1862.

Journal of the Confederate Congress. 7 vols. In U.S. Serial Set, Numbers 4610 to 4616, Washington, DC, 1904–1905.

Kautz, August V. "Memoirs, 1861–65." August Valentine Kautz Collection, manuscript, vol. 2, Library of Congress.

Kniffin, Gilbert C. "Raising the Siege of Knoxville." In *War Papers: Being Papers Read Before the Commandery of the District of Columbia, vol. 3, Papers 49–70. November 1903–November 1907,* pp. 359–375. Wilmington, NC: Broadfoot Publishing Company, 1993.

Ladd, David, and Audrey Ladd, eds. *The Bachelder Papers: Gettysburg in Their Own Words.* 3 vols. Dayton, OH: Morningside, 1995.

Lallemand, H. *A Treatise on Artillery.* Translated by James Renwick. 2 vols. New York, 1820.

Latrobe, Osmun. "Osmun Latrobe Diary." July 18, 1862–May 24, 1865. Typescript, Virginia Historical Society.

"Letter from the Second Battery." *Providence Daily Evening Press* (Rhode Island), vol. 5, no. 119, Jul. 31, 1861.

Lockett, S. H. "The Defense of Vicksburg." In *Battles and Leaders,* vol. 3, pp. 482–492. Secaucus, NJ: Castle Publishing, 1992.

Logan, Russell T. "Hampton and the Sabre." *Intelligencer,* Anderson, SC, May 22, 1895, p. 1, cols. 5–6.

Longacre, Edward G. *The Cavalry at Gettysburg: A Tactical Study of Mounted Operations During the Civil War's Pivotal Campaign, 9 June–14 July 1863.* Lincoln: University of Nebraska Press, 1986.

Longstaff, Major F. V., and A. Hilliard Atteridge. *The Book of the Machine Gun.* London: Hugh Rees Ltd., 1917.

Longstreet, James. "The Battle of Fredericksburg." In *Battles and Leaders,* vol. 3, pp. 70–85. Secaucus, NJ: Castle Publishing, 1992.

Lynn, John A. *The Bayonets of the Republic: Motivation and Tactics in the Army of Revolutionary France 1791–1794.* Chicago: University of Illinois Press, 1984.

Maxims, Advice and Instructions on the Art of War. Translated from the French by Captain Auguste F. Lendy. New York, 1862.

McClellan, Major General George B. *The Armies of Europe.* Philadelphia, 1862.

McClellan, Henry B. *I Rode with JEB Stuart, The Life and Campaigns of Major General JEB Stuart.* Introduction and notes by Burke Davis. New York: Da Capo Press, 1994.

McClendon, William Augustus. *Recollections of War Times, by an Old Veteran while Under Stonewall Jackson and Lieutenant James Longstreet: How I Got in and How I Got Out.* Montgomery, AL, 1909.

McLaws, Lafayette. "The Confederate Left at Fredericksburg." In *Battles and Leaders,* vol. 3, pp. 86–94. Secaucus, NJ: Castle Publishing, 1992.

Memphis Appeal (Tennessee). "Our Army Correspondence." Dec. 25, 1863.

"The 'Merrimac' Patented Forty-eight Years Ago." *Scientific American,* n.s., vol. 7, no. 21 (May 24, 1862): 328.

Meyers, William E. *The Sailor on Horseback, Personal Narratives of the Events in the War.* Series 5, no. 7. Rhode Island, 1912.

A Military Dictionary. Dublin, 1780.

Mingus, Scott L. *Flames Beyond the Susquehanna: The Gordon Expedition, June 1863.* Columbus, OH: Ironclad Publishing, 2008.

Monroe, John Albert. "The Rhode Island Artillery at the First Battle of Bull Run." In *Personal Narratives of Events in the War of the Rebellion.* Series 1, no. 2, Rhode Island, 1878.

Mordecai, Major Alfred. *Military Commission to Europe in 1855 and 1856, Report of Major Alfred Mordecai of the Ordnance Department to the House of Representatives.* Thirty-sixth Congress, 1st Session, vol. 1037, Washington, 1861.

Morgan, W. H. *Personal Reminiscences of the War of 1861–65.* Lynchburg, VA, 1911.

Moseley, Thomas Vernon. "Evolution of the American Civil War Infantry Tactics." Ph.D. diss., University of North Carolina at Chapel Hill, 1967.

Nesbitt, John W., ed. *General History of Company "D," 149th Pennsylvania Volunteers.* Oakdale, PA, 1908.

Nolan, Lewis E. *Cavalry: Its History and Tactics.* Columbia, SC, 1864.

Orr, Gustavus J. "The Eighth Georgia Regiment." *Daily Intelligencer,* Aug. 16, 1861, p. 2, cols. 2–6.

Osborne, William H. *The History of the Twenty-ninth Regiment of Massachusetts's Volunteer Infantry.* Boston, 1877.

Owen, William Miller. *In Camp and Battle with the Washington Artillery.* Boston, 1885.

———. "A Hot Day on Marye's Heights." In *Battles and Leaders,* vol. 3, pp. 97–101. Secaucus, NJ: Castle Publishing, 1992.

Phipps, Michael. *"Come on, You Wolverines!" Custer at Gettysburg.* Gettysburg, PA: Farnsworth House Military Impressions, 1995.

Poe, Orlando M. *Personal Recollections of the Occupation of East Tennessee and the Defence of Knoxville.* Detroit, MI, 1889.

———. "The Defense of Knoxville." In *Battles and Leaders,* vol. 3, pp. 731–745. Secaucus, NJ: Castle Publishing, 1992.

Polley, J. B. *Hood's Texas Brigade: Its Marches, Its Battles, Its Achievements.* New York, 1910.

———. "Polley Lost a Foot—A Furlough." *Confederate Veteran* 5 (November 1897): 569–571.

"Practical Warfare." *Scientific American,* n.s., vol. 4, no. 19 (May 11, 1861): 292.

Price, Isaiah. *History of the Ninety-seventh Regiment, Pennsylvania Volunteer Infantry.* Philadelphia, 1875.

Priest, Michael, ed. *Stephen Elliott Welch of the Hampton Legion.* Shippensburg, PA: Burd Street Press, 1994.

Providence Daily Journal (Rhode Island), vol. 32, nos. 177–182, July 25–31, 1861.

Puységur, Jacques Françoise de Chastenhat (Maréchal de France; Marquis de). *Art de la guerre par principes et par règles.* 2 vols. Paris, 1748.

Pyne, Chaplain Henry R. *The History of the First New Jersey Cavalry (Sixteenth Regiment, New Jersey Volunteers).* Trenton, NJ, 1871.

Rea, D. B. *Sketches of Hampton's Cavalry, Embracing the Principal Exploits of the Cavalry in the Campaigns of 1862 and 1863.* Columbia, SC, 1864.

R. E. C. [probably Raleigh Edward Colston]. "Modern Tactics." *Southern Literary Messenger* 26, no. 1 (January, 1858): 1–20.

Reed, John C. "The Journal of John C. Reed." Unpublished typescript. Alabama State Archives and History.

Regimental History Committee of the Third Pennsylvania Cavalry. Army Pennsylvania Cavalry Regiment, 3rd. History of the Third Pennsylvania Cavalry Sixtieth Regiment Pennsylvania Volunteers 1861–1865. Philadelphia, 1905.

Reichardt, Theodore. *Diary of Battery A First Regiment Rhode Island Light Artillery.* Providence, RI, 1865.

Rhea, Gordon. *The Battle of the Wilderness, May 5–6, 1864.* Baton Rouge: Louisiana State University Press, 1994.

———. *To the North Anna River, Grant and Lee, May 13–25, 1864.* Baton Rouge: Louisiana State University Press, 2000.

———. *Cold Harbor: Grant and Lee, May 26–June 3, 1864.* Baton Rouge: Louisiana State University Press, 2002.

Rhodes, Elisha Hunt. *All for the Union: A History of the 2nd Rhode Island Volunteer Infantry in the War of the Great Rebellion.* Edited by Robert Hunt Rhodes. Lincoln, RI: Andrew Mobray Inc., 1985.

———. "The First Campaign of the Second Rhode Island Infantry." In *Personal Narratives of Events in the War of the Rebellion.* Series 1, no. 1, Rhode Island, 1878.

Robbins, Major William. "With Generals Bee and Jackson at First Manassas." In *Battles and Leaders,* vol. 5. Edited by Peter Cozzens. Urbana and Chicago: University of Illinois Press, 2004.

Robertson, Robert S. *Personal Recollections of the War, A Record of Service with the Ninety-third New York.* Milwaukee, 1885.

Rochechouart, Comte de. *Memoirs of the Count de Rochechouart.* Translated by Francis Jackson. New York: E. P. Dutton, 1920.

Rogers, James B. *War Pictures: Experiences and Observations of a Chaplain in the U.S. Army, in the War of the Southern Rebellion.* Chicago, 1863.

Rome Tri-weekly Courier (Georgia), Aug. 1, 1861.

Ross, Steven. *From Flintlock to Rifle: Infantry Tactics 1740–1866.* Rutherford, NJ: Fairleigh Dickinson University Press, 1979.

Santa Cruz de Marcenado, Alvaro de Navia Osorio (Marquis de). *Reflexions militaires et politiques.* 13 vols. Paris, 1738.

Schmucker, Samuel Mosheim. *A History of the Civil War in the United States: Its Cause, Origin, Progress and Conclusion . . . and Biographical Sketches of Its Heroes.* Philadelphia, 1865.

Scoffern, Professor J. *Projectile Weapons of War & Explosive Compounds with Specific Reference to Rifled Ordnance.* Fourth edition. London, 1859.

Scribner, B. F. *How Soldiers Were Made, or, the War as I Saw It.* New Albany, IN, 1887.

Sentiments d'un homme de guerre sur le nouveau systême du chevalier de Folard. Paris, 1733 [generally attributed to Savorin].

Seymour, Digby Gordon. *Divided Loyalties: Fort Sanders and the Civil War in East Tennessee.* Dayton, OH: Morningside, 1963.

Sholes, Albert E. *Personal Reminiscences of Bull Run.* Read at the Thirteenth Annual Reunion of the First Rhode Island Regiment and the First Battery Association at Lakewood, Rhode Island, July 21, 1910.

Silber, Nina, and Mary Beth Sievens. *Yankee Correspondence: Civil War Letters Between New England Soldiers and the Home Front.* Charlottesville: University Press of Virginia, 1996.

Smith, Gustavus W. *The Battle of Seven Pines.* New York, 1891.

Smith, William Farrar. "Comments on Grant's 'Chattanooga.'" In *Battles and Leaders,* vol. 3, pp. 714–718. Secaucus, NJ: Castle Publishing, 1992.

Soley, James R. "The Union and Confederate Navies." In *Battle and Leaders,* vol. 1, pp. 611–631. Secaucus, NJ: Castle Publishing, 1992,

Southern Recorder (Milledgeville, Georgia), Dec. 15, 1863.

Starr, Stephen Z. *The Union Cavalry in the Civil War.* Baton Rouge: Louisiana State University Press, 1979.

Steadman, W. K. Letter to William G. Hinson, September 18, 1894. *Alexander C. Haskell Papers,* Southern Historical Collection, University of North Carolina.

"The Stevens Battery." *Scientific American,* n.s., vol. 5, no. 9 (August 31, 1861): 129–131.

Stocker, Jeffrey D. *From Huntsville to Appomattox: R. T. Cole's History of the 4th Regiment, Alabama Volunteer Infantry.* Knoxville: University of Tennessee Press, 1996.

Stone, Edwin M. *First Rhode Island Detached Militia Volunteers.* Providence, RI, 1866.

Strain, James L., and Adolphus E. Fant. *Found Among the Privates: Recollections of Holcomb's Legion 1861–1865.* Sharon, SC: Robert Jerald L. West, 1997.

"Suggestions from an Old Soldier." *New York Times,* vol. 10, no. 2993, May 1, 1861.

Sumner, George. "J. Albert Monroe: Recollections of Him as Commander Battery 'D' First Rhode Island Light Artillery." In *Personal Narratives of Events in the War of the Rebellion,* series 4, no. 18, pp. 5–25. Providence, RI, 1892.

Taylor, Frank. *Rifled Field Pieces, A Short History of What Is Known.* Washington, DC, 1862. Special Collections, Providence Public Library.

Tielke, Johann Gottlieb. *An Account of Some of the Most Remarkable Events of the War & A Treatise on Several Branches of the Military Art.* Translated by Captains C. Craufurd and R. Craufurd. 2 vols. London, 1787–1788.

Todd, William. *The Seventy-ninth Highlanders New York Volunteers in the War of Rebellion 1861–1865.* Albany, NY, 1886.

Treadwell, Daniel. *On the Construction of Improved Ordnance.* Cambridge, MA, 1862.

Trowbridge, Luther Stephen. *The Operations of the Cavalry in the Gettysburg Campaign: A Paper Prepared and Read Before the Michigan Commandery.* Detroit, MI: 1888.

Tyler, Captain. "The Rifle and the Spade, or the Future of Field Operations." *Journal of the Royal United Service Institute* 3, no. 10 (1859): 170–194.

Tyrrell, Henry. *History of the War with Russia.* London, 1858.

United States Government. *Reports of Experiments with Small Arms for the Military Service by Officers of the Ordnance Department, U.S. Army, Published by Authority of the*

Secretary of War. Washington, 1856. Reprinted by Thomas Publications, Gettysburg, PA, 1984.

United States War Department. *The War of the Rebellion: A Compilation of the Official Records of the Union and Confederate Armies.* 128 vols. Washington, DC: United States Printing Office, 1880–1891.

Upton, Brevet Major General Emory. "The Prussian Company Column." In *The International Review,* vol. 2, Jan. 1875, pp. 302–316.

Waitt, Ernest Linden, ed. *History of the Nineteenth Regiment Massachusetts Volunteer Infantry, 1861–1865.* Salem, MA, 1906.

Wallace, Lew. *The Story of American Heroism: Thrilling Narratives of Personal Adventures During the Great Civil War.* Indianapolis, 1897.

"War Frigates and Gunboats." *Scientific American,* n.s., vol. 4, no. 3 (January 19, 1861).

Wardner, T. B., and Jas. M. Catlett. *Battle of Young's Branch or, Manassas Plain.* Richmond, VA, 1862.

Warner, Ezra J. *Generals in Gray: Lives of the Confederate Commanders.* Baton Rouge: Louisiana State University Press, 1959.

"The Waste of Ammunition." *Army and Navy Journal,* vols. 1–3. New York, 1863–1865.

"The Weapons of This War." *Scientific American,* n.s., vol. 4, no. 24 (June 15, 1861): 379.

Webster, Dan, and Don C. Cameron. *History of the First Wisconsin Battery of Light Artillery.* Washington, DC, 1907.

Wheeler, Junius Brutus. *The Elements of Field Fortifications: For the Use of the Cadets of the United States Military.* New York, 1898.

Whittaker, Frederick. *Volunteer Cavalry: The Lessons of the Decade.* New York, 1871.

Whittemore, Henry. *History of the Seventy-first Regiment N.G.S.N.Y.* New York, 1886.

Wilcox, C. M. *Rifles and Rifle Practice as an Elementary Treatise upon the Theory of Rifle Firing.* New York, 1859.

Wilford, Lieutenant Colonel. "On the Rifle: Showing the Necessity for Its Introduction as a Universal Infantry Weapon." In *Journal of the Royal United Service Institution,* vol. 1, no. 3 (1857): 238–253.

Willie Workman Letters. Michael P. Musick Collection, U.S. Army Military History Institute, Carlisle Barracks.

Wittenberg, Eric J. *Protecting the Flank: The Battles for Brinkerhoff's Ridge and East Cavalry Field, Battle of Gettysburg, July 2–3, 1863.* Celina, OH: Ironclad Publishing, 2002.

Wolfe, General James. *General Wolfe's Instructions to Young Officers.* Second edition. London, 1780.

Woodbury, Augustus. *The Memory of the First Battle: A Discourse.* Providence, RI, 1889.

———. *A Narrative of the Campaign of the First Rhode Island Regiment in the Spring and Summer of 1861.* Providence, RI, 1862.

Wright, Captain Thomas J. *History of the Eighth Regiment Kentucky Volunteer Infantry.* St. Joseph, MO, 1880.

INDEX